GROTESQUE PROGENY

CULTURES OF CHILDHOOD

Susan Honeyman, Series Editor

GROTESQUE PROGENY

The Commodification of Dangerous and Endangered Children

MARK HEIMERMANN

University Press of Mississippi / Jackson

The University Press of Mississippi is the scholarly publishing agency of the Mississippi Institutions of Higher Learning: Alcorn State University, Delta State University, Jackson State University, Mississippi State University, Mississippi University for Women, Mississippi Valley State University, University of Mississippi, and University of Southern Mississippi.

www.upress.state.ms.us

The University Press of Mississippi is a member of the Association of University Presses.

An earlier version of chapter 1, "Innocent and Grotesque: The Child in *Sweet Tooth* and *The Girl with All the Gifts*," as well as a small amount of material from the introduction, appeared as "The Grotesque Child: Animal/Human Hybridity in *Sweet Tooth*," in *Picturing Childhood: Youth in Transnational Comics*, University of Texas Press, 2017, 234–50.

An earlier version of chapter 2, "'I'm Not an Animal': Grotesque Description and Chaotic Children in *The Power* and *The Flame Alphabet*," appeared as "Unsettling Language: Grotesque Description in *The Flame Alphabet*," in *Fantastika*, vol. 2, no.1, 2018, 41–53.

Library of Congress Control Number: 2024945510

Hardback ISBN 978-1-4968-5356-1
Paperback ISBN 978-1-4968-5357-8
Epub single ISBN 978-1-4968-5358-5
Epub institutional ISBN 978-1-4968-5359-2
PDF single ISBN 978-1-4968-5360-8
PDF institutional ISBN 978-1-4968-5361-5

British Library Cataloging-in-Publication Data available

For Lloyd, Dwight, Ramona, and Gus

CONTENTS

ACKNOWLEDGMENTS

From its early stages to its publication, this project benefited from the insight and knowledge of numerous people. I'm grateful for the support and feedback of Joe Austin, Ted Martin, Annie McClanahan, and Peter Paik, all of whom are dedicated scholars who helped me refine my work. I am especially grateful for Pete Sands's care and encouragement over the years. As this project has evolved, numerous people have listened to various conference presentations and provided feedback. There are too many to list here, and I know not all their names, but their interest and engagement helped strengthen my work and my thinking. In particular, I want to thank my colleagues at the International Association of the Fantastic in the Arts and the International Comic Arts Forum. I owe a debt of gratitude to Brittany Tullis. Her careful consideration helped strengthen my work, and her collaboration and friendship have been pivotal in the trajectory of my career. Were it not for the interest of Katie Keene and the University of Mississippi Press, this book wouldn't be in print today. I also want to thank my friends and colleagues at Lakeland University. Their support has been irreplaceable.

I'm also indebted to Kal Heck and Eric Herhuth, both of whom have been generous with their friendship, intelligence, and time throughout every stage of this project. Finally, more than any other, I extend my affection and gratitude to Becky Foster, whose unwavering love and encouragement enlivens me.

GROTESQUE PROGENY

INTRODUCTION

Childhood, Commodification, and the Grotesque

Winter's Bone, Daniel Woodrell's 2006 novel, is a coming-of-age tale set in the Ozarks. It follows Ree, who is sixteen years old and responsible for taking care of her two younger siblings and mentally ill mother. The plot involves Ree's desperate search for her father, who has disappeared after using the family's home as collateral for a bail bond. Ree must navigate a violent and drug-fueled rural community intent on keeping her father's fate a mystery. She refuses to relent even after she finds out her father was killed, and she is eventually taken to the pond in which his body was dumped, where she must help haul up the body and cut off his hands for proof that he is dead. While Ree clearly has adult responsibilities when the novel opens, the narrative includes the burgeoning respect adults begrudgingly give Ree as she demonstrates her determination and intelligence. This respect is echoed by the bondsman who, as the novel concludes, offers Ree a job she foregoes. The bondsman enjoins, "Listen, kid, you ain't old enough to hire legal'n all that, I know, but if you could get around, drive to town'n places, we'd sure use you. We go the bail for most every Dolly this side of the Eleven Point, you know. Almost all of you-all get bonded out by us. You'd be like gold to me" (192). This moment encapsulates the tension between Ree's age versus her experience. She's too young to legally hire, but it's clear she's capable of handling adult responsibilities. The bondsman calls her "kid" even as he recognizes the value she holds. The simile "you'd be like gold to me" positions Ree as an economically valuable commodity. Yet Ree is not valuable to the bondsman because she is an adolescent, but in spite of it.

Consider another example. "Babycakes" is a short comic written by Neil Gaiman, drawn by Michael Zulli, and lettered by Steve Bissette. In the comic, the narrator recounts how, after the extinction of animals, babies are now used for food, leather, and experimentation. When the babies run out, the elderly are next in line. This brief but dense narrative gets at a variety of issues, including the ethics of experimenting on animals, the ways in which society devalues certain groups of people, and the ethical blinders that people wear that allow horrible abuses to take place. The narrator begins his explanation of the abuses heaped upon children in Swiftian terms: "We made babies. And we used them. Some of them we **ate**. **Baby flesh** is **tender**, and **succulent**. We **flayed** their **skin**, and **decorated** ourselves in it. **Baby leather** is **soft**, and **comfortable**" (10). The dehumanizing verbs "made" and "used" blur the line between object and personhood. "Made" implies a logic of ownership that allows the adults to do with babies what they want, as if babies are objects. Terms like "baby flesh" and "baby leather" capture this objectification as "baby" simply becomes an adjective to describe component parts. Furthermore, the use of the verb "decorated" conjures up notions of fashion and ornamentation that move beyond the practicality of clothing and undermines the necessity to which the narrator will later appeal.

As the narrator continues, the abuses heaped upon children continue to pile up. The narrator explains, "Some of them we **tested**. We taped open their **eyes**, dropped **detergents** and **shampoos** in, a **drop** at a **time**. We **scarred** them, and **scalded** them. We **burnt** them. We clamped them and planted **electrodes** into their **brains**. We **grafted**, and we **froze**, and we **irradiated**" (10–11). This section amplifies the horror by listing the abuses heaped upon the babies. Furthermore, by moving from food to clothing to items that traditionally involve animal testing, the narrator continues to undermine their own case for necessity (and perhaps, by extension, the argument that animals ought to be test subjects). The cruelty feels overwhelming before we even get to verbs like "grafted," "froze," and "irradiated." Yet the narrator, rather than feeling remorse for what humans have done to other species and are currently doing to their own, appeals to necessity. The narrator asserts, "It was **hard**, of course, but it was **necessary**. No-one could deny **that**. With the animals gone, what **else** could we **do**? Some people **complained** of course, but then, they always **do**. And everything went back to **normal**" (11). The narrator's banality and list-like explanation seem to downplay the horror, but such a tone makes it more horrifying. Atrocity, fictional and real, is often justified as a necessity by those who perpetuate it, so it's no surprise that the narrator makes such an appeal. Yet despite the assertion of a unified belief that the actions are necessary, the narration soon gives way to the recognition that there were objections: "Some people **complained**." The claim that everything went back to normal is a fantasy. When the animals were driven extinct, normalcy vanished. Instead, the exploitation of the children creates a new status quo, a status quo enabled by the dehumanization of the children. Before the previous quotes begin, the narrator sums up this dehumanization. He claims, "A **baby** is not a **rational, thinking** creature" (10). This is the same claim that is often used to justify harm done to animals. Presumably, the narrator believes that rationality and thought are what makes a human unique. By denying babies access to rationality and thought, the narrator is then able to deny them an element of humanity and thus enable their dehumanization.

The narrator never grapples with the ethical implications of a dominant group maintaining its way of life at the expense of vulnerable groups. Yet the art of the comic reveals the artifice of the narrator's logic. The above quotes span the middle two pages of the four-page comic. On the third comic page, we see three panels on top of one another that gradually show the pain inflicted upon the abused child, as the child gradually disappears (figure I.1). The elderly man in the first panel, who also appears on the first and last pages, initially suggests someone who benefits from the exploitation of the children, but the last page of the comic shows him to be one of the people who is exploited when the babies run out, as he transitions from beneficiary to victim. The bottom panel, with its line of seemingly unconcerned women carrying babies into the USDA Redemption Center, suggests the act of handing over babies is routine and that the children are now seen as agricultural products. This is a society that refuses to acknowledge that past excesses were shortsighted and unsustainable and reorganize their society in more ethical ways. As a result, they sacrifice (among other things) their future, in the form of their children, for their misguided present. "Babycakes," like *Winter's Bone*, suggests the commodification of youths. Unlike *Winter's Bone*, however, where the commodification is not predicated on youth itself and is specific to one character, the exploitation of children because they are children is central to the narrative in "Babycakes," at least until they run out and another vulnerable group is sacrificed. Indeed, the title itself is a play on babies as commodities or products, which becomes apparent only as the horror of the narrative unfolds. The narrative identifies and critiques a mindset of exploitation that would understand children (as well as animals and eventually the elderly) as subject to the whims of a dominant class of adults. The previous examples provide instances, both subtle and overt, of the commodification of children and adolescents in fiction. Such commodification takes its cues from the real world. Both examples also metaphorically allude to the grotesque as they imagine people as commodities, but they lack the ontological uncertainty that is the hallmark of the aesthetic.

This project is an exploration of the exploitation of grotesque children and adolescents. It explores the commodification of children and adolescents by adult populations intent on wringing out whatever value such bodies might hold. In the subsequent texts under investigation here, the treatment of youths as commodities is mirrored in the bodily depictions of children and adolescents as grotesque, as animal-human hybrids or clones, for example. These are fantastical constructions of childhood, yes, but they build on the idea that childhood itself, though it includes lived experiences, is a construction which varies according to time and place (Jenks 7; Olson and Rampaul 23; Stearns 4). Therefore, understanding how childhood functions within a culture reveals as much about the culture as about childhood (Jenks 60). I argue that certain contemporary Western representations of grotesque children, based primarily but not exclusively in the United States, are a metaphor for the commodification of children and that these representations reflect cultural anxiety regarding a conceptual shift in the late twentieth and early twenty-first century of children from emotional assets back to economic ones. These grotesque depictions give form to concerns over shortsighted economic and political thinking, the exploitation of children, and the changing nature of childhood. The grotesque bodies of children not only provide both a metaphor and justification for the exploitation of children, but they also broaden our cultural understanding of childhood, commodification, and the grotesque by revealing the ways that these categories intersect. It is within this context that neoliberal darlings emerge, figures who are valued for their status as commodities in service to adult desires. This status is often legible on the grotesque progenies' bodies, which helps prevent adults from recognizing them as fully human. This affective distancing reifies their status as dehumanized commodities, as neoliberal darlings.

Figure I.1. Neil Gaiman et al. "Babycakes," *Taboo 4*, edited by Stephen R. Bissette, Spiderbaby Grafix & Publications, 1990, 11.

Childhood in Contemporary Western Culture

The Western world, particularly the United States and England, is dominated by two conceptions of childhood: the innocent or idealized child and the chaotic or even evil child. The innocent or idealized child is innately good and deserving of protection to help maintain its innocence. The chaotic or evil child requires strict regulation and oversight to restrain its natural tendency toward mayhem and disorder. Both constructions exist simultaneously.

I will begin by discussing the innocent child because it is perhaps more recognizable. The innocent child dominates the contemporary imagination despite evidence that its idyllic innocence cannot be maintained. People tend to see their own children and the children of their family and friends as innocent and deserving of protection and sheltering. Society, writ large, also tends to envision children in such a sense, even as society often fails to deliver protection and shelter to children in need. I will then discuss chaotic or depraved children, as there is a concurrent tendency in contemporary society to view children who undermine the artifice of innocence and protection as depraved, perhaps because such children speak truth to the lie that our society cares equally about all children.

Contemporary understandings of the innocent child owe much to Romantic conceptions of childhood. James Kincaid explains,

> For the Romantic poets, the child packaged a whole host of qualities that could be made into a poetics and a politics: the child was everything the sophisticated adult was not, everything the rational man of the Enlightenment was not. The child was gifted with spontaneity, imaginative quickness, and a closeness to God; but that's as far as its positive attributes went. More prominent were the negatives, the things not there. The child was figured as *free of* adult corruptions; *not yet burdened with* the weight of responsibility, mortality, and sexuality; *liberated from* 'the light of common day.' (*Erotic Innocence* 14–15)

The innocent child is defined by its lack of experience. This is why the innocent Romantic child is in need of protection (Pressler 19). It must be sheltered because experience chips away at the veneer of innocence and imbues a person with attributes and knowledge that work in opposition to the idea of innocence. The unburdened nature of childhood is also why Western society categorizes a child who begins puberty as an adolescent: he or she is henceforth burdened with sexuality. The Romantic child was a reaction against Enlightenment virtues such as "adulthood, sophistication, rational moderation, [and] judicious adjustment to the ways of the world. The child was used to deny these virtues, to eliminate them and substitute in their place a set of inversions: innocence, purity, emptiness. Childhood, to a large extent, came to be in our culture a coordinate set of *have nots*, of negations" (Kincaid, *Erotic Innocence* 15). Children's freedom from "adult corruptions" positions them as idealized cherubs unsullied by the unclean world. This, of course, is a fiction. Child illness, mortality, and labor, for example, did not end when the Romantics reconfigured childhood as a rebuttal to Enlightenment values.

The notion that the innocent child is made up in large part by what it lacks is central to its construction. For example, Anne Higonnet refers to the Romantic child as "naturally innocent," as it "makes a good show of having no class, no gender, and no thoughts—of being socially, sexually, and psychically innocent" (15; 24). Higonnet is specifically talking about visual depictions of innocent children, which began in the mid-eighteenth century with British portrait painters but proliferated during the nineteenth century due to the development of image technologies that expanded access to paintings and illustrations to a wider audience (9). She argues that the innocent child gradually gives way to the knowing child, a child cognizant of adult realities. However, her assertion that visual depictions of the Romantic child lack class, gender, or even interiority aligns with the idea that Romantic conceptions of the innocent child imbued it with certain virtues but kept it otherwise free of undesired attributes. The emergence of innocent children in British portraiture coincides with Jean-Jacque Rousseau's publication of *Emile* and *The Social Contract*. Both texts were published in 1762 and argue, "one finds in childhood humanity's original state of natural goodness. . . . Children, according to Rousseau, begin life neither brutish nor blank slates but naturally wise, just, and good" (Wall 22).

The imbued goodness of the child and the absence of undesirable elements creates a powerful cipher for adults. Jacqueline Bhabha believes that the need to protect the sentimentalized child says more about what society thinks adults should be like than what society actually does for children, especially those whose families lack resources (1,529). Adults have left childhood behind temporally but not emotionally. They've "gotten over it yet can't get over it" (Flynn, "The Intersection" 144). Marina Warner, who critiques the feasibility of childhood innocence, writes, "The nostalgic worship of childhood innocence . . . is more marked today than it ever has been: the difference of the child from the adult has become a dominant theme in contemporary society" (45). Warner believes the Western investment in the innocence of children is due to the desire of adults to live through children, "including Romantic and Surrealist yearnings to live through the imagination, with unfettered, unrepressed fantasy" (54). This is perhaps why the idea of the innocent child has been so irrepressible in contemporary times. It allows some adults an avenue of escape and makes no specific demands upon adults themselves.

Warner's assertion that adult desires shape cultural understandings of childhood is echoed across a range of scholarship. Perry Nodelman writes, "Childhood as we know it is an adult invention, a product of the adult imagination, and as such, it represents *adult* creativity," although he is also quite clear that this isn't necessarily bad ("Inventing Childhood" 14). Virginia L. Blum argues that psychoanalysis, with its narratives about how the adult self is subconsciously shaped by experiences in childhood, subordinates the child to adult needs. She notes that "in psychoanalysis's very articulation of the child as an object of study it tells the story not of the child itself but of why the adult talks about the child—what it is that the adult imagination pursues through the child" (4). This puts the child in service to his or her adult self. Blum continues, "In the effort to present the 'reality' of the child and its perceptions, we cannot help but interpret the child in light of adult motives; we cannot help but interpret *ourselves* through the child. The study of the child thus becomes a perpetual reenactment of the suppression of the actual child in favor of adult imperatives" (5). The study of the child, as undertaken by adults, is always viewed through an adult lens, and it becomes difficult to prevent this lens from becoming distorted by the imperatives, conscious or unconscious, of the adult.

The suppression of actual children and childhood in favor of adult imperatives is a common occurrence. Cindi Katz argues that concerns over various futures (political, economic, geopolitical, and environmental) are "in part channeled in and through concerns about children and the nature of childhood" ("Cultural Geographies" 6). The conflation of these concerns with children leads adults to think of children as bulwarks against disaster. For example, some argue society must improve conditions for future generations, while others believe future generations will be the ones to save or redeem society; children are also responsible for the future economy, and many expect children to take care of them later in life. These considerations blur the line between childhood and adulthood ("Cultural Geographies" 13). Some adults, however, want to cement the boundary between adulthood and childhood. Warner believes, "Grown-ups want [children] to stay [innocent] for their sakes, not the children's, and they want children to be simple enough to believe in fairies too, again, for humanity's sake on the whole, to prove something against the evidence" (54). The desire for children to remain innocent may be especially powerful when one believes childhood is threatened, like when boundaries between adulthood and childhood are blurred. Ellen Pifer notes that adults' relationship with childhood in contemporary fiction is an ambiguous one: we find children innocent and vulnerable, yet we sometimes see them as fearsome. This is because children are a mirror in which we see ourselves, but always from a distance. For example, fears over children and adolescents experimenting with drugs and sex are partly informed by some adults' own experimentation in the 1960s. Pifer observes that "the child represents the other side—original or shameful, beautiful or monstrous, forgotten or repressed—of the adult self" (16). In this articulation of the child, it is not glorified or denigrated because that is what the child deserves but because of the complex way that adults see themselves reflected in the child. What all these scholars have in common is the assertion that childhood is filtered through the adult imagination. Even actual children, rather than the ideal of the child or childhood, can be of service to adults, as in the latter half of the twentieth century, with its decline in public support for children and families: "[P]arents came to view their children as a form of personal expression" (Fass, *Children of a New World* 169).

Pifer's reference to the monstrous child also gets at the ambiguity surrounding children and childhood. She invokes the dark twin of the innocent child: the chaotic or evil one. Even as American society idealizes the innocent child, it also harbors its dangerous doppelganger, which is in large part a legacy of the Puritans. Puritans "emphasized original sin" (Pifer 20). Only through strict training and oversight could Puritan children overcome their tendency toward sin. Steven Mintz, in his meticulous account of the history of childhood in America and the active role children played throughout America's history, discusses the Puritan tradition. The Puritans left England in the early seventeenth century amid a host of challenges, including inflation, population growth, and a more youthful population (10). As real wages declined, many English children left their homes and sought employment or apprenticeships elsewhere.

This resulted in a rise in "youthful vagrancy and delinquency," which Puritans associated with "youthful vice" (10–11). As a result, many Puritans migrated in the hopes of improving their children's lives: "When English Puritans during the 1620s and 1630s contemplated migrating to the New World, their primary motives were to protect their children from moral corruption and to promote their spiritual and economic well-being" (10).

Although Puritans were not "unusually harsh" with their children, according to Mintz, they did not "sentimentalize childhood" either (10). Puritan discipline was meant to instill in children the attributes Puritan society valued in its members. Kathy Jackson writes, "The Puritans . . . regarded children as innately depraved and requiring strict control. Thus, they treated their children with little tenderness or affection; instead, they disciplined them, sometimes harshly, in order to teach them to be obedient, respectful, hard-working, and god-fearing" (14). Subsequent Romantic ideals that celebrate childhood precisely for being free of adult burdens are diametrically opposed to the notion that children's natural impulses should be suppressed.

The Puritans believed their attitudes toward their children were a benefit to both their children and to the larger society. Daniel Thomas Cook, in his analysis of the dialectical relationship between children and the United States's clothing industry in the twentieth century, notes that according to the Puritan minister Cotton Mathers, "Children, especially infants, are in a state of depravity and require *conversion*, and an early conversion at that, lest they die before they are saved. . . . Infants were seen as a danger to both the cosmic and social orders, their crawling placing them in postural proximity to members of the animal kingdom" (28). Not only did American Puritans have a different conception of childhood than the Romantics, but they saw the innocent conception of childhood as dangerous because "childish innocence and weakness were an invitation for Satan to do his works" (27). The Puritan construction of childhood requires adults to train children to restrain their natural tendency toward sin and disorder is what John Wall calls a top-down approach. A top-down approach "suggests that human nature starts out essentially unruly and therefore requires a higher moral purpose and order to be imposed throughout life upon it from above" (15). The Puritans' legacy remains strong. Mintz asserts, "Their legacy is a fixation on childhood corruption, child nurture, and schooling that remains undiminished in the United States today" (10). In fact, Warner asserts that "the Child has never been seen as such a menacing enemy as today" (56).

The Romantic and Puritan legacies leave us with conflicting ideas about the nature of childhood. Jackson notes, "On one hand, the child is wild and needing to be tamed; on the other, the child is tender and innocence. . . . In America, both of these images have persisted" (14). Chris Jenks uses the terms "Apollonian" and "Dionysian" to describe these two views. The Apollonian child is the innocent child who is naturally good, and the term associates such a child with the Greek god of art and knowledge (73). The Dionysian child is one who contains evil and corruption, and the term associates such a child with the chaotic Greek god of wine and revelry who is worshiped by centaurs and satyrs, beings who straddle the line between animal and human (70). Jenks writes, "These two images of the child that I have designated as the Dionysian and the Apollonian are not literal descriptions of the way that children intrinsically differ; they are no more than images. Yet these images are immensely powerful; they live on and give force to the different discourses that we have about our children" (74).[1]

It may seem contradictory that such diametrically opposed ideas regarding childhood still persist, even thrive, today. However, there are similarities between Romantic and Puritan conceptions. They both see the child as malleable. Puritans believe the child can change for the better by controlling their natural state; Romantic traditions believe the child becomes burdened by the erosion of its natural state and its contact with the wider world. Both traditions see childhood as a stage that is passed through; even if Romantics might embrace the innocent child, their experience tells them this is fleeting. Both conceptions also believe children require oversight. Puritan parents must prepare children to control themselves and become productive members of society, while Romantic parents should help preserve childhood innocence. Ironically then, Romantic and Puritanical conceptions of childhood share some general attitudes, though they radically differ in specifics. Both perspectives see something innate in childhood, but those innate attributes do not, or need not, continue to define children as they become adults.

Furthermore, these two conceptions are often reconciled within the same society by applying them simultaneously. For many people, their own loved ones follow Romantic trajectories, while other children, especially poor and minority children, may be "dangerous." Shirley Pressler explains, "Children are . . . seen as following a natural development aligned with a Romantic discourse—unless there is some deviation from the expected Romantic trajectory, in which they are constructed through a Puritan discourse" (22). In other words, all children are innocent until and unless they reveal themselves as evil or chaotic. Contemporary Western society can only allow so much deviation from Romantic conceptions. This is why when a child commits an especially gruesome act, like murder, he or she may be tried as an adult. Society cannot countenance such a heinous act from a youth, so it revokes the mantle of childhood.[2] The uneven application of Romantic and Puritan conceptions of childhood and the way such conceptions constrain children lead Pressler to argue that we ought to jettison Romantic and Puritan constructions of childhood and instead emphasize children as people in their own right, a position with which I agree.

Even when threatened, however, ingrained conceptions of childhood seem to stay with us. For example, configurations of childhood innocence have increasingly been under siege in American culture since the latter half of the twentieth century, as images of evil or knowing children proliferate (Bruhm; Heimermann; Higonnet; Jackson; Pifer). Steven Bruhm, for example, believes that twentieth-century Western culture increasingly depicts evil children because it has inherited or invented too many contradictory theories about children (98). He argues that society contains both the child of Rousseau and the child of Freud: the former full of innocence, the latter full of internal conflict. This conflict manifests itself in depictions of evil children. Bruhm writes, "The binary opposition between innocence and possession/corruption—which I am suggesting is no opposition at all, but rather a dialectic—produces in contemporary culture a panic about who children are and what they know" (103). Bruhm considers the innocent and evil child dialectical because innocence is only knowable in relation to corruption and vice versa (108). He also notes that we fear children in part because although adults might prefer children to absorb the best examples they provide and lessons they teach, there's no way to predict exactly what will stay with them (105).

While Romantic and Puritan ideas regarding childhood were passed down to contemporary Western society, these notions were influenced by earlier periods. Wall notes that bottom-up approaches like that of the Romantics, where innately good and wise children provide models for adults to follow, connect thinkers such as Rousseau and John Chrysostom, who share similar ideas about children. Rousseau thought children "naturally wise, just, and good," and Chrysostom championed "the ethical ideal that children are not objects to be molded by society but subjects toward which society should mold itself. He enjoins adults especially to recognize in children a deeper moral wisdom, wonder, and openness than adults themselves tend to attain" (Wall 21, 22). Wall explains that top-down approaches, like the Puritans', include philosophers like Plato, Augustine, and Immanuel Kant. Plato understands children "as irrational animals in need of rigorous ethical training" (Wall 15). Augustine uses "childhood as the prime example of his new doctrine of 'original sin.' . . . Augustine confesses that 'in your [God's] sight no man is free from sin, not even a child who has lived only one day on earth'" (Wall 16). Kant argues, "Childhood shows that the human will is first and foremost the plaything of want, instinct, and desire" (Wall 18).

Wall's emphasis on the range of thinkers who share similar conceptions of childhood demonstrates the prevalence of these constructions throughout Western history.[3] The Romantics and Puritans are simply the filters through which many of these conceptions most distinctly pass through to the contemporary Western world. Wall is not alone in recognizing the longer history of thinking about childhood, either. Pifer notes, "Since the Middle Ages, at least, children have been alternately regarded as innocent or depraved, the most vulnerable or the most vital representatives of humankind" (20). Ewa Kuryluk argues that childhood involves both "loveliness and horror: spontaneous goodness and equally sudden evil" and notes that both of these conceptions can be traced back to Christianity (160). While the Christ child is seen as innocent and children are sometimes praised for their wisdom within Christianity, the noncanonical Gospel of Thomas tells a story of Jesus as a child, killing another child who bumped into Jesus by reprimanding him that he would go no further. Kuryluk writes,

> The Gospel of Thomas expresses its concern with a child equipped with supernatural powers and points not to the innocent paradise of childhood but to the hell created for others by a selfish, juvenile god. As if unaware of good and evil, young Jesus takes advantage of his magical powers and behaves like a trickster. Like Childhood itself, the reverie of it is characterized by ambiguities and contradictions. (160)

Kuryluk finds this depiction of Jesus more accurately captures the ambiguities of children and childhood and the ambivalence adults may feel, both of which continue to this day.

Neoliberalism, Childhood, and Commodification

Contemporary ambivalence over childhood includes the changing nature of childhood under neoliberalism. In *A Brief History of Neoliberalism*, David Harvey outlines the rapid rise of neoliberalism and its transformation from a fringe theory to a mindset embraced by both major United States political parties and governments around the world. Harvey defines neoliberalism as "a theory of political economic practices" that involves "strong private property rights, free markets, and free trade" (2). Neoliberals and their theoretical forerunners argue that free and unrestrained markets increase quality of life while also spreading democracy and even providing a new way to understand social relationships (Becker and Murphy; Bhagwati; Friedman; Hayek). Critics note that the practice of neoliberalism diverges from these theoretical underpinnings. Rather than raising the quality of life for everyone, neoliberal globalization concentrates wealth in the hands of a few, increasing inequality and causing other deleterious societal effects (Colas; Giroux; Harris and Seid; Heilbroner and Milberg; Nieuwenhuys and de Kort; Saad-Filho and Johnston; Shaikh). For critics of neoliberalism, "corporate welfare substitute[s] for people welfare" (Harvey 47). This substitution destroys social safety nets and undermines communal values by emphasizing individuality and bringing all aspects of life under market control.

Neoliberal societal order is all-encompassing. Steven Shaviro observes that neoliberalism, along with its emphasis on commodification, privatization, and the transfer of wealth, also includes "the extraction . . . of a surplus from all social activities . . . the subjection of all aspects of life to the so-called discipline of the market . . . [and] the redefinition of human beings as the private owners of their own 'human capital'" (8). Shaviro finds the redefinition of humans as owners of their own capital especially lamentable because it forces people to constantly redefine themselves to maximize their value. He writes, "There is never enough . . . we always need to keep running, just to stay in the same place. *Precarity* is the fundamental condition of our times" (8). When Shaviro refers to "all aspects of life" being disciplined by "the market," he specifically means leisure activities, even sleep, but the dominance of the market and the interest in extracting "a surplus" from the social are central to understanding how children and childhood are being redefined (although many of the texts in this project posit a world where humans aren't "private owners of their own 'human capital'" because others already own or control them). This does not mean that everyone and everything is literally monetized under neoliberalism. Rather, the market serves as a model for other aspects of life (Brown 31). Annie McClanahan offers a slightly different take on neoliberalism, however, that helps unpack some of the baggage of the term. She opens up the possibility that neoliberalism works less as the idea that "formerly noneconomic" realms become so but instead that "economic exigencies" are introduced "into the lives of people once shielded from them" (118).

The economic colonization of the social, such as of humans themselves or of activities like raising a family or going to school, is what I am referring to when I use the term "neoliberalism." While McClanahan does not specifically discuss children, she focuses on adults with little or no access to banking as emblematic of the present; I believe the fact that children are subjected to economic imperatives when society has striven to keep them from such considerations is salient. To be clear, this is not a new development. As we shall see, children have had economic exigencies prior to our current moment, especially children of the poor and working classes. But McClanahan points out that there is an increasing number of people "for whom everything on which life depends is profoundly economic, precisely insofar as it is uncertain, precarious, and without guarantee" and that "growing portions of the population of the developing and developed world are finding themselves not 'entrepreneurs of the self' but no longer worth capital's investment at all" (121). I would specifically include children within these groups of people. In fact, the rise of people in precarious economic situations cannot help but include children and impact them negatively because "social class is the most significant determination of children's well-being" (Mintz ix).

Children from lower social classes are especially burdened by neoliberalism. Henry Giroux, for example, bemoans the placement of children into an increasingly privatized system of oversight that regulates their lives: a system that views children as commodifiable and disposable (4–5, 45). One way this neoliberal attitude toward children manifests is that rather than investing in educational and social systems, poor and minority children are increasingly placed into the criminal justice system, a system that is sometimes privatized, in which case the incarceration of children leads directly to the profit of companies. This disposability is due in part to the application of economic matrices to areas beyond the economy, a central tenet of American neoliberalism (Foucault 243;

Harvey 3). Under neoliberalism, it becomes acceptable to view children in increasingly economic terms, which contradicts the mid-to-late twentieth century's emphasis on the emotional and social value of children. This happens in a variety of ways. For instance, in many schools, standardized tests are emphasized so children can do well on exams, get into good colleges, and get good (well-paying) jobs. Of course, success on these exams can also mean more funding for certain schools. But many schools lack the investment necessary to effectively teach children, and these schools tend to be the ones that are responsible for teaching poor and minority students, which are populations the United States government, at least, is less interested in investing money and resources into, both in terms of education and their overall communities. Children are "product[s] and participant[s] in political—economic practices and thinking" (Sonu and Benson 235). The increasingly economic view of children and childhood reverses the trend of sacralization which took place in the late nineteenth and early twentieth centuries (Zelizer 11). The sacralization of children is the movement from valuing children as economic assets to valuing them as emotional assets. It was facilitated by economic and industrial changes including the advent of a living wage around the beginning of the twentieth century.[4] This movement came to a head with the transition of youth from the workforce and into the educational system: a transition that was hastened due to the lack of jobs during the Great Depression (Mintz 236).

Neoliberalism's relationship with children is fraught in other ways as well. Katz argues that children across the world are trained for professions that are disappearing as globalization spreads neoliberalism across the globe (*Growing Up Global*). Her observations of children in New York and Sudan demonstrate that the pace at which the political economy has transformed has left children without the skills, training, or access to succeed in a neoliberal world. Children often use play to internalize, practice, and develop skills they will need in their future professions, but for Katz, the heartbreaking reality is that the skills children develop are often related to careers that are or will soon be unavailable. Katz also argues that neoliberalism destroys social investment, which negatively impacts children. She writes, "Children, among others, suffer from these changes, as all manner of public disinvestments take place—including in education, social welfare, housing, health care, and public environments—as part of and in concert with a relative lack of corporate commitment to particular places ("Vagabond Capitalism" 710).

Helen Penn's study of childcare in England gives a specific example of how the disinvestment in social programs affects children and their families. Beginning with the Thatcher government and accelerating after the 1997 election of the Labor government, childcare has increasingly been a for-profit industry in England, as it is in the United States. This shifts the costs of childcare from the government to parents. Penn concludes, "In the case of the UK where the for-profit sector has been the main vehicle for implementing government policy, it is particularly problematic. For-profit care is volatile, dependent on local markets for uptake of places, expensive for parents, and frequently of poor quality" (159). The UK's privatization of this social service led to deteriorating, yet more expensive, quality of service. Furthermore, Penn believes the expansion of economic logic into social spheres undermines a vibrant society. She writes, "Market precepts have expanded into spheres where they have not previously operated—such as education—thereby undermining traditional social norms and values such as citizenship, social justice and social inclusion, and treating as irrelevant personal values and attributes such as sharing, caring, loving, intellectual curiosity, honesty, moral obligation or duty, etc." (Penn 158). These social and personal values and attributes are the sort of communal ideals that individualistic and short-term economic imperatives fail to nurture.

The preceding examples of the ways neoliberalism affects childhood has focused on the lack of investment in childhood, but neoliberalism can turn children themselves into economic vehicles. Many scholars discuss children being assigned economic value. When they do so, they are generally referring to the direct targeting of children as consumers. Markets geared toward children go back a long way. Children's literature in England emerged in the mid to late eighteenth century and was soon followed by other entertainment for children, like "circuses, puppet shows, exhibitions and educational games" (Grylls 20). However, over time, products for children were increasingly created for and marketed directly to them, sometimes due to external factors. From 1890 to 1940 in the United States, children were considered a new market because the mass-production of goods outpaced (adult) consumer demand (Chan 141).

The Great Depression contributed to the emphasis on children as an emerging market. Negative effects on jobs and wages "led financially hard-pressed marketers and manufacturers to target children as independent consumers," which in turn resulted in a variety of products geared toward youth, such as "comic books . . . movie serials . . . children's radio shows . . . and new kinds of children's toys" (Mintz 236) This had lasting repercussions for childhood: "By the end of the decade a new age category, the teenager, had emerged. . . . One of the Depression's lasting legacies was nationalizing and commercializing childhood" (Mintz 236). Since then, spending on products aimed at children also boomed. For example, toy sales in 1940 were $84 million. Two decades later, they were $1.25 billion (Mintz 277). The commercialization of childhood has only intensified. By 2002, four- to twelve-year-old children made $30 billion in purchases, and by 2004, advertising and marketing aimed at children was $15 billion (Schor 23; 21). The immensity of products aimed at children leads Warner to note, "The child, as a focus of worship, has been privatised as an economic unit, has become a link in the circulation of money and desire" (61).

The child as economic unit is not a cause for concern for everyone. David Buckingham writes, "Over the past few decades, children have become increasingly important both as a market in their own right and as a means to reach adult markets" and argues, "Contemporary childhoods are always-already commercial childhoods" (54, 59). Buckingham does not lament this because even as the market can shape "the meanings and pleasures that are available to children," children may "define and appropriate [the meanings and pleasures] in very diverse ways" (59). Cook argues that there is a dialectical relationship between children and the market. While children's clothing was originally meant to be purchased by adults for children, the market gradually began acceding to children. He argues that through the marketplace, "children become recognized, treated, and even deferred to as persons by adults on something other than an episodic basis (beyond the confines of the home, playground, or classroom)" and that "through consumption, children's 'wants,' 'needs,' and 'desires' . . . gain legitimacy as worthy of large-scale social action, such as the creation of business and industries based on them" (68). In this way, Cook "adds to the chorus of those who deny the pragmatic separability of culture on the one hand and markets on the other" (6).[5] So while Cook does demonstrate that the children's clothing market led to considerations of children and their preferences, he does not explore whether the marketplace is an ideal venue for this. What is insufficient about the home, playground, and/or classroom in legitimizing children's needs and preferences? What about other social arenas that might recognize children more directly, like the community or the government? While not Cook's intention, this lack of questioning about the appropriateness of the commodification of children leaves the integration of children into the market unchallenged, which may be cause for concern considering the ways that the market can create and distort relationships.

Juliet Schor explores some of the negative effects of the commodified or commercialized child. She writes, "Although children have long participated in the consumer marketplace, until recently they were bit players, purchasers of cheap goods. They attracted little of the industry's talent and resources and were approached primarily through their mothers. That has changed. Kids and teens are now the epicenter of American consumer culture" (9). Schor believes that the widespread influence of corporations on children is altering childhood in new ways. This is evident in the way advertising infiltrates schools and electronic media replaces other forms of play. She laments, "We have become a nation that places lower priority on teaching children how to thrive socially, intellectually, even spiritually, than it does on training them to consume" (13). For Schor, this consumption is not a potentially emancipatory exchange or relationship that cultivates children's agency. She writes, "Far from being a consumers' mecca ruled by diverse and rich choices, children's consumer culture is marked by bigness and sameness" (27). For Schor, the most ominous sign of the commercialization of children and childhood is in the way corporations have bought access to the captive bodies of children within the educational system via product placement and educational products. Overall, Schor finds that the more caught up in consumer culture children become, the greater the negative outcomes: they have lower self-esteem and are more prone to mental and physical illness. She writes, "The bottom line on the culture they're being raised in is that it's a lot more pernicious than most adults have been willing to admit" (173). The culture that causes Schor concern may have some upside: the emphasis on electronics in children's play, for example, may help prepare some children to participate in a post-Fordist economy and alleviate some of Katz's concern over children being trained in skills that are disappearing. Nonetheless, Schor provides a counterpoint to arguments that uphold the relationship between the child and the market.

While the relationship between childhood and consumption intensified during the twentieth century, the late twentieth and early twenty-first centuries have escalated this relationship and continue to transform it. Children are becoming even more entwined with economic logic and imperatives, and this transforms how society imagines them. Anne Higonnet writes, "The ideal of the child as object of adoration has turned all too easily into the concept of the child as object, and then into the marketing of the child as commodity" (194). Rob Latham, in *Consuming Youth*, sees the relationship between youth and consumption as dialectical. It involves both "exploitation and empowerment" (4). He analyzes the vampire and cyborg as metaphoric embodiments of "the consumerist ethos to which young people have systematically habituated during the contemporary period" (1). For Latham, consuming youth refers to the "consumerist values and practices" of youth, the metaphoric consumption of youth via "images and commodities," and "a general cultural obsession" with youth (5). Although youths may be courted as consumers and youth itself may be consumed and obsessed over, this doesn't guarantee a willingness to spend freely on children and adolescents. This is evident in Jules Gill-Peterson's argument that the neoliberal child is viewed in terms of futures trading. Investments in children and childhood are measured in future economic value, which is why society has disinvested in teaching poor and minority children. They have a riskier return on investment because of the systemic forces arrayed against them. Gill-Peterson writes, "The value of the future contracted through neoliberal child labor assigns and speculates on the future of kids as the incorporation of race, gender, and class—economic coefficients that materialize as the growing bodies of children. . . . Under this neoliberal social contract childhood becomes a form of futures trading" (185). The neoliberal child thus becomes an individual investment, which is subsequently how cuts to social programs like education are justified. This has an especially pernicious effect on poor and minority children. As a result of the lack of investment in children, they are sometimes cast as entrepreneurs who must demonstrate their earnings potential in ways outside the educational system, such as with YouTube "haul" videos (189–190). Katz also argues that children in the neoliberal world are an investment. They "secur[e] the economic future for their parents and other members of the extended family. . . . The child as commodity is niche-marketed to secure success in the insecure future" ("Cultural Geographies" 10). However, in increasingly uncertain times—when the environment is under consistent threat and the economic reality for so many is so bleak—there is no guarantee such an investment will pay off. Those children who do offer some economic or material relief are neoliberal darlings, even if such relief—perhaps especially if such relief—comes at the expense of their personhood.

Of course, the idea that children may contribute to a family's financial success is not new. The Industrial Revolution, for example, made childhood labor, which had already existed, more visible (Mintz 136). While middle- and upper-class families could shelter their children and provide them a lengthened childhood, farming and working-class families could not: "The demands of a market economy made their children indispensable economic resources, whose labor could be exploited in new ways" (134). This was not because these families were cruel but because the families' well-being required the children's labor. The income of children between ten and fifteen was often around one-fifth of families' income (136). Therefore, it is certainly not the case that neoliberalism invented the commodification of children. But some of the ideologies embedded in neoliberalism, such as short-term economic thinking and the dominance of a market-oriented system of thinking, exacerbate how society commodifies children and childhood. But beyond the relationships between children and consumption and children and labor, it must be recognized that children themselves are sometimes the product. For example, Jacqueline Bhabha observes a "market in babies and children . . . most apparent in poor and developing countries, where children are a tradeable commodity, though transnational adoption imports this commoditization of childhood into the developed world too" (1,528).

The transformation of children from economic contributors to emotional assets who consume to drivers of consumption and investments and eventually to commodities themselves undergirds this project. The utilization of children as economic assets challenges the dominant twentieth-century notion of the child as an emotional investment who should be sheltered, at least somewhat, from the adult world. Neoliberalism, by extending market logic into all aspects of life, including social arenas, facilitates this transformation. The texts in this project exhibit concern over the unrestrained economic or materialistic transformation of childhood: the "commodification of . . . children" referenced in my title. "Commodification" refers to a specific type of objectification. Martha Nussbaum defines objectification as "the seeing and/or treating of someone as an object" (251). Nussbaum complicates this definition by insisting on the need to understand objectification within specific contexts, as well as objectification's various manifestations (256–57). For example, the denial of a child's bodily integrity, a type of objectification, whether involving "battery or sexual abuse," is morally reprehensible (262). On the other hand, parents usually deny their children autonomy to varying degrees, and the denial of autonomy is also a form of objectification (262). However, not granting children complete autonomy is acceptable parenting in the contemporary United States. Commodification involves objectification but is more specific. In the context of this project, commodification treats a person as a commodity: a valuable entity capable of generating monetary, scientific, or material benefit for others, someone forced into an objectifying system of exploitation. The term "commodification" as opposed to "objectification" emphasizes the type of *thing* the children are turned into.

The Grotesque and Childhood

Because commodification involves seeing a person as a thing, whether an abstract thing like a market or a material thing like an object, it is grotesque. The grotesque comes from the word "grottesco," which initially described paintings on the walls and ceilings of Nero's Golden Palace, which was unearthed "around 1480" but built as early as 100 BC (Chao 1). The paintings "offered images of a jumble of human and animal forms, strangely interwoven with fruit, flowers, and foliage" (1). Key to this description of the grotesque is the combination of human forms with animal and natural forms and images. The Renaissance understood "grottesco" as an ornamental style that was "playfully gay and carelessly fantastic, but also something ominous and sinister in the face of a world totally different from the familiar one—a world in which the realm of inanimate things is no longer separated from those of plants, animals, and human beings, and where the laws of statics, symmetry, and proportion are no longer valid" (Kayser 21). The marriage of disparate forms not only refers to the playful marriage of seemingly incompatible elements but also the dreadful imposition of chaos upon order. Interest in the grotesque spread throughout Europe over the sixteenth century and became prominent in a variety of artistic forms including drawing, engraving, painting, and sculpture (22). As the adjective "grotesque" came into use, it retained similarities to its origin. Its first German usage recalls "the monstrous fusion of human and nonhuman elements as the most typical feature of the grotesque style" (24). The use of the term "grotesque," in both art and literature, remained popular for centuries, and its conceptual underpinnings were relatively stable, even though "new perceptions and conceptions of the grotesque occurred with every new generation of artists and critics;

each created its own grotesque art, understood the past in its own way, and invested the world with its own meanings" (Barasch 152).

Successive generations employ the grotesque in their own, often unique ways because the grotesque, like childhood, is culturally constructed (Carroll, "The Grotesque Today"; Cassuto, *The Inhuman Race* 6–7; Connelly, *The Grotesque in Western Art* 4; Edwards and Graulund 11–12; Schulz 3). This can make it difficult to apprehend the grotesque, as what is considered grotesque in one cultural-historical moment may not be grotesque to others. For example, some African and Indian art was considered grotesque by Europeans but not the makers (Connelly, "Introduction" 5). Another example is how Francisco Goya's *Los Caprichos* has irretrievably lost some of its meaning over time (Schulz 3). Despite the importance of context in discerning the grotesque, it retains some common associations. The grotesque challenges our conceptual categories. For Paula Uruburu, it "derives its effectiveness from paradox, from the fusion of numerous and seemingly incompatible elements—the horrible with the laughable, the sinister with the ludicrous, the mundane with the bizarre" (8). "The fusion of numerous and incompatible elements" undermines ontological divisions by combining what society thinks of as separate.

The combination of seemingly disparate elements recurs in definitions of the grotesque. Justin Edwards and Rune Graulund write, "Grotesque fiction, in a general sense, violates the laws of nature. Here, clear-cut taxonomies, definitions and classifications break down and, as a result, there is a built-in narrative tension between the ludicrous and the fearful, the absurd and the terrifying" (4). By undermining ontological divisions, such as that which separates animal from human, the grotesque inspires ambivalent emotional reactions, even if these reactions might not register to the same degree. A human with a pig's head may be laughable because of its incongruity but also fearsome because of its unnatural existence. The grotesque takes the familiar (the human, the pig) and makes it strange (the human/pig or the pig/human). This estranges us from the world we thought we knew and re-creates the world as a place where ontological categories are blurred and rules no longer apply; this is central to definitions of the grotesque. Scholars of the grotesque emphasize the juxtaposition or fusion of the familiar with strange or oppositional elements, or the transformation of familiar elements into something strange (Cassuto, *The Inhuman Race* 6; Edwards and Graulund 3; Gysin 28; Harpham 9). The grotesque's unsettling juxtapositions and combinations are often lauded for their disruptive and subversive qualities because they have the potential to force viewers and readers to reexamine the ways that they order the world (Cassuto, *The Inhuman Race* 8; Edwards and Graulund 3; Gysin 28; Harpham 12).

The grotesque may be received in different ways. For Kayser, the grotesque is violent and destructive. He writes, "The grotesque world is—and is not—our own world. The ambiguous way in which we are affected by it results from our awareness that the familiar and apparently harmonious world is alienated under the impact of abysmal forces, which break it up and shatter its coherence" (37). Kayser's description privileges order and considers its violation dangerous, but Mikhail Bakhtin glorifies in the disruptive and subversive qualities of the grotesque. Bakhtin identifies these qualities within the carnivalesque: a cognate to the grotesque involving medieval carnivals. Medieval carnivals provided people with respite from the feudal and ecclesiastical hierarchy that dominated the political landscape (5–6). In the carnival, with its emphasis on folk humor and laughter, hierarchies are upended (10). The legacy of the carnivalesque and its subversive folk humor carries into subsequent iterations of the grotesque, such as grotesque realism, which Bakhtin argues is primarily concerned with positive images of bodily excess (18–19). Kayser and Bakhtin present two starkly different conceptions of the grotesque. Kayser's emphasis on the infernal and disorienting is a far cry from Bakhtin's interest in laughter and excess. What they have in common, however, is an interest in fusions or juxtapositions (human/nonhuman, high/low) and systemic subversion of the natural order. Furthermore, while the grotesque is often associated with bodies, any fusion or juxtaposition that subverts the "natural" order or calls into question the schema on which we categorize the world may be grotesque. As Istvan Csicsery-Ronay Jr. so eloquently puts it, "The grotesque is life set free of law" (*The Seven Beauties* 190). It refuses to acquiesce to the political, religious, or cultural norms and instead creates the space for challenging them.

Twentieth-century American culture is rife with the grotesque. It's present in some comic strips and comic books (Berger 113, 199). Certain American modernist authors utilize the grotesque "to foster a social criticism that explored issues of class, ethnicity, and gender" (Bombaci 134). The grotesque was the dominant mode of Depression Era theater as a result of the world "not-making-sense" to audiences at the time, a common feature during times of "rapid social change" (Fearnow 7). This upending of the world coincides with the argument that the satiric grotesque is the dominant mode of the twentieth century because "the ideal of inevitable progress came terribly crashing to the ground, shattered by monumental world wars, revolutions, indeterminacy, atomic energy, the Freudian id, and the Holocaust" (Clark 18). As the world changes and our ideas are increasingly challenged, the grotesque represents these distortions. It has also been argued that the metaphysical grotesque, with its juxtaposition of concepts like life and death, is the thread that runs throughout American literature (Meindl 2), and that the grotesque is an "informing principle" in American literature and the dominant motif in Flannery O'Conner's work (Muller 4). The grotesque is arguably the "dominant sensibility of modernism" and postmodernism, the difference being that "anomalous deviations" were monstrous during modernism but became the norm during postmodernism (Csicsery-Ronay Jr., "On the Grotesque" 72–73). The grotesque has subsequently proliferated in contemporary American culture and has become mainstream (Carroll, "The Grotesque Today" 293). The grotesque is also one of the mechanisms by which contemporary fiction discomforts readers. Kathryn Hume writes, "Novels presenting the grotesque drive home the point that our conventional ideas about meaning are inadequate. Meaning, after all, frequently comes from predictable form, both in plots and in physical shape; it relies on firm boundaries. The grotesque exists to break patterns, in particular the pattern of what it is to be human" (166). These examples demonstrate the range of ways some scholars understand the frequency and importance of the grotesque.

I argue that a strain of the grotesque, as depicted in certain speculative narratives, represents concern over the changing nature of childhood and the increasing awareness that parents cannot always shelter and protect children as much as they may prefer. The grotesque bodies of children in the narratives within this project represent the way in which the proliferation of neoliberal values have overtaken what were recently considered social realms, thus changing conceptions of children and childhood. Children are often idealized as innocents and are currently a dominant symbol in political discourse, ciphers through which politicians and other adults assert their own values (Edelman). The ability of neoliberal logic to invade the supposedly sacred space of childhood is symbolized through the warped and unfamiliar bodies of grotesque children. As society's ideas about childhood change, grotesque progeny metaphorically embody this change. Grotesque depictions of children have the power to show the extremes to which neoliberalism dehumanizes people by showing its invasion of one of society's most sacred institutions: childhood.

At the same time, however, the metaphor ends up justifying the exploitation of children by depicting them as radically different from our idealized conceptions of children. Thinking about children as economic assets validates itself by transforming children into bodies some find suitable for exploitation. Therefore, the grotesque bodies used to illustrate dehumanization also create a systemic loop where they end up providing the justification for their abuse. The grotesque children are often not considered *fully* human. In this way, the logic of the grotesque in these texts offers the means to consider the humanity of the characters while always effacing this humanity, just as neoliberalism always becomes the solution to its own problem. When neoliberalism creates economic disparity, neoliberals call for *more* neoliberalism, thus worsening economic inequality. When grotesque bodies illustrate the horror of neoliberal commodification upon the body, they cannot help but acknowledge the plausibility that these bodies *need* economic justification because they are different.

The grotesque is suited to representing tension over the commodification of children in part because the grotesque can already be understood in relation to the economy. Tensions rooted in "categories of religion, polity and commerce" may be displaced into the grotesque (Webb and Enstice 96). Indeed, the vast economic inequality and government spending on war and defense rather than combating poverty may also be understood as grotesque (J. L. Adams 72). The grotesque and childhood also share an interest in liminality, which makes the grotesque an even more apt metaphor for the contemporary distortions of childhood. In *Childhood*, Jenks observes, "The child is familiar to us and yet strange, he or she inhabits our world and yet seems to answer to another, he or she is essentially of ourselves and yet appears to display a systematically different order of being" (3). Jenks's description of the child emphasizes his or her liminal nature as a creature existing between worlds. This liminality is strikingly similar to definitions of the grotesque. For example, Leonard Cassuto writes, "The grotesque is born of the violation of basic categories. It occurs when an image cannot be easily classified even on the most fundamental level: when it is both one thing and another, and thus neither one" (6). Cassuto's definition of the grotesque is akin to Jenks's definition of childhood in its emphasis on the problems of simply categorizing something as one thing or another. But Jenks's description of the child does not challenge our ability to classify children because of startling juxtapositions or fusions. It relies on the liminal nature of childhood itself. However, Kuryluk directly connects childhood to the grotesque. She considers childhood a grotesque "anti-world" governed by adults, and she notes that children, along with women and animals, are often positioned in opposition to the church and state (3, 319). Of course, talking about children as a separate group apart from adults is a model of childhood belonging that emphasizes differences. Such models "stress the radical alterity or otherness of children" (Gubar 451). These models become self-fulfilling prophecies in that by exploring differences, one can't help but notice and emphasize differences. This can be addressed by prioritizing a kinship model that recognizes and foregrounds the relationship between children and adults (453). The texts to come, however, depict the divides between children and adults, divides caused by adults who see children as hybrid objects. It is the conceptualization of children as grotesque, as creatures belonging to multiple categories (social and economic, child and adult) but fully belonging to none, that this project engages to better understand contemporary depictions of childhood. In part, concerns over the idealization of economic imperatives and values get shunted onto the bodies of children as a way of exploring how such a practice invades social spaces and alters our perceptions of children and, ultimately, ourselves.

My reading of the characters as grotesque is utilized in part as a way to explain how adult characters may be both attracted to and repulsed by the child characters and how that metaphorically resonates with the process of commodification and serves as a description of the behavior of those who objectify others. I also believe that the grotesque is an increasingly appropriate way to understand a world where the distance between the haves and the have-nots seems insurmountable and meaningful efforts to combat climate change are foregone so as not to upset the capitalist class. Many of the subsequent characters may also be seen, however, as posthuman. Posthumanism uses potentially radical or emancipatory forms to push against our understanding of what makes us human, in part by dissolving borders and hierarchies. It's not that borders do not exist within posthumanism, but that posthumanism "both exposes and ironically establishes boundaries between the human and the non-human, to facilitate a dialogue as to how these very borders might become more fluid" (Jaques 2–3). Posthumanism rejects the humanist interpretation of the boundaried human as a creature that stands above and apart from other animals and the environment (Tarr and White xi). In this context, the presence of borders between humans and nonhumans or humans and the environment, for example, are recognized in part as a way to better understand exactly what they keep apart and why, and how we might reimagine our world and ourselves by undermining such divisions. In children's literature, which is obviously resplendent with depictions of children and childhood, posthumanism, specifically in relation to humans and animals, can be used to "denaturalize concepts of difference, in order to enhance a sense of equality" (Jaques 12). While this can help us better value other creatures, posthumanism's potential is often restrained in its reconfiguration for children (13–14).

Kinga Földváry identifies contemporary English texts in which the child is futureless, which signifies an anxiety over the future (207–8). She also reads the child as posthuman in a literal sense, in that they come after current generations and have "a story waiting to be told" (210). Földváry is not arguing for an association between children and apocalyptic imaginings, so much as a pessimism associated with such child characters. The novels about which she writes, "which were written by and for adults," are "a warning rather than a call for identification" of a world on the decline that lacks the opportunities previous generations had (219). While the texts I write about sometimes do end up with relatively happy endings, many of them are quite bleak and foretell not just lost opportunities but suffering and death. Despite the range of endings, the following texts all indicate an anxiety over the direction the world is heading and show a persistent interest in how changing conceptions of children and childhood transform both bodies and relationships.

Within the context of the preceding framework, the following chapters explore texts illustrative of how the grotesque depiction of children or childhood embodies the transformative aspect of commodification. Sometimes this commodification involves money, sometimes it provides adults with materials, like organs or test subjects, but it always sacrifices children for the benefit of adults. The grotesque pervades all these instances of commodification.

This project follows the example of Karen Renner and considers childhood to be anyone below the age of eighteen (5). Any attempt to draw a clear-cut division is fraught with issues, of course. Most people consider children to be those who have yet to reach puberty, after which children become adolescents. However, puberty comes at different times for different people, and grouping adolescents with children acknowledges another political dimension of childhood, where anyone in the United States under age eighteen cannot vote and is not automatically tried as an adult if they commit a crime. It also helps smooth over the problem of aging in the narratives. The characters in the texts under examination are often depicted over a period of years. Some narratives spend more time on the characters as adults than others, but it is in childhood where the characters are forged in the crucible of exploitation and commodification.

Each chapter tackles two fictional narratives: one with a more sustained analysis and the other to help illuminate the issues at play. Because the discussions of childhood, as we have seen, are dominated by two traditional conceptions, innocence and chaos, the subsequent chapters start by engaging specifically with those concepts. In the first chapter, I analyze the comic book series *Sweet Tooth* and the novel *The Girl with All the Gifts* as texts that use the hybridity of transformed children to imagine societies that transform under the pressures brought about by a society that sacrifices its own children. Jeff Lemire's *Sweet Tooth* draws on the discourse of the innocent child but shows how borders are incapable of preventing crossing, which metaphorically represents the impossibility of preserving childhood innocence. The comics eventually replace the hegemony of humanity with a community of animal/ human hybrids, but this community is similar to previous conceptions of human communities as it reestablishes children as social creatures to be protected from exploitation. M. R. Carey's *The Girl with All the Gifts* offers a more radical ideology that forces a generational break with abusive adults. In this example, chaotic children who are nonetheless innocent of causing the issues the world faces are scapegoated, and, as a result, a child makes the decision to start society anew. Chaotic depictions are expanded upon in the second chapter, which analyzes the novels *The Power* and *The Flame Alphabet*. Naomi Alderman's *The Power* explores the shift in power dynamics that takes place when the abused become the abusers, as teenage girls, and eventually grown women, gain the ability to channel electricity and threaten patriarchal power. Ben Marcus's *The Flame Alphabet* takes chaotic depictions a step further as it emphasizes the capacity of language and metaphor to depict the grotesque and to explore what happens when meaning breaks down. In doing so, it more fully epitomizes the grotesque transformation between victims and victimizers. Both texts also include depictions of chaotic youths who are innocent of causing societal shifts that threaten adults, but in these cases, the youths often embrace their chaotic and violent nature from the outset, as opposed to a character like Melanie from *The Girl with All the Gifts*, who tries to suppress her chaotic nature until she realizes she has to act for children to survive and thrive.

After establishing the exploitation of grotesque children within the context of innocent and chaotic depictions, I shift to an emphasis on various ideologies or institutions at the forefront of exploitation. The third chapter explores patriarchal, capitalist methods of commodification in the short story "Reeling for the Empire" and the novel *Geek Love*. Karen Russell's "Reeling for the Empire" takes place in Meiji era Japan during its transition to industrialization. Katherine Dunn's *Geek Love* takes place within the latter half of the twentieth century in a traveling carnival. Both see children and adolescents, almost exclusively girls and young women, as a means of capitalistic accumulation at the expense of the characters' individual autonomy. These texts, ultimately, posit methods of resistance to such patriarchal dominance over exploited bodies. On the other hand, the comic book series *Elephantmen*, the focus of the next chapter, explores the lives of corporate ownership of children and adolescents groomed to be soldiers. It employs the racial grotesque as it demonstrates that the attempt to dehumanize a person or group of people is a process that can never be fully completed. The comic series, written by Richard Starkings and drawn by a platoon of artists, draws upon the experiences of slaves and immigrants and mashes them up into a postmodern pastiche, where the specifics of the unique experiences of various marginalized groups are forsaken for a collective emphasis on relatively homogenous outsiders trying to leave their pasts behind and forge their own futures. This amalgamation of the postmodern and the grotesque is further developed by Starkings and his cocreators of the comic book series *The Beef*. The final chapter draws upon the novels *One of Us*, by Craig DiLouie, and *Never Let Me Go*, by Kazuo Ishiguro. It argues that biopolitical considerations of human life by governments end up disenfranchising and commodifying some groups of children and adolescents. Both these texts understand grotesque children as in debt to the state for what limited and self-serving services it provides to such children. In doing so, the state argues that children are ultimately only valuable if they can repay these debts. I end with a coda that offers some final thoughts on reproduction and nonreproduction as well as how to potentially reorient society away from the commodification of children. Of course, there are many connections and affinities between and across these texts beyond the way in which they are currently grouped into chapters, but this organization allows for some introduction to conceptual understandings of children and childhood and highlights a range of institutions complicit in the exploitation of children. They demonstrate the perverseness of the commodification of children by depicting it in relation to adults serving in military and scientific communities as well as corporations, the family, and the state. In every instance, the children, regardless of whether they veer toward innocence or chaos, are not responsible for the environments in which they find themselves grotesquely dehumanized. In this way, the texts as a whole reveal that all children, regardless of how they behave, are at risk for exploitation.[6]

The texts' commodification of children causes anxiety by reflecting a disturbing reality where children are valued more for their current or future potential as commodities than as humans. The grotesque provides a way of thinking about childhood in uncertain and confusing times due to the relationship of the grotesque with incongruity and opposition. All the chapters demonstrate that not only are the children grotesque metaphors but that adults can be metaphorically grotesque when they commodify children and therefore violate boundaries between people and things. In this way, the theoretically value-neutral concept of the grotesque also works in tandem with the linguistically pejorative adjective "grotesque." The texts draw upon Western conceptions of childhood but situate them in worlds that posit how neoliberalism fundamentally changes our understanding of humanity and social relationships. This is done by estranging us from children, who are commonly considered symbols of reproductive futurity but are simultaneously some of the people most in need of protection in the present. Because of the emphasis on Western understandings of childhood and on the Western tradition of the grotesque, the texts under exanimation are mostly from and about the United States, although they also include Canadian and English connections, all places where the invasiveness of neoliberalism transforms and dehumanizes.

In foregrounding the way youths are commodified, it may seem as if the children in the texts to follow are passive recipients with no control over their lives, but it's more complicated than that. The characters' reactions to the situation they find themselves in are varied. Some texts do position the children and young adults as relatively powerless, while others depict them exerting agency and fighting back. It is widely recognized among childhood studies scholars that children can and do exert agency and actively engage with the world around them. Of course, adults do tend to have more power than children, but that doesn't mean that children have no power or that relationships between children and adults are "inherently oppositional" (Flynn, "What Are We" 256). However, the texts under consideration here tend to be by and for adults, although some are more clearly geared toward adult audiences than others. This is not to say that young adults don't read these texts, but the potential audience is important because these texts engage in a dialogue about the way society is perhaps not only failing children but actively harming them. This failure is the fault of adults—both in the present and past. When I assert the texts being by and for adults, I base this primarily on the fact that, as far as I can tell, these texts aren't marketed predominantly as children's or young adult literature. Often, there are associations between genre literature and the form of comics as childish fare, but these associations are often inaccurate, although it depends upon the specific text. I do not emphasize adult readerships to denigrate young readers or the texts targeting them (as well as adult readers, like myself, of texts aimed at younger audiences) but simply to note the texts I'm writing about here don't automatically fall into that group. Some of them may straddle that line, but just because they involve stories of children and childhood doesn't mean youths are the primary audience. Even the comic *Sweet Tooth*, which has been adapted as a Netflix show with a TV-14 rating, was functioning differently in its original form—a common occurrence between source materials and adaptations. Again, it is likely there were young readers, but the comic was originally published by the Vertigo imprint of DC Comics, which was an imprint with a history of publishing more mature fare, and the material within the *Sweet Tooth* comics is often more brutal and pessimistic than the show.

This book braids together multiple discourses to better understand grotesque children, and it primarily employs childhood studies in one of the ways identified by Richard Flynn. It "examines the representation of children and childhood throughout literature and culture" ("The Intersection" 144). In doing so, it reveals anxiety and discomfort over some of the ways children are dehumanized through commodification. This gets at the significance of the subsequent texts being written and consumed by adults, who may share concern over the myriad ways that children are commodified for the benefit of adults like themselves.

CHAPTER 1

Innocent and Grotesque
The Child in *Sweet Tooth* and *The Girl with All the Gifts*

Under late or neoliberal capitalism, almost all aspects of life are commodified or understood in terms of market value. This results in alienating and dehumanizing effects. Yet because people are immersed within market society and much of its working is obfuscated, it is sometimes difficult to grapple with its specific impacts or to register its dehumanizing effects. Amid this dehumanization, there is a turn to grotesque, hybrid characters in some speculative fiction who metaphorically embody dehumanization. In this context, child characters are especially meaningful for two primary reasons. They represent the future, and there is a tendency, at least initially, to shelter them from the present. Therefore, the commodification and subsequent dehumanization of child characters reveals anxiety over the future, specifically the direction society might be heading. Furthermore, because society likes to believe it protects children, narratives that depict the opposite also illustrate unease with the contemporary moment. This chapter analyzes the comic book *Sweet Tooth* to demonstrate the way innocent child characters cannot be sheltered when adults want to utilize them as resources. The use of children as resources is a form of grotesque dehumanization that the child characters metaphorically embody via their grotesque bodies. The chapter then shifts to a shorter analysis of the novel *The Girl with All the Gifts* to reveal how the act of sacrificing children to maintain the present is an act of biopolitical supremacy. These texts pair well because they both involve hybrid child characters commodified at the hands of adults wielding violence under the guise of military and scientific legitimacy.

Sweet Tooth, a serialized comic book that followed a monthly publication schedule from 2009 to 2013, is compiled in six volumes of trade paperbacks and three volumes of deluxe editions. The comic was written and mostly drawn by Jeff Lemire,[1] although occasionally other artists contributed.[2] *Sweet Tooth* takes place in a postapocalyptic United States approximately seven years after a plague decimates the human population. The beginning of the plague coincides with human newborns being born as animal/human hybrids who are immune to the plague. Some hybrids appear predominantly human, some animal, but all blur the line between the categories of animal and human, unsettling their ontological status. The titular character, Gus (nicknamed Sweet Tooth), is a mostly human-looking hybrid with antlers and deer-like ears. Gus is raised in isolation in Nebraska by his religious father, Richard, who hides him from hunters. These hunters trade the hybrid children, alive or dead, to a military/scientific compound for resources. In the compound, pregnant women and hybrid children are experimented upon in the hopes of unlocking a cure for the plague. These experiments often kill the women and children. The narrative emphasizes the survival of the hybrids amid the decline of humans. The series utilizes the animal/human hybridity of the children as a metaphor for contemporary anxiety over the exploitation of children. The exploitation of children and other vulnerable groups is not unique to the contemporary moment, but the depiction of grotesque children whose bodies are sacrificed to potentially benefit adults actualizes the relationship between exploitation and a political economy seemingly uninterested in future societal well-being.

Theories of the grotesque emphasize transformation. Shun-Liang Chao asserts that the grotesque involves a "perpetual, never-ending metamorphosis of one substance into another" (45). A human princess turned into a frog is not grotesque; a human princess who is part frog is grotesque. For Chao, another way to think about the state of transformation and its relationship to the grotesque is to consider perpetual metamorphosis as incomplete (168). Chao understands perpetual metamorphosis as incomplete because the metamorphosis appears to never end. It exists in a state of in-betweenness (26). Chao's understanding of the grotesque as a state of never-ending transformation is well suited to his use of classical mythology. For example, he describes Scylla as grotesque because she exists between human and monster but rejects Daphne as grotesque because her transformation into a tree completes (45). Mikhail Bakhtin is also interested in metamorphosis. He writes,

> The grotesque image reflects a phenomenon in transformation, an as yet unfinished metamorphosis, of death and birth, growing and becoming. The relation to time is one determining trait of the grotesque image. The other indispensable trait is ambivalence. For in this image we find poles of transformation, the old and the new, the dying and the procreating, the beginning and the end of the metamorphosis. (24)

Bakhtin highlights the way that transformation, by virtue of its in-between status, suggests both its beginning and its end. That the metamorphosis is "as yet unfinished" leaves the possibility for its completion, even though a metamorphosis may never be complete. Bakhtin writes, "The grotesque body, as we have often stressed, is a body in the act of becoming. It is never finished, never completed; it is continually built, created, and builds and creates another body" (317).

In *Sweet Tooth*, the grotesque manifests in both the hybridity of the child characters as part animal/part human as well as their treatment as commodities. These grotesque bodies also represent a transformative shift for humanity. What is significant about grotesque transformation in *Sweet Tooth* is that the individual bodies do not exist in a state of transformation; they only appear to, whereas humanity itself is transforming. The hybrids exist as complete biological entities who blur categories as they generate new ones. But readers understand the hybrids by comparing them to what they know: the imagined separate, although increasingly complicated, domains of the animal and the human.[3] The hybrids share elements of both animal and human but are not fully accepted by either group. The hybrid boy Gus cannot be immediately classified because he looks like a cross between animal and human, even though the comic leaves little doubt as to his humanity. Furthermore, he often looks older than his age. He is under ten years old, but the long, sometimes angular line work of Lemire ages Gus, which reinforces some adults' refusal to see Gus as a child (figure 1.1). This refusal is partially because Gus has animal elements, but it is also because, in the society in which Gus lives, adults are always cognizant of Gus's value as a commodity. While Lemire's use of long lines when drawing faces is a common aesthetic across his work, the style works particularly well here: Gus's older appearance

Figure 1.1 Jeff Lemire. *Sweet Tooth, Vol. 1: In Captivity*, DC Comics, 2010, 10.

reflects the harsh world in which he lives, where hunters trade children for resources and adults battle each other.

Slippage between the animal and the human is captured in two early scenes that speak to the grotesque nature of the characters due to the difficulty in situating them ontologically. Early in the narrative, Gus encounters a buck (figure 1.2). The first panel is a large, establishing image of Gus and the buck, which takes up most of the page and depicts an initial confrontation followed by narrow panels emphasizing the eyes of the characters. In the large panel, the buck seems to be creeping exceptionally close to Gus. There is a palpable sense of slowness. The antlers, of course, tie these two creatures together. The mirroring of the antlers ties Gus to the animal kingdom, but it is the emphasis on the eyes that truly connects them. In the second and third panel, the eyes of Gus and the buck are similar in appearance, as are their other features, such as the angle of their noses and slope of their ears. These panels flatten the difference between Gus and the buck even more. Furthermore, the placement of these panels beneath the image of the buck potentially advancing on Gus creates a pause allowing for recognition to take place. As opposed to the potential for movement in the top image implied by the buck's upraised hoof, the narrow panels lack any implied movement. The lack of movement provides the space for consideration between the two beings. This page highlights the ontological gray area hybrids inhabit. However, the second and third panel, although they emphasize the similarities between Gus and the buck, make the buck resemble a human more than Gus resembles a buck in that they excise both their antlers and the buck's quadruped body.

The inability to fully place the hybrids as animal or human is inverted when shortly thereafter Gus encounters a hunter, Jepperd (figure 1.3). Jepperd tracks Gus to his home. He convinces Gus to go with him to an animal sanctuary, then instead takes him to the compound where the experiments are taking place and trades him for the body of his wife, who died giving birth to a hybrid in the same compound, a trade that treats Gus as a commodity. Jepperd eventually experiences regret, stages a breakout, and becomes Gus's protector, but at this moment, Jepperd is a predator. Jepperd observes, "I ain't never seen a deer-one before" (*Out of the Deep Woods* 36). He says "one" rather than "child" or "kid" or even "hybrid," which emphasizes Gus's animal aspect while refusing to recognize the human aspect. It also reflects the estrangement necessary for Jepperd to harm him.

Figure 1.2. Jeff Lemire. *Sweet Tooth, Vol. 1: In Captivity*, DC Comics, 2010, 23.

The panel composition is reminiscent of that between Gus and the buck. In the first, large panel, which occupies the top two thirds of the page, Jepperd grips Gus by the antler with one hand while holding a gun in the other. The next panel is small and thin, focusing on Jepperd's eyes. Like the panel, they are narrow, and the suspicion he feels is made evident in their glare. The next panel, which has the same size and basic composition, cuts to Gus's eyes, which are widened in fear. Despite the longer ears, Gus looks just as human as Jepperd does, especially because in this narrow framing, his antlers are no longer visible. The fourth and final panel returns again to Jepperd's eyes, which are now widened in belated recognition of Gus's humanity. In the first panel on the next page, he says, "Relax kid . . . I ain't gonna hurt you" (37). Of course, Jepperd will take advantage of Gus, but at this moment, Jepperd's physical dominance of Gus ends. Over the course of their journey, Jepperd

Figure 1.3. Jeff Lemire. *Sweet Tooth, Vol. 1: In Captivity*, DC Comics, 2010, 36.

bonds with Gus, which sets the stage for Jepperd's rescue attempt. That bond begins here, with Jepperd seeing Gus's humanity through his expressive eyes and recognizing him as a "kid" rather than a "deer-one." Looking solely at a hybrid's animal aspects may allow some characters to overlook the hybrids' humanity, but, when confronted with Gus's humanity, Jepperd cannot ignore it. Even so, Gus's grotesque nature initially makes it difficult for Jepperd to connect with him.

Despite their differences, these scenes are both about potential connections, even if for the briefest of moments. The initial example involves Gus's identification with the deer, but because the page also makes the buck appear more human, it reinforces the connection between different forms of alterity. Showing Gus looking like a buck and the buck looking like a human is one way to emphasize that the distinctions some make between humans and other animals are not as gaping as they might first appear. This fluidity between human and nonhuman animal gets the buck killed, as hunters who are trying to capture Gus accidentally shoot the buck instead. The inadvertent killing of the buck represents the dehumanizing way hybrids are hunted like nonhuman animals, yet paradoxically, the buck would have lived had it been recognized as a buck and not a hybrid. Gus's interactions with the buck and Jepperd highlight the uncertain nature of Gus's ontological status, but they also allow for the possibility of recognizing different forms of being based on similarity rather than difference.

The notion that the hybrid characters exist along a spectrum of grotesque alterity resonates with what little current scholarship there is on the text. Katherine Kelp-Stebbins argues that the series participates in a posthumanist renegotiation of what it means to be human by destabilizing traditional hierarchies, such as word/image and animal/human relationships. This destabilization involves the hybridity of the comic's form and the comic book's narrative. This renegotiation allows for a posthumanist reimagining of being. Kelp-Stebbins notes, "The boundaries between nature and culture, human and animal, man and god, and mind and body are sketchy and seamy . . . expectations about the diegetic world are frustrated or overturned so that the knowledge of the world it presents is always only speculative" (339). This speculation is the result of the indeterminacy of the narrative. Because boundaries in the narrative are "sketchy and seamy," clearly classifying the "diegetic world" is difficult. Kelp-Stebbins extends the liminality of the narrative beyond the posthuman bodies of the animal/human hybrids, but such hybrids are appropriate vehicles in part because "intersecting the human and animal is crucial to visualizing the posthuman" (Castro 255). This is in part due to the way such intersections help humans recognize the relationships between themselves and nonhuman animals as interconnected.

Furthermore, *Sweet Tooth* embodies and extends the relationship between animals and otherness in comics. While Kelp-Stebbins sees posthuman possibilities inherent in the text, Michael A. Chaney notes that animal representations tend to be traditional or conservative. Chaney is not writing about *Sweet Tooth* specifically, but his analysis still illuminates the text. In "Animal Subjects of the Graphic Novel," Chaney explores the role of the animal in comics and finds that animal/human figures reinscribe the superiority of the human, which coincide with *Sweet Tooth*'s emphasis on Gus's humanity despite his association with the animal realm. Chaney notes that the animal has been a common theme in comics throughout their history and that this trend continues unabated. Evidenced by his analysis of autobiographical graphic novels, Chaney asserts, "[T]heorizing the animal has become (and indeed always has been) essential to sequential pictorial narratives of identity and otherness" and that "the animal referenced in comics is more generally a ludic cipher of otherness" (129, 130). He further declares that the anthropomorphized animals or humans with animal attributes are always understood in relation to the idealized human body: "The animalized human body is visually legible and fictively pleasing, therefore, precisely because it is neither legible nor pleasing in relation to the norm or to the 'real' that the comic fantastically suspends yet constantly and invisibly produces as an essential effect of that suspension" (132). In other words, the animalized human body may appeal or work on its audiences through its differences, but such a body evokes the traditional human body precisely because it alters it. That this is not a random side effect but integral to the workings of such depictions is evident in Chaney's choice of words, "the animalized human body," not the animal/human body or hybrid body. Indeed, Chaney is cautious of even using the term "hybridity" because it implies a relationship that lacks the coercion that the constant reification of the human represents (131). He notes, for example, the rarity of "a talking or magical quadruped that actually walks on four legs" (131–32), an observation that applies to the protagonists of *Sweet Tooth*. It is not that Gus fails to see himself in relation to nature or animals, but he is, at his core, a human, despite his radical alterity. However, his form allows for his estrangement from adults. Because his difference is legible through his body, his otherness becomes the defining element on which villains in the series choose to focus, rather than his humanity, and thus exploit him and his ilk. For readers, Gus's form may reinforce the dominance of the human body, but in the diegetic world in which he exists, his body is a grotesque form of otherness due to its hybridity, even if that hybridity is weighted toward his human elements.

Childhood Innocence

Part of the reason the hybrids are so sympathetic is the association of childhood with innocence. Lemire states, "*Sweet Tooth* was about childhood and innocence and the things that destroy them. Making the children animal/human hybrids added yet another level of innocence to it. What's more innocent than animals[?] They aren't good or evil. They just are[.] They are nature" (Lemire, email). While the hybridity of the animals has ramifications beyond innocence, innocence and its destruction are central themes of the narrative. The innocence of children to which Lemire refers is one of the dominant constructions of childhood in the Western world. However, Lemire's assertion that animals, as part of nature, represent innocence is interesting because it associates innocence with existence unconstrained by morality.[4] In this light, the innocence of nature can be maintained indefinitely because it is not only free from adult burdens and corruptions but from questions of good and evil entirely.

Lemire establishes the threat to innocence early on by evoking concerns over protecting children from strangers. Gus's father, Richard, seeks to completely shelter him from the outside world in the hopes of protecting him. Gus is raised in isolation because Richard fears Gus will be kidnapped for experimentation. At the beginning of the series, Gus, who has never interacted with anyone other than Richard, finds a candy bar and takes it. Richard, who is sick and dying, finds out and chastises Gus because candy is sometimes used to lure hybrids. "Where did you get this?!" Gus's father asks. Gus responds, "In the woods." Richard warns, "They'll try to trick you with these. . . . You have to be more careful. It's in me bad now . . . you know I'm going soon" (*Out of the Deep Woods* 15–16). This incident highlights Gus's sheltered upbringing and the limits of parental protection. Richard will soon die and leave Gus alone, and Richard's teachings cannot keep away others who would do Gus harm.

This initial connection in *Sweet Tooth* between candy and predators demonstrates how sometimes the protection of children and the maintenance of innocence are at odds, even though they are both part of the discourse surrounding childhood, and that the grotesque may reside within the liminal spaces of children's knowledge of the horrors of the world (Wanzo 140). The 1980s were the beginning of an intense period of anxiety over children and child safety, and middle-class children had less freedom of movement than children in previous decades (Fass, "The Child-Centered Family?" 14). Abduction was perhaps the most central issue of child safety on adults' minds at this time (Abate 409). Parents tried to warn children to be on their guard, even as they sought not to frighten their children. It was common practice when I grew up in the 1980s and early 1990s, and remains so today, to warn children not to accept candy from strangers or talk to strangers due to fears of adult predators luring children into their automobiles. Speaking of candy, persistent warnings also crop up every year relating to potentially harmful Halloween candy. Reporters warn parents that hostile adults might slip razor blades or other dangerous items or substances into candy. The paradox of these warnings is that when they are relayed to children, they destabilize the innocence of children in the hopes of protecting them. This is not to say that knowledge should neither be shared to protect children nor withheld until they might process it more effectively. Rather, it illustrates the tension between innocence and protection. By conditioning children to be on their guard, society also creates the conditions by which potential innocence gives way to awareness of the dangers of the world. This awareness undermines constructions of innocence because it entails knowledge of the world that is at odds with innocence unburdened by knowledge. As Rebekah Sheldon notes, "The task of managing innocence—contaminated by questioning, forbidding examination—generates a quest that can only spoil what it seeks to verify" (9–10).

Another way that the comic metaphorically represents the destruction of childhood innocence is through the disintegration of borders, which represent the inability of society to completely shelter children indefinitely. After Gus's father dies, Gus must leave the protection of his childhood home, a place where he already knew of certain dangers but was able to avoid them. Jepperd lies and offers to take Gus to a wilderness preserve where hybrids are kept safe. Gus takes a chance and goes with him. This moment of transition is exemplified in Gus's passing of the borders of his former home (figure 1.4).

Figure 1.4. Jeff Lemire. *Sweet Tooth, Vol. 1: In Captivity*, DC Comics, 2010, 40.

Despite being alone, Gus originally refuses to accompany Jepperd, so Jepperd starts to leave without him. The top half of the page shows Jepperd on the highway, saddling his horse, no cars in sight. The highway cuts through the image. The fence that keeps animals from crossing the highway and people from entering the forest is missing a section. Telephone poles are leaning and broken. Modern society has collapsed.[5] This section of the page shows the porous nature of the divide between worlds. The fence is ineffectual, and no figurative walls could prevent illness from claiming Gus's father. But this image also shows the encroachment of nature onto society, which the hybrids also represent. Despite the clear planting lines and hollowed spaces humans made, the trees surround the highway, and while the wooden telephone poles crumble, the trees stand erect. The lone tree, particularly, rises prominently above the graves of Gus's parents. These images metaphorically demonstrate that nature cannot be completely subjugated to civilization, in much the same way that civilizing influences cannot completely shelter children. Gus must leave behind Richard's legacy and the shelter he provided. Inset within the top right of the page are speech bubbles relaying Gus's thoughts. He recalls his happiness and his isolation. However, as Gus tells Jepperd, "I don't wanna be alone no more."

The top third of this page is structurally similar to the page where Jepperd leaves Gus at the compound (figure 1.5). A fence crosses this page diagonally. The compound's fence is certainly more secure than the highway fence and keeps hybrids *in* rather than hunters *out*. Yet the fence cannot protect against the plague, and Jepperd will eventually breach it. The difficulty maintaining borders and boundaries exemplifies how children, and others, cannot be sealed off from the outside world. It provides a metaphor for the impossibility of sheltering children from the outside world for extended periods; borders are unable to keep people either in or out. Roads and streets also serve as borders, especially for younger children. In this light, the crossing of the boundary of Gus's childhood home is not just about the movement into a more dangerous area because of the failure of the boundaries in keeping potential predators out. It is also about the failure of regulation and structure to guarantee safety. It was only a matter of time before Gus's cabin was discovered, regardless of the rules restricting Gus's movements. The implication of this is that the rules Gus's father initially put in place to protect Gus, like not to wander off or to take candy from strangers, carry short-term benefits, but they lack long-term viability because others do not

Figure 1.5. Jeff Lemire *Sweet Tooth, Vol. 1: In Captivity*, DC Comics, 2010, 124.

abide by Richard's rules or share his concerns. They will eventually invade his space. The necessity of protecting children and ability to transgress borders provide insight into the impossibility of keeping childhood separate from adult realities—in Gus's case, adult predators and the knowledge of death and destruction within the wider world.

Interest in children and spatial borders has historical precedent. Viviana Zelizer argues that around the turn of the twentieth century, children in the United States began being valued increasingly for their emotional worth rather than as economic contributors. She writes, "While in the nineteenth century, the market value of children was culturally acceptable, later the new normative ideal of the child as an exclusively emotional and affective asset precluded instrumental or fiscal considerations" (11). This shift involved changes in the way children were raised, as adults increasingly sheltered children. For example, concern over automobile accidents in cities led to familial regulations on children's activities:

> Saving child life meant changing the daily activities of city children, pushing them indoors into playrooms and schoolrooms or designing special "child" public spaces, such as playgrounds. Streets were not only physically danger-ous, but socially inadequate; the proper place for a "sacred" child was a pro-tected environment, segregated from adult activities. (52)

These motivations for protecting children's lives connect to the transgression of boundaries in *Sweet Tooth*. Sheltering children involves the structuring, or restructuring, of their environment. Children were pulled off the streets to protect them from cars and from people whom they might encounter outside, including adults (52). Not that all adults were unsavory, but children's lives were increasingly structured so their encounters with adults dwindled. The rise of forced schooling in the early twentieth century, which culminated dur-ing the Great Depression, helped reinforce this separation and played a role in creating an adolescent culture and life stage distinct from adults (Mintz 239).

Despite societal attempts to shelter children through the restructuring of their environment, children cannot be kept distinct from the rest of the world. Marina Warner argues, "Childhood doesn't occupy some sealed Eden or Neverland set apart from the grown-up world: our children can't be bet-ter than we are" (60). That Eden or Neverland cannot be sealed is indicative of the porous nature of borders. We cannot provide children with a world unfettered by sin or enlivened by perpetual youth. The metaphor of Eden, however, is more attainable than Warner gives it credit for, when we factor in the Fall. After all, we can initially protect children from the outside world. We just cannot maintain it. This is a moment where theory and practice may clash. Most parents probably do recognize that too much sheltering can be harmful to childhood. Yet the idea of the innocent child, for however long parents may reinforce it, is still a powerful symbol. In this light, Eden is the appropriate metaphor; it represents the innocence that can initially be preserved until children inevitably encounter knowledge and thus can no longer exist in their sheltered Eden. This is not to make the loss of innocence sound sinister; children simply grow up, sometimes sooner than some would prefer.

Not everyone agrees with the assertion of a disappearance of childhood innocence. Perry Nodelman believes that in light of the "increasingly repressive surveillance of and protectiveness toward children and of ongoing commodification of the cuteness of childhood innocence in the marketplace," the notion that "we are moving beyond our cultural commitment to the idea of childhood as a safe preserve" is unconvincing ("The Disappearing Childhood" 156). Nodelman is specifically critiquing handbooks on children's literature studies for downplaying the relationship "between children's literature, children, and childhood" ("The Disappearing Childhood" 156). While the texts I explore are not specifically aimed at children, I do want to address the idea that increased oversight and commodification of childhood innocence signifies, at least in part, an investment in such an ideal. When the sanctity of childhood innocence is threatened, there is a desire by some to retrench and protect it. There *is* a remarkable cultural investment in maintaining childhood innocence, but that's in part because people see childhood as increasingly under threat for a variety of reasons, including via commodification. Indeed, childhood innocence is commodifiable partly due to people's obsession over it, in addition to the current trend of selling consumers on nostalgia for their own childhoods. In this light, the relationship between childhood innocence and its destabilization is dialectical. As childhood innocence is threatened, some seek to further protect it, but this is a reaction to the threats, both real and perceived. Nodelman also reminds us that the idea of childhood innocence probably does keep many children safer from danger due to adults' policing of children "just like the people who live behind the walls of gated communities" ("Inventing Childhood" 15). But people in gated communities likely cannot stay within them forever, and dangers can always lurk within the community itself, as exclusive as it may be. This reinforces the idea that children cannot be sheltered as long as many would like, perhaps not even to adolescence for some, although perhaps longer for others, but also that eventually people must venture out beyond the gates, even if one is privileged enough to be able to have such a sheltered space as a home.

The inability to shelter children from the outside world echoes throughout *Sweet Tooth*, but the porous nature of borders is not the only way that the comics accomplish this. Before Jepperd betrays Gus, they encounter a run-down building where a couple preys on other human survivors and forces women into prostitution. Jepperd and Gus are initially unaware of the purpose of the building; they enter after seeing what appears to be a hybrid in a window. The hybrid turns out to be a teenage prostitute wearing animal ears. The ears facilitate the fantasy of having sex with a hybrid, which is a fantasy of child abuse. Other than Gus, who is approximately nine at this point, the oldest hybrids are only seven years old. No humans are younger than the hybrids, so the hybrids are the beings most imbued with perceived innocence and purity. James Kincaid argues that constructing childhood innocence simultaneously creates the desire in some adults to possess such innocence (*Child-Loving* 5). Kincaid's emphasis is on how childhood innocence leads to child sexual abuse, but more benign forms include adults who simply desire to have and raise innocent children of their own. The purity of the hybrid child carries additional connotations because of their immunity to the plague. Children are ideally uncontaminated from the adult world; hybrids are uncontaminated from sickness. In fact, Richard sees Gus as a "New Adam" who will lead a "new race . . . forever innocent and pure" (*In Captivity* 113).

The first clear image of the prostitute, Becky, reinforces the ways in which innocence and purity are a façade, a construction easily undermined (figure 1.6). Becky is positioned slightly to the left of center, and her eyeline gives the impression she is looking at the reader. Like Gus's peeping over Jepperd's shoulder, the reader peeps over Gus to see Becky. This positioning highlights the seedy nature of the situation in which Gus and Jepperd find themselves, particularly in that the reader is, at this moment, a voyeur seeing something both private and upsetting. Despite Becky's pink makeup and negligee, which reinforce her sexuality, she appears distant. Her bunny ears look realistic, but they are fake, a mockery of Gus's antlers. The juxtaposition of Becky and Gus is highlighted by their mirroring positions. Becky, however, at fifteen, has long

Figure 1.6. Jeff Lemire. *Sweet Tooth, Vol. 1: In Captivity*, DC Comics, 2010, 77.

ago lost her innocence despite her adolescent age. She is a dark harbinger of one of the ways hybrids might be exploited, of youth forced into a system of exploitation. The dingy room, with muck on the bed and a broken spring protruding, emphasizes the artificiality of this pretend innocence. The walls are crumbling and the landscape picture is askew, subtly reinforcing how nature and society are both off-kilter.

This moment helps demonstrate the impossibility of maintaining childhood innocence, but it also connects to commodification. To her pimp, Becky is valuable solely for her body's ability to generate income. While Becky is not as young as Gus, she is still an adolescent controlled by an adult. It is made clear that Becky and the women in the house are forced to be there. By depicting Becky with the bunny ears (a nod to the role *Playboy* plays in commodifying female bodies), Becky's commodification evokes the hybrids. Becky is sexually commodified; the hybrids are scientifically commodified. Both are valuable because of their youth and their closeness to innocence and purity (even though this pairing is not tenable). Some hybrids are not aligned with innocence and its loss but are instead associated more with chaotic or feral depictions, such as some canine/human children who consume flesh. But even these siblings are harnessed and used as tools by their father. They are innocent in the sense that they are acting within their nature. But I would argue that *Sweet Tooth* is not arguing that there is only one construction of childhood, that of innocence, but rather that children are punished for issues of which they are innocent. The series reasserts the desire for childhood to be protected, sheltered from the dangers that adults can pose to children and childhood by treating them as commodities. Barring a prolonged period of sheltered innocence, children at least deserve to be safe and free of the violence and dehumanization that certain adults inflict upon them.

Exploitation

Gus and the children's grotesque hybridity creates provocative tensions that speak to larger social questions and concerns about childhood. There is a clash between what society may or may not condone that becomes complicated by the hybrid nature of the children. In one panel, for example, Gus and five other hybrid children are caged and waiting for their captors to return (figure 1.7). The caging of animals is troubling but widely accepted in the

Figure 1.7. Jeff Lemire. *Sweet Tooth, Vol. 2: Out of the Deep Woods*, DC Comics, 2010, 21.

United States. However, the caging of children is clearly perverse, even if it is currently the policy of the United States government. When Gus introduces himself to the rest of the hybrids, Wendy, the human/pig hybrid, calls the other hybrids "ignorants" because they cannot effectively communicate (*In Captivity* 19). That some of these child characters are incapable of language begs consideration of when the dehumanization of others' bodies is acceptable. For some, what separates humans from other animals is intellect, which can be conveyed through speech or other forms of communication. Yet even the hybrids who can effectively communicate are denied their humanity

Figure 1.8. Jeff Lemire. *Sweet Tooth, Vol. 2: Out of the Deep Woods*, DC Comics, 2010, 44.

because their victimizers are not interested in communication. One particularly evocative image of the dehumanization that hybrids experience depicts a horse/human hybrid on an operating table in the compound (figure 1.8). His or her chest cavity is ripped open, and blood is sprayed throughout the room. This panel would be shocking if the hybrid had no human attributes, but adding human elements, like the human-like body and the positioning of the hybrid on his back, makes the image even more upsetting. What strikes the reader as grotesque about this panel is not the hybrid, but the hybrid's victimization. The panel is especially disturbing because the mutilated body is out in the open and blood is splattered across the floor and walls. These elements reveal the butchery underneath the clinical setting of the tiled room and dissection table, an artifice meant to add an air of legitimacy to the experimentation taking place on the hybrids. Lemire intended for this butchery to shock and contrast with Gus's personality and innocence (email).

The hybrids' exploitation is complicated by their uncertain ontological status. Their value is tied up in their immunity to the plague ravaging the adult populations. While their bodies and behaviors constantly reify the human form, for the antagonists, their bodies provide a distancing effect whereby they can be treated as nonhuman. Yet while the legal institutions that might have advocated for them have crumbled into the ruins of the new world, they remain the heirs of humanity. *Sweet Tooth* leaves little doubt that the exploitation of the hybrids is morally reprehensible. At the same time, their exploitation opens up space for consideration of readers' own complicity in the exploitation of others. People want to reject exploitation but also accept or ignore it, which can make people complicit via their inaction.

The comic books interrogate readers' complicity by utilizing direct address. One example of this is the earlier image of Becky looking at Jepperd and Gus but also at the reader. Another example is the previously mentioned caged hybrids, all facing Gus, who also face the reader, as if challenging the reader regarding his or her own complicity in what is transpiring. Of course, the reader is an observer and has no power over the narrative; at the same time, however, the reader's enjoyment of the narrative is predicated on the exploitation of the hybrids.[6] The hybrids' persecution heightens the satisfaction of their escape. When Gus is subsequently questioned by Dr. Singh, the scientist running the experiments, the comic book depicts a series of mostly alternating point-of-view panels as the characters take turns speaking, although Singh's dialogue intrudes into Gus's panel in the second row (figure 1.9).[7] In the last row of panels, however, Singh has the first two panels, and Gus has the last one. The break in the alternating images extends Singh's narrative space as he continues articulating his reasoning for why he is not a "bad man" (*In Captivity* 65). Singh asserts, "We are the only semblance of order left in this world. And I know it's hard to understand . . . but the things we do here . . . we are humanity's last hope." Gus rejects Singh's rationalization: "You cut up animal kids . . . I saw it! You think you're doing good, but you're just a sinner . . . the worst sinner" (65). Gus's response is part of a panel where Gus is drawn directly facing the reader and pointing his finger in accusation. The alternating panels are broken so that Gus's rejection is in the final, rather than the middle, panel. This ends the page in rebuttal and subtly reinforces Gus's stance over Singh's. The use of "you" in Gus's accusation, combined with the pointed finger, further confronts the reader. Gus's moral position is all the more powerful because of the tag on his ear, which catalogs him as an object of experimentation and study.

Lemire notes that direct address was not his intent here but an effect of the POV. Yet Lemire describes his art as "expressive" and meant to capture "emotional truth." This may contribute to the feeling of being directly addressed (email). Singh does not give up rationalizing his behavior: he explains that

Figure 1.9. Jeff Lemire. *Sweet Tooth, Vol. 2: Out of the Deep Woods*, DC Comics, 2010, 65.

he has done horrible things, but that "we must keep trying" because "soon we'll be gone . . . all of us." Gus responds, "Not me. . . . Not us animal kids" (*In Captivity* 66). Gus's response is incisive. By carving up hybrids and pregnant women, these adults are engaging in shortsighted thinking that forestalls future generations and terrorizes current populations.[8]

For many people, harming others requires some sort of estrangement. Singh excludes Gus from his vision of collective humanity—Gus is not included in Singh's "us"—because Singh does not consider him fully human. It is striking, then, that Gus's critique takes up Singh's rhetoric of difference. By reminding Singh that the "animal kids" will survive, Gus's rebuttal undermines Singh's rationale on two registers. Metaphorically, it rejects short-term ideologies that sacrifice futurity for the sake of the present by announcing that the desires of one generation are not always in line with the desires of subsequent ones; literally, it also reorients the rationale for exploiting hybrids—that they are different—as an argument for not exploiting hybrids: the problems of the humans are not the problems of the hybrids. The term "animal kids" is also deceptively complicated. The hybrids are not the children of animals, and their appearance is not exactly that of animals. If anything, the protagonist hybrids are closer to humans than animals, yet nonhuman animals shouldn't be treated in such a way either.

Even when Gus uses a clear term, "animal kids," to describe himself and his peers, it still cannot help but convey the uncertain ontological status of the hybrids. The hybrids are not always depicted as humans who happen to have some of the physical features of animals. Some are almost exclusively animal, like a bird/human hybrid and dog/human hybrids, and there is Bobby, a groundhog hybrid who feels the need to hibernate in the winter. Yet in the major cases, Gus and Wendy, the hybrids are shown to be different from humans physically, but not intellectually or emotionally, and this humanity is present in Bobby as well. Even animalistic hybrids or nonhuman animals do not deserve mistreatment. The ability of adults to see children as nonhuman objects of study and experimentation arises from some adults' objectification and is aided by the grotesque representations of the hybrids, but it also represents the ways society exploits children and others in contemporary society. Treating humans as objects is itself a grotesque hybridization that often benefits the economic elite at the expense of lower classes.

The experimentation on the hybrids is a perverse continuation of Western society's experimentation on not just animals, but humans who have been treated as such due to certain conditions, disorders, or situations. A Western history of exploitation is in large part a history of commodifying the marginalized, and the United States has an abject history involving experimentation on those who lack the power to speak for themselves, literally and metaphorically.

Mike Stobbe details some of this history in an Associated Press article preceding a 2011 biomedical ethics commission. In his abbreviated history, Stobbe notes experimentation on United States prisoners increased dramatically in the 1940s and 1950s as the pharmaceutical and health care industries grew. These experiments were driven by economic considerations: "In 1973, pharmaceutical industry officials acknowledged they were using prisoners for testing because they were cheaper than chimpanzees" (np). Backlash in the 1970s over the use of powerless populations in experiments led to their decline.

Examples of the types of experiments being conducted on humans kept separate from mainstream society abound. American scientists conducting a study from 1946 to 1948 at a mental hospital in Guatemala "infected prisoners and patients . . . with syphilis . . . to test whether penicillin could prevent some sexually transmitted diseases" (np). Stobbe also notes that from 1963 to 1966, administrators of one study at the Willowbrook State School infected children who had intellectual disabilities with hepatitis to test a potential cure. Professionals administering these tests may feel the benefits outweigh the risks. Saul Krugman, who was involved in the Willowbrook hepatitis study, defends it. He notes they obtained permission from parents and that most of the child subjects would have contracted the virus anyway in the course of their stay. He also asserts that those who were infected were kept separate from the general population and thus avoided contracting other viruses that were present in the population. He writes, "The fact that the children were mentally retarded was relevant only to the extent that society placed them in an institution where hepatitis was prevalent. The primary objective of our studies was to protect the children and employees while acquiring new knowledge in the process" (160). Even if one accepts Krugman's rationale, the tests were still only administered on vulnerable populations. Were the children not vulnerable already, they would never have been there. Furthermore, it is apparent that not everyone was concerned for their test subjects. Faculty members in the dermatology department of the University of Pennsylvania Medical School, including Dr. Albert Kligman, had a "cavalier attitude toward using institutionalized groups as research subjects" and would sometimes joke about them (Hornblum 35). Dr. Kligman was the force behind experiments on prisoners in Holmesburg Prison from the 1950s to the 1970s. Upon entering the prison for the first time, he recalls, "All I saw before me were acres of skin. It was like a farmer seeing a fertile field for the first time" (Hornblum 37). The emphasis on people's skin rather than their personhood and the comparison to farming, where soil is tilled (sometimes violently), situates the prisoners as objects and resources to be used for the sake of others. This figuration of the vulnerable as resources to be exploited until they are no longer useful connects to the use of the hybrid children in *Sweet Tooth*.

Despite the horrific treatment of the hybrids, the series offers a hopeful ending. Earlier, I noted the transformative element of the grotesque. This transformative aspect eventually extends to society itself. In the end, traditional humanity gives way to hybridity. At the end of human society, the hybrids escape their exploitation. They establish a haven where hybrids exist peacefully with the dwindling number of humans. Doctor Singh lives among them and teaches the children of the hybrid humans. These youths are no more or less hybrid, no closer to a completed transformation to an animal state or return to a human one than previous hybrids.[9]

The conclusion resolves contemporary anxieties over the exploitation of children. The new hybrid community does not appear to exploit any subset of their community on behalf of another subset (although there is an initial argument over whether remaining humans should be killed or integrated). *Sweet Tooth* demonstrates that a society sacrificing its children for the benefit of adults is a society on the brink of destruction. Society can be redeemed, however, when it reevaluates its relationship between generations. This reevaluation is made possible in *Sweet Tooth* because of the hybrid's grotesque bodies. The animal/human hybrids exist along a spectrum of alterity that challenges one's ability to classify what it means to be human. By highlighting humanity in the midst of dehumanizing characterizations, *Sweet Tooth* challenges processes of dehumanization. The children are grotesque yet remain children, and while their grotesque nature may repulse adult characters, for the readers, the grotesque elements beg consideration of their altered states even if they ultimately reaffirm the human.

Biopolitics and *The Girl with All the Gifts*

Michel Foucault defines biopolitics as "the attempt, starting from the eighteenth century, to rationalize the problems posed to governmental practice by phenomena characteristic of a set of living beings forming a population: health, hygiene, birthrate, life expectancy, race" (317). For example, a nation may institute policies to raise birth rates as a means of preparing for economic growth over generations. Or it may imprison those who refuse to conform to its laws or institutions. Foucault understand biopolitics and liberalism as intertwined (317), and Michel Senellart, who edited Foucault's *The Birth of Biopolitics*, states, "Liberty and security: it is the procedures of control and forms of state intervention required by this double exigency that constitute the paradox of liberalism" (329). Biopolitics is, in part, the attempt to reconcile or at least navigate this paradox. The state curtails liberty for the sake of security or at least the perception of security, if not the reality. The state asserts that such restrictions on individual liberty benefit its citizenry, and there are examples of where this is the case, but it is more accurate to state that restrictions on individual liberty are for the benefit of those running the state, not necessarily its citizens, though these categories can overlap. What is significant about biopolitics is that it highlights the fact that countries have histories of managing populations, populations often, though not always, within their borders, and such biopolitical management is often done in the name of the citizens, but the reality is that it is instead often done at the expense of the citizens. The assertion in *Sweet Tooth* that hybrid children and pregnant women can be experimented upon for the benefit of those adults in positions of power is an assertion of biopolitical supremacy.

This abuse is aided by the dehumanization of the hybrids, and while the hybrids are physically different, anyone can be dehumanized. Carey Wolfe argues,

> To live under biopolitics is to live in a situation in which we are all always already (potential) "animals" before the law—not just nonhuman animals according to zoological classification, but any group of living beings that is so framed. Here, the distinction "human/animal"—as the history of slavery, colonialism, and imperialism well shows—is a discursive resource, not a zoological designation. (10)

Wolfe goes on to discuss the lack of attention paid to nonhuman animals, but this quotation is also helpful in thinking about the hybrid children. For Wolfe, animalization is used to dehumanize others by casting them as nonhuman, which is also what is happening with the hybrid children, whose humanity is rejected due to their ontological differences. The dehumanization of the hybrids is a discursive tool that enables those in power to experiment on and sacrifice hybrid children even though these children were conceived by human parents. Humans maintain an attitude of sovereignty over others, even as their world slips away. In fact, this slippage causes humans to cling even tighter to what little authority they still have.

The exploitation of children by adults is often biopolitical in that those who execute or sanction it accept the exploitation as politically or economically worthwhile or at least believe stopping the exploitation is not worth the effort and/or capital. In *Sweet Tooth*, the humans' willingness to experiment on hybrid children derives from what they perceive to be a biopolitical authority. The exploitation is specifically enacted by those who claim military and scientific imperatives in the face of societal collapse. This cling to institutional legitimacy does not validate the behavior, but it seems to allow characters the perception that it does. The assertion of institutional superiority and the claim to work on behalf of survivors is what gives the villains in *Sweet Tooth* a biopolitical slant. The brief period Gus spends inside the compound speaks to this authority, but the latter half of the novel is about evading the villains, and so the biopolitical angle gets relegated to the background in some respects, even as it pervades the narrative.

This biopolitical slant is not unique to *Sweet Tooth*. M. R. Carey's *The Girl with All the Gifts*, despite its differences, is quite similar to *Sweet Tooth*. Both are about hybrid children who are experimented upon by adults claiming military and scientific authority in a misguided attempt to save older generations. Those children who are less able to effectively communicate are depicted as chaotic, but they also remain innocent of causing the zombie infestation and do not deserve to be sacrificed due to it. Both narratives also imagine a world that must give way to new conceptions of humanity. In doing so, these texts reject biopolitical assertions of power over others. Furthermore, *The Girl with All the Gifts* foregrounds the biopolitical elements of the narrative by pairing the child protagonist with her military and scientific overseers throughout the novel.

The novel is set in a postapocalyptic England where zombies created by a contagious fungal infection run rampant. The surviving humans are driven out of most of England and into zones they are able to control. Some adult humans experiment on hybrid zombie/human children in the hopes that they can find and create a cure. Zombies are often understood as metaphorical representations of larger societal issues; perhaps the most popular reading, based on George Romero's *Dawn of the Dead*, understands zombies as emblematic of rampant, unthinking consumption and consumerism. However, Evan Calder Williams argues that zombies are radical metaphors in that they work against capitalist forms of ownership (104). *The Girl with All the Gifts*' rejection of ownership is not specifically about consumerist practices, but rather the ownership or control of bodies. This is because the novel, like *Sweet Tooth*, focuses on hybrid children. The adults who experiment on these children do so with the imprimatur of the military and scientific remnants of society, who have formed a sort of government dominated by the military. This project contends that the adults' experimentation on the hybrid children, as in *Sweet Tooth*, envisions a sort of last-ditch biopolitical program that sacrifices those who embody a new conception of humanity for the sake of a status quo that is no longer tenable. This has catastrophic effects as one of these children escapes and punishes the adults for their crimes against the hybrids.

In the novel, humans have been increasingly hedged in by hungries for two decades. Hungries are created by exposure to a fungal parasite that spreads through blood and saliva. Once infected, the fungus grows and weaves threads into a person's brain and throughout their body, and the parasite propagates itself by forcing the hijacked body to attack and infect others. There also exists a second generation of hungries, born of women who become hungries while they were pregnant. These children are born with the fungus, but in the second generation, the fungus lives in a symbiotic relationship with the host rather than a parasitic one. For example, it does not damage and destroy the brains of the second generation, like it does when the fungus is spread through an attack. As a result, these posthuman children are driven by the same hunger, but they are also capable of thinking, learning, and communicating. Humans at a military compound some distance away from Beacon, the human base, experiment on these children. They lock them in cells and only cart them out in restraints to feed and teach them. Meanwhile, some of these children are removed and vivisected in the hope of finding a cure for the infection. The hybrids are dangerous to the humans in that they will attack them if they smell them, but humans have developed a compound that blocks their scent from hybrids and hungries, although it needs to be reapplied.

Sergeant Parks, the ranking military official at the compound, does not initially see any humanity in the hybrid children. He has the following exchange with one of their teachers, Helen Justineau: "'Not everyone who looks human is human,' he says. 'No,' Miss Justineau agrees. 'I'm with you on that one'" (14). What is unsaid is that she agrees not because she thinks the children nonhuman but because she rejects the inhumane treatment of the children by Parks and others. This tension between treating the main hybrid character, Melanie, as a human and/or a threat carries throughout the novel. Melanie is a second-generation hungry and a ten-year-old genius. She demonstrates restraint throughout the novel and is able to manage her condition so as not to attack those she cares about. She is drawn to Helen because Helen is the only person who has ever shown her affection.

Early in the story, the military compound is attacked, and a group of characters is forced to flee south and hope to make it to Beacon. This group includes Melanie and Helen Justineau. It also includes Dr. Caldwell and Sergeant Parks, who represent the scientific and military communities and see the children as inhuman monsters, and a soldier named Gallagher. Justineau wants to bring Melanie with them because she does not want to leave the child alone to die. Dr. Caldwell wants to bring the child along because of Melanie's perceived importance to Caldwell's research, the rest of which was destroyed when their base fell.

Those running Beacon, and by extension Dr. Caldwell, clearly believe they have the moral authority to guide and protect themselves and the humans under their control and protection from hungries and other humans who challenge their authority. This in itself seems perfectly reasonable. But the humans sacrifice their moral and institutional legitimacy through their experimentation on the second-generation hungries. These hybrid children represent a posthuman condition whereby they have adapted to the changing environment. Instead of taking samples in nonviolent ways or from dead hybrids, Caldwell saws open their heads and removes their brains, without even rendering them unconscious or giving them anesthetic. This is because Dr. Caldwell and others in power refuse to see the hybrids as human, and Caldwell refuses to "waste" limited resources on them.

Of course, those exerting authority over others do not see their actions as illegitimate. If anything, they assert that the dire circumstances facing what is left of society necessitate such actions. Dr. Caldwell argues that her experiments are imperative because they are about survival. As she explains, through these experiments, she hopes to help develop "some hope for a future. Some way out of this mess" (46). But her inability to imagine some sort of collaboration with the hybrids,[10] a way to test them without murdering them, or even a future that isn't an attempt to recreate the past as best she can, reveals that for Caldwell, the future is a nostalgic mirage, aimed at returning humans to their past superiority over their environment. To truly adapt to a new world would mean giving up their viselike grip on the past and facilitating the transition to a posthuman conception of the future. While many postapocalyptic narratives explore what lengths people are willing to go to protect what they hold dear, this logic is often used by characters to whitewash violent and totalitarian impulses.

The character who best embodies the future is Melanie, of course, as both child and posthuman. Melanie works together with the adult humans to help ensure the survival of their group, even as some continue to look down on her. Upon encountering a group of feral, second-generation hungries, Melanie recognizes that the future that adults envision is not a future for the children, so she forcefully asserts her vision of a new world. When the initial group of survivors travel through London, they encounter hungries within whom the fungal infection is so advanced that it has sprouted from their decomposed bodies. They first encounter "a hungry, lying full length on the ground. . . . Its chest . . . forced open from within by . . . a white column, at least six feet high, flaring at the top into a sort of round pillow things with fluted edges—and with bulbous growths on its sides like blisters" (250). These columns are fruiting, and the growths contain spores that, if released into the atmosphere, could infect surviving humans around the globe, but the growths are tough to open. Later, they come upon a forest of these that is forty feet high and goes on for miles. This forest becomes a tool for Melanie to help secure the future of the second-generation hungries.

Dr. Caldwell, on her deathbed, explains her research, including the logistics of the columns, to Melanie with the hope that Melanie will communicate this to the adults at Beacon when they arrive. Instead, Melanie later convinces a recently infected Sergeant Parks to burn the forest of fungal spores without telling him why. When Parks realizes that by burning the forest, he's released the fungal spores rather than destroyed them, he asks Melanie why she had him do it. Melanie tells him it is because of the children. The plague will become its own cure by turning all remaining humans into hungries who will eventually be overtaken by the next stage of the fungal infection as it transitions from a reliance on human hosts to forests of fruiting bodies. Melanie shows remorse over the infection of the remaining humans, but she justifies it because "their children will be okay and they'll be the ones who live and grow up and have children of their own and make a new world" (399). But this can only be achieved if adults "*let* them grow up" instead of killing them (399). She ends by stating, "[T]hen the children will grow up, and they won't be the old kind of people but they won't be hungries either. . . . They'll be the *next* people. The ones who make everything okay again" (399). The novel then ends with Justineau exiting a mobile laboratory they have found. She is enclosed in a protective suit, beginning to teach a lesson to the feral children Melanie has gathered together. Presumably, the best aspects of human contributions to the world, like knowledge and culture, will remain. This liberal arts education will presumably transform the lives of the feral hybrid children as they will be given the cultural tools to recreate society but in a more sustainable fashion. The novel's ending is an emancipatory gesture meant to break clean with abusive and shortsighted ancestors for the sake of future prosperity. Kimberly Hurd Hale and Erin A. Dolgoy find Melanie's decision to be justifiable. It's true not all humans deserve to be infected, but Melanie is acting out of necessity to save herself and those like her (357).

The Girl with All the Gifts opens up space to consider the ways in which biopolitical policies that rationalize violence and destruction are not legitimate, and it argues that there needs to be a drastic reconfiguration of power and of whom power serves. Such a reconfiguration should actively privilege the needs of future generations so that society is always in a state of improvement. This emphasis on long-term prosperity would paradoxically improve life for many in the present because of its emphasis on creating a just and healthy world. The children in the novel are applying a similar logic to what the adult humans use to justify harming the posthuman children but only after it is made clear that most adults do not see a place among them for the posthuman children. While the sequel walks back some of the finality of the first novel's final gesture, it is no less significant that Melanie is willing to kill off almost all adults to save all hybrid children.

The hungry children can be read as symbolically representative of exploited children today, but the emphasis on the well-being of children and future generations is not meant as a conservative argument that people and spaces must be censored to make all of society appear child-friendly. Not all spaces need include children and what is appropriate for children and adolescents of various ages is contested. Rather, I mean that biopolitical support must be extended to ensure that vulnerable populations like children, and by extension any and every vulnerable population, be given the protection and resources they need to thrive.

Conclusion

In her article on the fictional depiction of children in zombie apocalypses, Lisa Nevárez notes, "Theoretically, were they to be protected, in the world of the zombie apocalypse, children should be at the frontlines of the new world order. They are malleable, and without a strong or *any* recollection of the destroyed world, can forge ahead and craft a new existence and society" (89). This insightful observation is deceptively simple. Of course children are often the most capable of adapting to new societal figurations because former societal structures are less engrained in them. Yet as Nevárez correctly observes, theory does not always match practice in such narratives. Children in these narratives are often unable to defend themselves or survive the mental trauma of what they encounter during and after catastrophe. *The Girl with All the Gifts* evokes this idea when Helen Justineau considers dead children:

> She thinks about all the children in the world who ever died without growing up. There must have been billions of them. Hecatombs of children, apocalypses, genocides of them. In every war, every famine, thrown to the wall. Too small to protect themselves, too innocent to get out of the way. Killed by madmen, perverts, judges, soldiers, random passers-by, friends and neighbours, their own parents. By stupid chance or ruthless edict. (152)

Both *Sweet Tooth* and *The Girl with All the Gifts* are narratives where children overcome "stupid chance [and] ruthless edict" to survive and even thrive. They fight for worlds that are different and more sustainable after an apocalyptic event, and in both instances, their primary antagonists are old-guard adults so caught up in eradicating what plagues them that they also eviscerate the future as embodied in children.

The new worlds both texts establish are not as radically altered as one might imagine a new society to be. They still look very similar to previous conceptions of society. In addition, both involve feral children, more akin to animals and/or lacking the civilizing influence of culture, who represent a more total collapse of society or a drastically different future. But both narratives choose not to center on the feral children and instead pin their hopes on the more recognizably human child innocent of what they are punished for, an ennobling figure who represents new hope. This new hope comes in the form of an alternative to adults unwilling to release their viselike grip on their current course, which is always an attempt to maintain or return to the status quo for the benefit of the adults, not an attempt to guide the world in a new, brighter direction. In both texts, adults seek to turn children into currency for their own purposes, but children reassert themselves as individuals who deserve to exist outside the bounds of such a corrupt market.

CHAPTER 2

"I'm Not an Animal"

Grotesque Description and Chaotic Children
in *The Power* and *The Flame Alphabet*

Introduction

The previous chapter focused on narratives with protagonists who are grotesque and, despite the inclusion of wild or chaotic depictions of children,
emphasize the characters' innocence and its loss before re-establishing a safe
and stable society. This chapter focuses on two novels with adolescents who
embrace the chaotic elements within themselves: Naomi Alderman's *The
Power* and Ben Marcus's *The Flame Alphabet*. The youths in these texts are
innocent in the sense that they are not responsible for what plagues adults,
whether it be a literal plague or the fears adults have, but the novels in this
chapter choose not to emphasize or linger on that innocence. Rather, they
highlight the unpredictable nature of adolescence that some overacting adults
fear, as well as the fact that adults themselves can be a danger to children
and adolescents and vice versa. This shift in emphasis resides in part on the
nature of adolescence compared to childhood. Adolescents have had more
time to lose their innocence, even though chaotic conceptions of childhood
do account for young children, even infants. In one sense, the chaotic youths
of these texts are not necessarily opposed to an innocent construction of
childhood. Instead, they have grown out of it. Their age and experience make

innocence increasingly impossible to maintain. As a result, the subsequent texts highlight fears over unrestrained and unrepressed adolescents.

The first novel this chapter takes up, *The Power*, involves adolescents who become threatening to patriarchal power structures as they develop new powers and adults who behave grotesquely as they seek to commodify the adolescents. This sets the stage for the chapter's emphasis on chaotic depictions of youth. Then the chapter takes up Ben Marcus's *The Flame Alphabet*. This continues the focus on chaotic children, but it extends the argument of the chapter in two ways. It associates the grotesque with language and metaphor, and it highlights the grotesque slippage between the categories of victim and victimizer.

The central conceit of *The Power*, Naomi Alderman's electrifying exploration of gender and power, is that adolescent girls develop the ability to channel electricity from a skein near their collar bone. This ability gives girls a source of elemental power that allows them new opportunities to both protect themselves from violence and inflict it on others. Girls can also awaken the power in adult women. This upends traditional gender roles in violent ways. The novel includes adult authority figures commodifying the power, eventually at the expense of those who possess it. While the novel does not emphasize the chaotic child throughout the text, it does show that the power leads to frenzied and violent, even animalistic, attacks, including episodes of sexual assault against men.

These scenarios are meant as a commentary on the ways in which women and girls are required to navigate a society that fails to protect them from male objectification and assault. As soon as the power arrives, instances of gendered violence abound, and it is my contention that these moments coincide with animalistic depictions of children and adolescents. Ultimately, this critiques men and boys who behave in such ways, as well as the higher value society seems to place on men. But in the context of this chapter, it connects to a wider theme of animalistic portrayals of children and adolescents who are different. Almost immediately upon the arrival of the power, there are concerns for boys' safety. Boys and girls are separated at school; boys are told not to travel alone or go too far; school buses are segregated by gender. A woman interviewed on TV explains, "I saw a girl in the park doing that to a boy for no reason, he was bleeding from the eyes. The *eyes*. Once you've seen that happen, no mom would let her boys out of her sight" (23). The girls also fight with one another: "There have been injuries and accidents; one girl has been struck blind by another. The teachers are afraid" (23). There are also calls to lock up these girls, who are mostly about fifteen at this point. The references to fighting, scared teachers, and calls for imprisonment paint a portrait of a group of adolescents run amok and inciting fear. The hysteria over these kids is also an overreaction, but it contributes to the sense that these young women are uncontrollable and unmanageable due to their power and inability or unwillingness to control it. Later, three young women sexually assault a brother of one of the main characters, Roxy. They sodomize him with jolts of electricity, which causes excruciating pain even as it keeps him sexually aroused. After the assault, Roxy is asked to retaliate: "Roxy knows why they haven't called Bernie [their father and a mobster] home. He'd hate Ricky for this, even if he tried not to. This is not what happens to a man. Except now it is" (218). This moment gets at the gendered expectations society has for violence: that men are more likely to commit it and women to experience it. But despite concerns over the newfound power, adult authority figures seek to benefit from it.

In the early stages of the discovery of the power, an American politician named Margot, whose own power has been inadvertently awakened by her daughter, proposes training the girls to use the power effectively and turns them into a private military force. Margot parlays this military force into increasing political influence and ascendance. The military force is mostly relegated to the background of the novel, so even though Margot benefits from the adolescents and their power, this example lacks the severity of, for instance, *Elephantmen*, which I will turn to in a later chapter. But this is an example of how a power initially appearing in adolescents is used as an opportunity for others.

The more unsettling example, however, comes from Bernie Monke. His daughter Roxy has larger reservoirs of power than most and is one of the mightiest executors of her newfound capabilities. Early on, Bernie sees potential for profit. The text reads, "All over the world people are going crazy about this thing, but a few people always look at anything and go, 'Where's the profit in this, and where's the advantage?'" (53). Bernie first takes advantage of the situation by having a drug developed that heightens the impact of the power, which he and Roxy sell. However, his desire for profit does not stop there. He has men ambush Roxy and surgically remove her skein. Roxy escapes, but her skein is implanted into her brother Darrell. Bernie tells Darrell, "And if we can get it to work on you, this operation, think of who we couldn't sell it to. Chinese, the Russians, anyone with a prison population. Skein transplants ... everyone's going to be doing it" (288). Bernie removed his own daughter's organ because he believed it to be commodifiable. They will sell it to governments to facilitate the violent repression of their citizens. Darrell's response, "We'll make a killing, Dad" (288), refers to the obscene profit they could make, but the dark underside of Darrell's response is it would likely involve the actual killing of young women to harness the power and further killing by those who purchase the power. Roxy only survives because she escapes, not due to any largesse on the part of her captors.

Though the basic premises are not reminiscent of each other, *The Power* and Ben Marcus's *The Flame Alphabet* have striking similarities. Both explore worlds where power structures are upended by the explosive appearance of new powers that first surface in children and adolescents. Both involve adults' attempts to commodify their children. Both explore power dynamics between youths and adults. Both also include chaotic depictions of children. But whereas *The Power*'s use of the grotesque centers on the grotesque behavior of people in power or seeking power and some initial feelings of adolescent difference, *The Flame Alphabet* leans more heavily into the chaotic depictions, and it uses the grotesque as an aesthetic throughout the text. In doing so, it marks the grotesque's capacity to reside in language.

The Flame Alphabet

The Flame Alphabet takes place in a world where language becomes toxic to adults. The language plague is monstrous: it breaks down a person's body, causing an "intolerable squeezing in the chest and the hips" and an unyielding lethargy (4). Tongues harden and faces become "slightly smaller" (22). Bodies eventually decompose into pillars of salt. The poisonous language is first attributed solely to children because of their immunity to the disease, but eventually, the plague is understood to encompass all spoken and written communication, no matter who produces it. The novel is divided into three parts, all of them from the narrator Sam's perspective. In the first part, Sam recounts the plague's onset and the disconnect between himself and his daughter. The second part explores Sam's time at a compound where adults experiment to come up with new ways of communicating and counteracting the devastating effects of the plague. These tests are conducted on children and other adults. The third part follows Sam, now outside the compound, as he seeks to reunite with his family.

The novel highlights language, so it is appropriate that critical reviews of the novel, while mixed, all address Marcus's imaginative prose to a greater or lesser degree. The *New York Times* review calls Marcus's sentences "excessive" (Lennon np); *NPR*'s review agrees, calling entire sections "superfluous" (Diamond np). These negative comments come after disclaimers that stylistic prowess is generally one of Marcus's strengths. The *Guardian* review, on the other hand, praises the "cold beauty of [his] prose" (Lezard np); and the review from the *Los Angeles Times* asserts, "[T]here are rich pleasures in Marcus's words" and that Marcus is "wildly inventive in his imagery" (Barton np). The emphasis on Marcus's vivid prose is in line with his categorization as an experimental writer. In a nonfiction article, Marcus carves out a place for experimental fiction amid the dominance of literary realism by emphasizing experimental fiction's capacity to challenge readers and stimulate critical thinking ("Why Experimental Fiction"). Thus, it is no surprise that critics also note the difficulty of interpreting *The Flame Alphabet*. There are "so many arresting yet confounding details that the reader is left to puzzle over their meaning" (Barton np). The "allegory or message . . . never becomes clear" (Diamond np). The novel is "laden with metaphor; everything might mean something, but nothing is certain" (Lennon np); It "both invites and strongly resists allegorical interpretation" (Lezard np). The reason for this interpretive quagmire is Marcus's use of the grotesque.

Mikhail Bakhtin argues that grotesque bodies transcend their normative limits. This is why the grotesque is often concerned with "apertures or convexities, or on various ramifications and offshoots" (26). It "ignores the impenetrable surface that closes and limits the body as a separate and completed phenomenon" (318). *The Flame Alphabet*'s plague exemplifies this tendency, as it primarily spreads from the mouth and enters through the ears. For Bakhtin, the ability of the grotesque to exceed boundaries has the potential for renewal, but Marcus turns this on its head. Instead of renewal, the grotesque leads to debilitating deterioration. Marcus's grotesque imagery provides the diegetic space where abstract concepts are imprinted onto physical bodies, transforming them. Marcus's application of the grotesque involves an apprehensive approach, where grotesque figures may be feared because of their disruptive potential. Yet these grotesque transformations mark both victims and victimizers, as Sam and his ilk eventually conduct abhorrent experiments on others as they seek a cure.[1] The ambiguity between victim and victimizer reveals how easy it is to objectify and harm others, often while operating under the illusion of self-preservation. This uncomfortable reality is part of the novel's use of the grotesque to actively cause discomfort in the reader, which coincides with Kathryn Hume's argument that contemporary American fiction "offends and upsets willfully and deliberately" so that readers might question their values and critically engage with a text's message (8). For Hume, the grotesque is one of the ways aggressive fiction achieves such an effect.

Metaphor, the Grotesque, and Childhood

The Flame Alphabet's use of the grotesque resides in language. It is toxic language that transforms people in grotesque ways, and it is people's capacity to use language or attempt to resist its debilitating effects that reveals their grotesque nature. Therefore, this section takes up the relationship between language, the grotesque, and, eventually, the child to understand how language and the grotesque function in the novel.

In *Metaphor*, David Punter writes,

> Metaphor makes us look at the world afresh, but it often does so by challenging our notions of the similarity that exists between things; how alike they are; and in what ways, in fact, they are irreconcilably unalike. Thus metaphor represents a basic operation of language: it seeks to "fix" our understanding, but at the same time it reveals how any such fixity, any such desire for stability and certainty, is constructed on shifting sands. (9–10)

Metaphor may help us see the world anew, but it does so not only by emphasizing similarity but also by highlighting difference. This is similar to the grotesque, which creates an ambiguous tension. Perhaps something evokes simultaneous laughter and terror, even if not in equal measure, or straddles animal and human realms. The ability of the grotesque to challenge classification disrupts social order, which might be emancipatory or terrifying, depending on one's perspective. Bakhtin observes that the carnivals during the Renaissance and Middle Ages were places that allowed for a period of freedom and equality not known in day-to-day life because social hierarchies and prohibitions could be suspended (9, 15). The power of the grotesque to upend our conceptions of the world has potentially far-reaching consequences. Leonard Cassuto writes, "The grotesque is hard to apprehend because it doesn't fit neatly into a category. This makes it a threat to the entire system" (*The Inhuman Race* 8). Later, he notes, "A threat to established categories is an attack on the basis of comparison. The grotesque does precisely this, which makes it a phenomenon of great cultural consequence. The grotesque is felt in the form of anomalies that bridge categories and resist integration. It consequently questions the basis on which knowledge rests" (11). Notice the similarities between Punter's explanation of metaphor and Cassuto's explanation of the grotesque. Metaphor helps us see the world anew through its emphasis on both similarity and difference, but in doing so, it demonstrates the instability of language and certainty. Metaphor has the capacity to simultaneously illuminate the world and make the world appear more unknowable by undermining the knowledge humanity has constructed to explain it. The grotesque does not fit neatly into conceptual categories, which undermines our construction of knowledge. The grotesque, then, is a concept that can deconstruct, although not all comparative language is grotesque. Rather, comparative language that challenges us simultaneously with distinctive acumen and previously unthinkable juxtaposition has unsettling potential.

The grotesque's instability resonates with Punter's discussion of dissimilarity and metaphor, so it is perhaps no surprise that metaphor and the grotesque are closely related. Dieter Meindl acknowledges the relationship between the grotesque and metaphor. He writes, "The kinship between metaphor and the grotesque should be noted" (81). He goes on to note that Paul Ricœur "emphasizes the factor of categorical transgression in metaphor, which results in a redescription and redistribution of reality. The grotesque conflates categories and is notable for the effect of defamiliarization and estrangement it produces in the reader" (81). Shun-Liang Chao, who also invokes Punter, argues that metaphor is what makes "the grotesque, which is primarily visual or pictorial . . . also verbal" (14). In other words, metaphor is what brings the grotesque into the world of language. Chao situates the grotesque as "a corporeal, or flesh-made, metaphor which produces within itself (and within the reader/viewer's response) intellectual uncertainty, emotional disharmony, and hermeneutic indeterminacy" (14). Chao understands the grotesque "as a metaphor whose literalness tampers with its structural unity or totality" (14). Metaphor and the grotesque share the ability to conflate categories and estrange readers, and metaphors are ideally suited to the literary grotesque because they are predicated on the yoking together of disparate elements to provide fresh insight, even as they might foreground incongruity. Yet the grotesque is also metaphoric itself in its conflation of dissimilar elements. These unrelated elements do not seem to belong together in actuality or lack the cohesiveness to coexist without drawing attention to themselves and so they appear incongruous.

The focus on metaphor is especially appropriate in relation to the powerfully evocative imagery of *The Flame Alphabet*. While not all its stunning images are metaphors, the effects of language on the body and the unique and sometimes horrifying images often generate their power through comparison. The novel is about grotesque transformations, both physically and psychologically. These grotesque transformations are brought on through language, and the text's unsettling description helps readers visualize this strange but familiar world. While the grotesque metaphors are not always corporeal—the children, for example, are not physically grotesque even though they are compared to animals—the novel draws its power from evocative and grotesque imagery.

The grotesque metaphor of children and adolescents as dangerous or chaotic has roots in antiquity. For example, John Wall notes that Plato saw "that humanity starts out uncivilized and barbaric" (16). Wall observes this line of thinking can be found in much of Western religious thought but is perhaps best epitomized by Augustine: "If babies are innocent, it is not for lack of will to do harm, but for lack of strength" (17). Much current American discourse on childhood is filtered through the Puritan perspective, which asserts that children require shaping and regulation because their natural instincts are animalistic and chaotic. As previously noted, Daniel Cook writes, "Infants were seen as a danger to both the cosmic and social orders, their crawling placing them in postural proximity to members of the animal kingdom" (28). The idea that crawling children are bestial situates some of their natural impulses as animalistic, which is the same rhetoric on which *The Flame Alphabet* draws with its depiction of animalistic children. Furthermore, the Puritan legacy contains ambivalent "hope and fear" for the future that the Puritans saw embodied in children. Mintz observes,

Beginning in the 1660s and 1670s, Puritan presses and pulpits produced a stream of jeremiads lamenting the sins of the rising generation and the

degeneration of the young from the religion and godliness of their fore-
bears. Young people were made to carry an awesome psychological burden.
Morality, religion, indeed the future, depended on them. In secularized form,
it is this mixture of hope and fear about the rising generation that remains
Puritanism's most lasting legacy. (31)

The lament over the degeneration of children may be cliché to contemporary
audiences, and the notion that children are emblematic of the future is as
prominent as ever. This notion is partially why it can be so disturbing to see
our metaphoric future scavenged for the present.

The Flame Alphabet's unruly youths represent fears over unrestrained
impulses run amok (even as the hope for a cure is located within the bodies
of children). Rather than strengthening the society of their parents, the youths
actively undermine it. The parents cannot control their children, and the result
is catastrophic: children discipline adults, and they do so in seemingly capri-
cious fashion. Sam and his wife Claire initially do their best to relate to their
daughter Esther, but Esther will have none of it. The parents' emotional labor
is lost in a void of rejection and thinly veiled animosity. Yet they keep giving
until their physical health no longer allows for it because Esther's language,
and the language of all children, physically breaks them down.[2]

As children and adolescents begin actively harming adults, they are
increasingly described as animals. They form "feral pack[s]" that attack
strangers by yelling and screaming at them: "And together, when they spoke
in unison on their nighttime tours, their weapon was worse" (54). Fairly early
in the novel, Sam and another man are caught outside at night when a group
of children and adolescents approach:

> A din rose out of the north field beyond the school, and as the sound
> bloomed it grew piercing, wretchedly clear, borne so quickly on the wind, we
> shuddered when it hit. Voice-like, childlike, a cluster of speech blaring out of
> the field. The sound crushed out my air. Behind the noise ran a pack of kids,
> so shadowed and small at that distance, they looked like animals springing
> across the field. Coming right toward us. In front of them came a wall of
> speech so foul I felt myself burning. (74)

This troubling moment continues an ongoing metaphor of children as nonhuman, as monstrous animals trampling adults underfoot. They are a pack

that springs rather than walks. While they are still "like" animals, their "cluster of speech" is also "childlike," which metaphorically positions the children as neither animals nor children, but like animals and children. They exist in something of a liminal state: familiar yet strange due to their capacity for physical harm and increasingly predatory behavior. Markus P. J. Bohlmann and Sean Moreland dissect the term "childlike." They argue the adjective is "imaginatively empowering," as opposed to the adjective "childish," which is an "infantilizing" description (14). Because of the preexisting connotations of the preceding terms, Bohlmann and Moreland thus propose "childness" as a way of apprehending the "elusive quiddity" of the child and the way it is perceived, while providing distance from "the reality of *actual* children" (15–16). "Childness," then, is about how society imagines children to be and what qualities it ascribes to them without describing actual children. Bohlmann and Moreland are correct that it is important to understand that children's lived experiences are not the same as theoretical understandings. At the same time, theory does shape people's perceptions of children, both in their day-to-day interactions and the way in which adults discuss children, such as in political arenas.

Separating the theoretical child from the actual child can provide clarity; at the same time, however, divorcing them too much may make it more difficult to understand how theory and practice intersect. Nonetheless, Bohlmann and Moreland's proposal is compelling. Their distinction between "childish" and "childlike," however, is worth further examination. "Childish" is an infantilizing pejorative because it embodies regression. Idealized attributes like innocence that are associated with childhood cannot be reattained. Calling someone "childish" is in essence an assertion that a person has gained no knowledge or perspective despite their loss of innocence and exposure to the wider world: a poor trade. Calling someone "childlike" (as opposed to "like a child," which is sometimes closer in meaning to "childish") is a more neutral descriptor that depends upon what is "childlike" regarding one's behavior. Bohlmann and Moreland's assertion that the term "childlike" is imaginatively empowering hinges on the idealized child. For example, saying someone has a childlike imagination is an association with a positive quality. This bestows on a person a desirable attribute that stays with him or her despite maturation and its corresponding knowledge and perspective. Saying someone has a childish temper is an association with a negative quality, which ideally should have been shed as one matures and learns how to better control themselves.

Perhaps "childlike" isn't used as a pejorative because the "like" emphasizes similarity, and thus the insult would sully the idealized understanding of the child, whereas "ish" leaves enough comparative distance to not fully challenge our romantic image of the child.

Of course, when *The Flame Alphabet* tells us that the "cluster of speech" was "voice-like, childlike," it is functioning differently from Bohlmann and Moreland's description. It shows the ontological slippage among the children, who, at this moment, are closer to animals behaving as humans. The difference in Marcus's usage of "childlike" compared to Bohlmann and Moreland's is not a critique of Bohlmann and Moreland's assessment; rather, the difference helps illustrate the conceptual baggage that Marcus is unpacking in such a brief comparison. Describing children as animalistic and their speech as "childlike" divorces children from their privileged status in the social imagination. Everything the children do could reasonably be described as "childlike" because children are doing it. At the same time, describing children as animals who sound childlike is a comparative move that both divorces children from, and points out, their ontological underpinnings. In doing so, the novel asserts the constructed and ambiguous nature of both language and childhood. Here, children exist in between the world of animal and human, fully belonging to neither.

This ambiguity resurfaces as the scene continues. One kid catches a man and attacks him with speech. The attack is described "as if a cattle prod shot electricity from [the boy's] mouth" (75). This reference to language in electrical terms is reminiscent of *The Power*, and this moment also inverts societal assumptions about gendered violence because the attacking boy is actually Esther: "When the boy stood up we saw his face in the streetlight, so long and solemn and awful to behold. Except the kid wasn't a boy. It was my Esther. Her hair was wild and she wore an outfit I didn't recognize, some long coat that was too big on her" (75). Esther's grotesque transformation becomes so complete that she is initially unrecognizable to her own father. Her wild hair and unfamiliar, ill-fitting coat speak to the transition of Esther from alienated daughter to feral other. Her transformation is imprinted upon her body and clothing, which can now be read as a metaphor for her ontological shift. Of course, the children are not literally transformed into part human/part animal. This ontological blurring is created through the extended use of comparisons that associate the children with animals, which imbues them with a sort of wildness that intersects with their transgressive behaviors. It is also significant that the violence is gendered male even though a female commits it. This suggests a further blurring between notions of masculinity and femininity even though the subversion of this binary division is not maintained throughout the novel, and it briefly coincides with *The Power*'s gender dynamics.

Significantly, the novel's association of youth with animality harkens back to before the language plague even arrives. Early in the novel, Sam recounts a time when he was with his family at a picnic before the onset of the language plague. At the picnic, "kids would devour their food" before they "formed a roving pack, moving like one of those clusters of birds that seem to share a single, frantic brain" (27). "A roving pack" connotes animals like dogs or wolves. The image of the bird cluster is another animal comparison, and it highlights groups that operate as a single unit (which hunting canines may also seem to do). There is, of course, a significant difference between kids moving "like" a cluster of birds and being such a cluster, a difference of comparative degree that Marcus utilizes throughout. Children may be behaving as part of a cluster without individual autonomy, but their individuality is still their own. They are not animals; they are just like them. The references to pack and cluster mix animal metaphors regarding biological type, but they share an emphasis on nonhuman animals acting on instinct rather than emphasizing individuality. For this reason, Sam's adolescent daughter, Esther, refuses to play with the other youths. She tells her parents, "I'm not an animal. I don't follow people around simply because their asses smell good to me" (28). Esther's rebuke encapsulates a disaffected teen's angst. Her reproach also rejects behavior that impinges on her distinct personhood. Esther does not want to be someone who follows the crowd—especially a crowd predicated on instinct. However, eventually Esther becomes part of the adolescent pack and encapsulates the tension between similarity and dissimilarity, animal and human.

The animal comparisons eventually extend beyond children. Sam, for example, receives a package from an associate. The materials Sam receives, known as *The Proofs*, include drawings where "germs were people or beasts, and viruses looked like the world seen from miles away. Speech from the faces of children was rendered in ugly rushes of color, with each color coded to some kind of distress" (81). *The Proofs*' association of the plague's germs with "people or beasts" seems to differentiate between human and animal. In reality, it continues the association between these two diverse groups. In this case, "or" conjoins the terms. It can be one or the other. They are almost interchangeable in this context. But this is not actually true. Beasts, lacking the capacity for language-based communication, do not spread this particular language-based plague. Therefore, although the reference to beasts evokes animals, the reference can also metaphorically represent the liminal boundary crossing of humans behaving in bestial fashion. The use of "people" encompasses more age groups than "children" and extends the blame for the plague's progression to all humans. The novel later admits this more specifically, as it reveals, "The toxicity had spread beyond children" (116), but *The Proofs'* movement from depicting germs as "people or beasts" to showing the "ugly rushes of color" coming from children resituates the plague as primarily child-based. Nonetheless, this moment starts to expand the connection of the metaphor of the chaotic other to people aside from children. It also foreshadows future events, such as when Sam and Claire's town is evacuated. Claire jumps out of the car she is riding in because she cannot leave Esther behind. There are adults with dogs monitoring the area to make sure everyone evacuates. "From the woods trotted a pack of dogs," the novel reads, "like old men in animal suits, barking with human voices. Behind them trudged a human chain of jumpsuited rescuers, arms linked so they'd miss no one" (142). The term "pack" is now directly associated with animals, as opposed to people behaving like animals, but now the animals are like humans. Or, depending on how one interprets that sentence, dogs are like old men pretending to be dogs. The comparison of dogs to men dressed as dogs is practically an ouroboros of a metaphor. It circles around on itself. The novel compares humans to animals, and then compares animals to humans behaving like animals. The subsequent image is of a human chain or humans behaving as an object.

The way the language of the novel blurs the lines between human and animal and undermines constructions of the idealized child provides the conditions by which people harm each other. Although it begins with children harming adults, this eventually extends to adults harming children and each other. Prior to the evacuation, Sam encounters a group of children while in his car. He narrates, "A pack of children tore across a yard, fled from sight. I locked my doors" (117). He feels his car lifting and revs the engines, but something blocks the car. Next, "One of them pressed his little face into the driver's side window, so close. He smiled, his lips moving, as if he were singing. With his finger he tapped on the glass, made a twirling motion for me to roll down the window. His hands formed a posture of prayer under his chin and I believe he mimed the word *please*" (117). Sam lays on the gas and is able to drive over "whatever had been blocking [the car]" (117). In his rearview mirror, he sees "them. . . . They formed a circle, went to their knees and that was all I saw" (117). Sam's constant refusal to use the term "child" or "children," or to confront the fact that what is stuck underneath his car is a child—not animal roadkill or an object—marks the full-scale conversion of children to things in his mind. The animal comparisons are minimal here; just one ambiguous use of "pack," but the danger they pose is salient. This danger is predicated on the appeal to innocence from the child at the car window. His smile, pretend prayer, and miming of "*please*" are all things a child might do to get their way, and they manufacture an image of an inno- cent child that belies the danger the child represents. The child is appealing to the innocent conception of childhood to try to get Sam to roll down the window. This encounter highlights the danger that the child is able to deceive others by drawing upon idealized depictions of childhood to hide his or her true, dangerous self. Sam tells himself, "It was just kids, out in the street after suppertime. That's all it was. Kids playing in the road" (118). Yet even when he thinks of the children as kids, he still refuses to consider he ran over a child. He reaches for a sense of normalcy, as if he may not have just murdered a kid; perhaps for that reason. Sam's initial dehumanization of the children and subsequent refusal to grapple with what happened allows him to avoid confronting his role in what occurred. He escapes, but he risks losing his own humanity in the process. While his actions are understandable, at some point, one must question whether the ends justify the means. How much harm can a person do in the name of self-preservation before they become an abomination? This is not an easy question to answer, but Sam crosses the line somewhere. These depictions of children and adolescents as animals are significant to the novel because it causes adults to feel under threat by unfamiliar forces. This threat becomes the cover for abusive and exploitative behavior. Of course, people *are* facing a crisis, but readers realize that it is not only youths who are capable of behaving like animals.

The Grotesque Transformation from Victim to Victimizer

In *The Flame Alphabet*, after initially situating children as grotesque and the deteriorating bodies of the adults as a metaphor for their victimhood, adult bodies subsequently become a metaphor for their monstrous actions. The grotesque runs throughout the novel, but initially, the decomposition of the adult bodies demonstrates how objectification breaks down a person by stripping them of their vitality. At the same time, however, the disturbing appearance of the adults also provides a grotesque metaphor for those who victimize both adults and children. Their monstrous behavior is written onto their features as some adults become inhuman monsters.

Exposure to language transforms adults into grotesque, pitiful creatures. This gives them a monstrous appearance. For example, Claire's face is "the weight of clay," and "a shadow had spread under her gums, a darkness inside her mouth" (98; 99). Her body is dry. She has "rank-smelling hair" and wears a mouth guard "to keep her from gnashing into the exposed nerve pulp of her teeth" (132). The "darkness" residing in Claire's mouth and her disgusting hair and exposed "nerve pulp" position her as monstrous, yes, but even more specifically as a zombie. The decomposing mouth, combined with the emphasis on the gnashing teeth and the inability to prevent them from doing harm, is reminiscent of zombies. Indeed, Claire is literally the walking dead: her lethargy and decomposition cause her to move slowly and spend much of her time in bed, uncommunicative. She does not live so much as exist in a state of perpetually worsening decay. Adults in the novel become grotesque due to their monstrous appearance and how the novel's language positions them as both human and object. In this way, their broken bodies provide a metaphor for how, as Evan Calder Williams writes, "real abstractions affect real bodies" (73).[3] Outside Forsythe, the place where experiments are taking place in the hopes of recovering some form of language and finding a cure for the plague, "hordes of people sought entrance. . . . A mob of bodies swelled before the gate as if suspended in emulsion" (168). This horde is evocative of zombie imagery in contemporary narratives. Contemporary zombie narratives often focus on which ethical lines survivors are willing to cross to survive. What morals are worth sacrificing for an additional indeterminant amount of time among the living dead? Although zombies are the literal monsters in the genre, many of the humans behave in ways that seem far more monstrous. *The Flame Alphabet* is interested in similar questions as zombie narratives, and these zombie references help establish that connection.

The bodies of the adults are horrifying, but the monstrosity of the adults is also emblematic of how Marcus explores the grotesque slippage between language and meaning. For example, there are also hints that the monstrous adults can be associated with vampires.[4] There is Claire's bruised neck, which is not unique to vampires or their victims, but is more directly associated with them than zombies. An early description of the plague's onset compares it to a bite: "At first we thought we were bitten. Something had landed on our backs and sucked on us. Now we would perish" (14). The vector for the disease and the subsequent lethargy Sam and Claire experience is tied up in the draining of their vitality.

The vampirism metaphor resonates in other ways. Some adults, in an attempt to combat the plague, establish a testing facility called Forsythe in an abandoned school. Various language-based experiments involving reading and exposure to multiple languages and scripts are conducted in an attempt to understand what is causing the plague and how to counteract it. These experiments are largely in vain because they are done in isolation and even reading written language damages people. However, there is some success. A serum that grants temporary immunity is developed at Forsythe. It involves draining the essence of children, which is metaphorically similar to what the children do to the adults with their speech. When Sam first sees a demonstration of an adult able to withstand the deleterious effects of speech, that adult is with a child, and there is "a bag of *fluid*" that "dangled from the little neck of the child, puckering from his skin into the tube. From this it flowed directly into the man. Allowing him to speak, one presumed. *A fluid drawn directly from the child*" (192). The withdrawal of children's fluids for the sustenance of adults (from their neck, no less) is metaphorically vampiric. The adult is even dressed in a tuxedo, "*almost* a gentleman" (191), which coincides with aristocratic depictions of vampires. The vampire logic here differs from the logic of the vampires of Rob Latham's analysis, who seek perpetual youth and who reveal the exploitation inherent in consumer culture. While exploitation is clearly present in *The Flame Alphabet*, the draining of the essence of children is not part of a consumerist ethos. It is part of an ethos of self-preservation at the expense of youth. The vampiric sacrifice of the children here is also an inversion of the first section of the book, where Esther, as a standoffish adolescent, metaphorically drains her parents' vitality. Because vampires subsist on the blood of others, they provide an appropriate metaphor for a text where adults are willing to sacrifice children to save themselves.[5]

Marcus's text constantly explores the changing nature of people and how they shift categories, which is what makes the grotesque such an appropriate aesthetic category for analysis. In addition to the monstrous zombie and vampire metaphors used to describe the appearance of the adults, their monstrosity also surfaces in their behavior, as Sam shifts from victim to victimizer. In this way, the monstrous appearance of the adults becomes a grotesque metaphor with dual resonance: adults are both grotesque subjects and objects, capable of exerting agency in grotesque ways and transforming into grotesque creatures via exposure to the plague. The plague does not just transform the bodies of adults—though it certainly does that—it also causes some to engage in horrific behavior.

The grotesque behavior of the adults becomes more horrific as the novel progresses. When the plague starts, Sam engages in what he calls "smallwork" (18). He constantly measures and tests what he can, hoping to find ways to discover the causes and effects of the plague and to contain its damages. His smallwork eventually encompasses his attempts at Forsythe to create a new language, as well as his extraction of children's essence. Initially, he runs tests on Claire, but Claire stops willingly participating. Sam observes, "She stopped appearing in the kitchen for night treatments, declined the new smoke. When I served infused milk she fastened her mouth shut. If she accepted medicine from me she did so unwittingly, asleep, whimpering when the needle went in" (97). Calling his concoctions "medicine" implies a palliative effect that belies the amateur and speculative nature of his smallwork, and it masks his abuse of Claire. Sam's penetration of an unwilling Claire with a needle metaphorically registers as rape and reinforces the vampiric quality of Sam. He is denied consent but does what he wants, regardless.

Sam's transformation into a monster continues. As Sam and Claire become increasingly sick, Esther goes on a tirade, harming Claire and Sam with her foul language. Sam enters the room late, but imagines the tirade started with Esther "climbing up on her mother and assum[ing] a feral crouch, opening her throat for the pure injury to pour out" (132). This continues Esther's depiction as a dangerous animal. In a moment of desperation, Sam jams a needle into his own ear. The needle is supposedly capable of providing temporary immunity from language, but it works for Sam in another way. It shocks Esther into silence: "My activities with the needle had rendered her mute. She stood watching me, a mostly convincing look of fear on her face. An effective display of crying, soft crying that she seemed to want to suppress, came next. She performed her grief for my benefit" (133). When the scene starts, Sam fears Esther and her ability to harm Claire and himself. This scene is evocative of a common parenting scenario, where an adolescent child lashes out at her parents. When Sam slams the needle into his own ear, power dynamics shift. "I would literally stab my own ears out," his actions scream, "rather than be subjected to your tirade." Sam shocks Esther into submission, causing her to become fearful and cry. Sam's distrust of Esther's actions, which he interprets as performative, reveals the widening void opening up between Sam and his daughter. Sam's distrust may be warranted, but it is also a sign of his own transformation. Esther becomes dangerous and animal-like, but she controls herself after witnessing her father's actions. If this encounter is understood, at least in part, as a metaphoric representation of a challenging parenting scenario, Sam's behavior is also callous and chilling. This monstrous transformation demonstrates Sam's shift from victim to victimizer, which emphasizes his grotesque nature.

Sam's monstrous transformation becomes even clearer when Esther approaches Sam and signals to him that she will be quiet. She tries cleaning up some of the fluid from Sam's ear. Sam rejects this help and drags Esther from the house. Marcus writes,

> Esther stood outside our house with her head down, shoulders small. I rushed her again, moved my daughter yet farther into the yard, and she slumped over me, let herself be carried. At the sidewalk I dropped her and with my hands I made the most terrible gesture I could. It was the most fluent I'd ever been without speech. *Stay, stay there. Do not come in this house again. You are forbidden from here. We do not know you.* Esther looked up at me and nodded. With her little finger she crossed her heart. (133)

Esther is diminished: her "shoulders small," she slumps and is carried. She lacks the will to resist but is unwilling or unable to move away unassisted. Sam is violent and aggressive. He drops her and makes "the most terrible gesture [he] could." This gesture indicates a moment where nonverbal communication succeeds while language fails. What single gesture could be so terrible as to contain all the hurt that Sam communicates? Any actual description of the gesture would fail to render its full power. A description may even lower the terrible power of the gesture to a joke, as the description may fall so far short of communicating the precise language Sam believes it entails. Esther's understanding leads her to a heartbreaking moment of acceptance. The subtle nod is understated. The crossing of her heart is a childlike promise—*cross my heart and hope to die*—that reinforces the nod. This is a gesture that can be understood without explanation. Esther's gestures communicate something like, "I understand, and I promise to honor your wishes." A narrative description of Sam's gesture would fail because no gesture can encapsulate such a specific and terrible meaning as he wishes to communicate. On the other hand, Esther's gestures succeed because they are familiar. These gestures illustrate the difficulty in creating meaning disconnected from context. They also show a reversal between Sam and Esther. Now Sam is the metaphoric monster. This moment is significant because this scene subtly embodies Sam's shift from victim to victimizer. One might argue that Sam is just doing what he must to survive, but this argument does not account for Claire, who would rather not separate from Esther despite Esther's harmful presence. Claire would sacrifice herself and forego survival. This is demonstrated when the adults evacuate the town and Claire jumps out of the car because she would prefer to stay near Esther.

Sam's shift from victim to victimizer coincides with the plague becoming part of everyone's language. Children are still immune, but adults also harm each other by communicating. This makes it even more difficult to find a cure, but adults at Forsythe continue to search for one by experimenting on children and adults. Adults are tricked into coming to Forsythe because they are shown pictures of their missing children. It is implied that families will be reunited. Instead, the adults are used as test subjects. Sam reveals, "There was a healthy supply of subjects on hand. People lined up for this work. They volunteered, fought to be first, scratched at each other without mercy, as if they'd been profoundly misled about what waited for them at Forsythe. Which of course, well, they had" (171). The adults are misled because they would not be willing to participate of their own volition. Sam observes, "From my office the specimens were brought downstairs and readied for testing against people, people already shattered and near death, overexposed to the very thing I made more of every day" (169). Sam's description of the people as specimens is part of the process of objectification where people are dehumanized. At the same time, Sam is not able to complete this objectification in his own mind, as he subsequently uses the word "people" twice. This tension between thing and person is omnipresent in discussions of children and test subjects. Children are referred to as "the ultimate asset" and Sam observes the people at Forsythe "struck gold in those kids," thus situating children as commodities and currency (180; 193). This commodity-based language also obfuscates that because the serum is derived from the children themselves, the "struck gold" is a metaphor but the "in those kids" is literal, which illustrates how metaphor may be able to help people see the world in new ways, but it can also obfuscate reality. Here, beginning the comparison as metaphoric lends a comparative element to the entire moment. This moment is emblematic of the way the adults in power value children as commodities.

The adults at Forsythe are able to engage in abuse and exploitation of children and other, less powerful adults because the victimizers dehumanize those they victimize, and Sam refuses to confront the terrible nature of the facility and his involvement. When Sam first witnesses a demonstration of the child serum that provides temporary immunity to language, it involves two test subjects: an adult and a child. The adult enters first, and it is clear he is one of those who have been overexposed: "Onto the stage came an old man, his head draped in testicle skin. When he rubbed it and blinked into the lights I saw it was merely his face, beset with a terrible, taffy-like drop. I did not want to reflect what sort of experiments, or what sort of life, had led to possessing a face like that" (190). The image of a man with testicle skin draped over his head is both absurd and gross, but it also highlights Sam's willful ignorance regarding the test subjects. Sam does not wish to confront how the experiments transformed him, and then he hedges further by noting it could be the life the man led instead of the experiments. Even though Sam also does not want to reflect on the sort of life that would cause such deformity, this is a mental maneuver that deemphasizes the suffering the man endured at Forsythe. This self-justification and willful disconnect consistently manifests in the author's use of euphemisms and constant understatement. After the demonstration is finished, "[t]he child had to be carried off, but first they threw a sheet over him" and Sam notes that in further demonstrations, "[t]he child was never the same one, though sometimes the man was" (192). The unstated detail is that the children are killed in the process of creating the serum.

In the final section of the novel, Sam completes his transformation into a monster objectifying children. Sam abandons Forsythe to search for Esther. While outside the compound and before he finds who he thinks is Esther, Sam hunts children and experiments on them; his hope is to unlock the secrets of the immunity serum. He recounts stumbling onto the cure by accident: "One of my subjects, strapped to an old bottled respirator, so large it dwarfed his little face, began the rapid breathing one never likes to see in a small person. Too often it foreshadows the unproductive kind of stillness" (281). It is then that Sam notices some powder in the respirator, which he distills into the serum. Sam's use of the term "specimen" situates the child as an object, not an individual, and recalls Sam's time at Forsythe. It positions him as a scientist or expert, something he has been playing at the entire novel. The image of the large machine dwarfing the small child highlights the power differential between Sam, his experiment, and the child. When Sam laments the fact that rapid breathing "too often" leads to "unproductive stillness," it is a euphemistic lament for the inconvenient loss of a test subject. "Unproductive" is often used to describe workers who fail or refuse to generate as much value for their employer as is desired. In this instance, the term also situates the child further in the realm of the objectified, as it refers to a lack of productivity based on the fact that it prevents others from extracting value from the body. Even Sam's terminology for his actions is euphemistic. "Smallwork," while initially an accurate portrayal of the scale of his amateurish tests, fails to encompass the harm it does to others. The serum made from children is called Child's Play, thus associating something created through a harmful and laborious process with connotations of both ease (making it was *child's play*) and harmless play (the play of a child). Like in *Sweet Tooth* and *The Girl with All the Gifts*, a defense might be mustered for the experiments on behalf of the human race, but the issue of consent remains. Subjects are tricked and forced into the experiments, and there seems to be no qualms about killing those who are being tested. Sam deludes himself into thinking he can make a difference, but all he accomplishes is to add to the pain and misery of others.

Sam's grotesque dehumanization sometimes involves the ontological dehumanization of the children he objectifies. For example, having associated children with threatening animals or nonhuman objects for so long, it is less of a jump for him to experiment on them. After finding "the first child" upon leaving Forsythe, he starts his "project with assets, with person-derived inhibitors" (277). In this example, the inhibitors, which temporarily suppress language's toxicity, are the assets. But the children are also assets. The inhibitors are derived from them. In this way, the children are not only valued for their status as fungible commodities used to produce more valuable commodities, but they are also seen as less valuable than their parts. Sam later says, "When I need some [language serum], I pull it out of little ones. I used it first at Forsythe. The crude kind, the roughly gained immunity, drawn on the priceless account of the child's person" (278). The initial reference to "little ones" rather than "children" is an abstraction that is no less horrifying than simply saying "little children." Sam's behavior has become so abhorrent that euphemisms begin losing their understated power, including the "roughly" in the subsequent sentence, which acknowledges some violence but not the full scope. Sam's observation that the serum that provides him immunity is "drawn on the priceless account of the child's person" is a direct subversion of the emotionally priceless child. Viviana Zelizer argues that children are imbued with emotional value and kept separate from economic worlds (11). She reveals this conception of children is the result of a transition away from valuing them for their economic potential. This transition helps reify the figure of the innocent child, which makes it easier for many people to shelter children from work and other adult realities. Children may be "priceless" in the sense that they have unique and irreplaceable emotional value to their family and friends, but they have become literally "priceless" in Sam's world because money is worthless, whereas children's bodies have immense value.

The book ends with Sam abducting the young adult he thinks is Esther, who, having aged, is now susceptible to the poison of language. But it is highly likely it is not Esther. She looks different and they cannot effectively communicate. Sam grants, "It was marginally possible I'd rescued, instead of Esther, a stranger with a different name" (257). Sam's inability to know whether he has found his daughter or not speaks to the extent of his grotesque transformation. The loss of one's identity is sometimes associated with the grotesque. Bernard McElroy argues, "The world intuited by the grotesque is one in which identity may be wholly or partially lost through transformations of the individual into something subhuman" (16). Wolfgang Kayser also associates "the loss of identity" with the grotesque (185). Sam's loss of his identity surfaces not only to Sam's inability to recognize Esther but the monstrous transformation he has undergone himself. Not just physically, but psychologically. His physical transformations change how he appears, but his willingness to harm others changes who he is on a deeper level.

Having captured Esther/not-Esther, Sam continues hunting for other children so that he can create Child's Play. He says, "What I was seeking is small and it has a face and it breathes so prettily, in little wet gusts of air. Often it comes along willingly. It harbors a medicine inside its delicate chest" (255). The constant repetition of "it" adds to the horror by demonstrating the child stalker's objectification of his victims. Here the child is almost completely objectified, and Sam is at his most monstrous. By making Sam's appearance match his grotesque behavior, the novel provides a visualization of how the adjective "grotesque" is often used to position heinous human behavior as inhuman.

It is especially ironic that Sam experiments on others because he was once placed in the position of dehumanized other by the Forsythe researchers. When he arrives at Forsythe, he is violently brought in for examination and study, disrobed and prodded, and language is tested on him (151–52). Sam is hung in a room where "mesh baggies of hair hung from the ceiling, repelling flies. Possibly the hair attracted them instead" (153). This marks Sam's setting as grotesque. The strange containers of hair make no sense, and the uncertainty over what the bags of hair would need to repel flies from is discomforting. However, the uncertainty over their function gets at the ambiguity within the grotesque itself. Philip Thomson observes that the modern era "view[s] the grotesque as a fundamentally ambivalent thing" (11). Justin D. Edwards and Rune Graulund corroborate this view. They observe the grotesque can both attract and repulse (78). Sam's grotesque body is always a sliding signifier, shifting between a physical representation of his own objectification and the objectification he inflicts on others. That Sam can so easily experiment on others is especially upsetting perhaps because we want to believe that people who have been mistreated would not mistreat others. Sam's transformations encapsulate the novel itself, where the grotesque shifts from child to adult, animal to thing, subject to object. These transformations are downplayed through the extended use of euphemisms.

The novel's simultaneous invitation to interpret and its refusal to validate interpretation is its most confounding and rewarding attribute, and it achieves this by engaging with the grotesque on multiple levels. The plot is grotesque in its ambiguity and the discomfort it creates within the reader, which challenges them to consider the way in which the grotesque permeates our own world. Grotesque images often have the potential to inspire both attraction and repulsion, though the novel prefers repulsion. *The Flame Alphabet* takes the grotesque a step further by revealing the grotesque within us all. Everyone in the novel is grotesque to varying degrees, and our sympathies shift as the novel progresses. In this light, we may be faced with a chilling reality: the grotesque, rather than being an intrusion into the natural order, may itself be the natural order. The grotesque in all its forms and functions suffuses the world. It seeps into our relationships, both familial and communal. This thought might repulse us, yet it should also engage us. Not everything or everyone will always be grotesque in their actions, but the capacity is always there, beneath the surface, festering: a rot under the skin. If there is any hope in the novel, it is that the novel's metaphoric world challenges us to reconsider our own relationships so that we might cleanse or excise that within us which threatens to transform us into monsters.

Conclusion: On Parenting

The Flame Alphabet and to a lesser extent, *The Power*, get at issues pertaining to the grotesque and the commodification of children and adolescents, but they also get at contemporary anxieties over parenting. In the latter, Margot deals with her daughter Jocelyn's advent of the power and Jocelyn's struggles with it, as well as more mundane aspects of lifelike dating, which, of course, is impacted by her power. Allie, a messiah character, flees an abusive foster family, and Roxy's story begins with her mother's murder and becomes in large part about how Roxy navigates her role working with her male family members. The only major character who gets multiple chapters devoted to him who does not have significant narrative threads pertaining to family is the male reporter Tunde, which captures the notion that domestic spaces are traditionally coded female. In the former, Sam reflects on raising Esther and the struggles involved, and Claire tries to abandon the evacuation of the town because she would rather stay with Esther, even if it kills her. At one point, Sam and Claire hide in a bathroom, waiting for Esther to leave them alone. Ostensibly this is because Esther's speech harms them, but metaphorically, it also gets at the exhausting work of parenting. In fact, Sam connects parenting itself back to the animality of children. For example, he notes, "Perhaps it is better now to liken a father to an animal parent. Certain caretaking is observed, but when the offspring matures, alienation and estrangement set in" (256). This connects back to the chapter's initial discussion of chaotic children, and it harkens to how many parents and guardians encounter less extreme versions of chaotic children. Most people who have consistent interactions with children or adolescents have probably encountered an unruly child. The societal danger is not that children can act unpredictably or chaotically (after all, adults do so often), but when society really does dehumanize children and adolescents and treats them as dangerous. This dehumanization has been particularly harmful to minority youths, and the notion that children can be dangerous can be seen, for example, in the relatively recent shift toward placing police officers in schools, although, as noted, the novels in this chapter are interested in the parent-child relationship specifically. Naomi Morgenstern posits a posthumanist wild child who exists

in a physical or ideological space in which the easy distinction between the wild and the civilized or rational has collapsed. The child in contemporary literature appears at the center of an ethical or ontological wilderness that allegorizes the relationship between parents and children and registers, in displaced fashion, particular forms of cultural anxiety about reproduction and futurity and about the relationship between the human and what has traditionally been quarantined as "the animal." (2)

Morgenstern is particularly interested in how reproductive technology and postheteronormativity often obscure the ways that such advancements risk taking us closer rather than further from an "animal" world (2). Morgenstern's wild child is posthumanist partly in that it comes at a time when reproductive technology has advanced significantly and partly because the ability to reproduce the social world in which we live is under greater strain. Yet the posthumanist child is still part of a tradition of centuries of thought related to the "classically humanist (wild) child" that "functions . . . as a way to cordon off the wild animal from the civilized, rational adult" (192). Like the posthumanist wild child, the humanist wild child, I think, also registers "cultural anxiety about reproduction and futurity" and humanity's relationship to "the animal" (2). Anxiety over reproduction and futurity may also be fed by declining birthrates in some parts of the world, unprecedented climate change, and a related fascination with the postapocalyptic. Morgenstern notes that there is a "panicked intensity" to the parenting of the late twentieth and twenty-first century and connects this to "the commodification of reproduction as with the child's dwindling capacity to signify a space immune to capitalization" (11). This is a point of intersection between this project and Morgenstern's. The texts which I write about are also connected to the "dwindling capacity [of the child] to signify a space immune to capitalization." However, I use the term "commodification" because it better evokes the nature of some of the exploitation I analyze, whereby children and adolescents are valued for what can be extracted from them. Of course, the children and adolescents in these texts are also grotesque in that they embody an otherness that sets them apart from the adults. The grotesqueness of the characters in *The Flame Alphabet* and *The Power* is not due to bodily or ontological differences, such as in *Sweet Tooth* or *The Girl with All the Gifts*. Rather, the former texts' grotesqueness is twofold. It is in the capacity of their characters to easily shift into villainous roles, and it resides in the uncanny abilities that set youths apart from adults; abilities that both repel and entice those in power.

CHAPTER 3

"We Are Masterpieces"
Child Labor in "Reeling for the Empire" and *Geek Love*

Child Labor in the US

Child labor has been part of the United States economy since before the country's inception, as it was a common occurrence in colonial times. At that time, child labor was not seen as a problem because there was a fundamentally different understanding of children's relationship to work. For example, children engaged in preindustrial agricultural work, but this work was also considered educational (Hindman 14). Indentured servitude could be seen in a similar light, and this labor theoretically allowed for upward mobility, although how often upward mobility actually occurred is unclear. Yet indentured servitude helped alleviate economic stress on poor families by cutting down on the number of mouths they had to feed (17). There was exploitation of children's labor in such environments, but the fact that children worked did not automatically mean they were being exploited, except in the case of children who were enslaved, who were forced to work as soon as they were able (17).

Child labor underwent a transformation during industrialization. Child labor morphed from "a social and economic good . . . into not merely a social and economic problem but a moral evil" (13). Prior to industrialization, the household or community was the site of both production and consumption. During industrialization, however, production was severed from consumption. Labor became a marketable commodity that generally took place outside the home, and individuals, rather than families, competed for work (22–23). Furthermore, the industrialization of America was driven by women and children, as large numbers of them made for abundant and inexpensive labor in the Northeast, which was part of the reason that industrialization in America began there (33–34). Children worked in a dizzying assortment of industries including agricultural, canning, mining, textile, and newspaper industries, among others, and "by 1900, over two million children under the age of sixteen held jobs, earning low pay for long hours" (Rosenberg 1). At that peak, over 20 percent of children ages ten to fourteen worked (Hindman 32). In some industries, such as the cotton textile industry, work consisted of sixty- and seventy-hour weeks (5). Families often had little choice, however, in requiring their children to work. For example, "In 1890, most families in America earned less than \$400 a year, with \$550 needed for a decent life. Dire necessity drove parents, especially immigrant parents, to send their under-age children to work" (Rosenberg 5). Alternatively, wealthy families simply were not driven by necessity to require their children to work. Some children did desire to work. During times of war, for example, numbers of children have lied about their age to work in the military as soldiers and support staff. For example, up to half a million boys enlisted during the Civil War by stating they were eighteen when they were not, and an estimated two hundred thousand of these boys were sixteen or younger (155). I point this out because it is important to remember that children sometimes exert their own agency in relation to work even though adults may reasonably consider them too young to fully understand the ramification of their decisions, just as it is important to consider that most families or children worked by necessity, not choice.

Child labor is not as prominent as it once was in the United States. Historian Chaim M. Rosenberg notes that "child labor wilted under the assault of reformers, raised living standard, civil rights, legislation education, and technology" even as he warns against the possibility of its resurgence and the need for "tools of change, especially economic progress . . . to rid the world of child labor" (210). The emphasis on economic progress as a tool to combat child labor makes sense considering the historical reality that children worked, and continue to work, to help support their families and that child labor is associated with "economically underdeveloped nations" (Hindman 4). Poverty is the biggest necessitating factor for child labor (Schmitz et al. 2). But economic progress alone is not enough to combat child labor. Scholars note, "Strategies to reduce child labor focus on poverty reduction *and related issues,* including education, support services for children and families, and the elimination of gender oppression" (2; emphasis added). Furthermore, while economically advanced countries all went through periods of "pervasive child labor on the path to advancement," that does not mean that such periods were or are required for economic progress (Hindman 4). Globally, child labor is currently driven by economic and political systems. In fact, "The economic policies established by Western governments and financial institutions foster the development of global systems in which parents in poorer countries must rely on the labor of the children" (Schmitz et al. 7). A reimagining of current economic systems might privilege ending child labor if those with power were so inclined, or pressured enough, to do so.

Nonetheless, child labor still exists. Partly, this is a definitional issue. Child labor is often "used to denote employment that is harmful to a child's physical, cognitive, emotional, social, and moral development. In the United States, work that is detrimental to children's well-being is called *oppressive child labor* in the Fair Labor Standards ACT (FLSA) of 1938" (Pieris 186). Oppressive child labor, as defined under the FLSA, does still exist in the United States, especially in the agricultural industries (187). Yet child labor in the United States is much more widespread than just oppressive child labor because nonoppressive child labor goes by other terms, such as child or youth employment. This employment supposedly exposes young workers to the value of work and the management of finances, although some teens still work to contribute to their families' economic survival as well.

In multiple articles for *The Guardian,* Michael Sainato chronicles the rise and impact of child labor in the United States. He reports that many child labor laws are being rolled back to allow children to work in a variety of more dangerous industries, work longer hours, and receive subminimum wages. This is coming at a time when lawmakers are also trying to reduce enforcement amid an increasing amount of child labor violations ("Dumb and Dangerous"). A July 2023 article notes that the US Department of Labor found 4,474 cases of children working illegally and was investigating 700 more cases since the start of the fiscal year, which was a 44% increase from the year prior. The article registers the deaths of a sixteen-year-old boy working at a slaughterhouse in Mississippi, a sixteen-year-old boy working at a sawmill in Wisconsin, and a sixteen-year-old boy working at a landfill in Missouri ("US Labor Department Condemns Surge").

It is clear, then, that child labor in the contemporary moment has not gone away and may be resurging, even as its meaning and parameters have shifted over time in economically advantaged nations like the United States. Oppressive child labor is thought to be a relic of an unenlightened past, when in actuality, it perseveres and is even necessary for some families due to political and economic realities. In the neoliberal moment, it is not difficult to envision a more complete return to such oppressive practices either, especially because education at every level is placed under increasingly severe scrutiny with fewer resources allocated. Some politicians and voters would refuse investments in children and adolescents because economic and social returns-on-investment fully fruit in the future rather than ripen immediately. It may come as no surprise, then, that while the United States currently lacks widespread oppressive child labor, this has not stopped authors from considering child labor in the contemporary moment. Karen Russell's "Reeling for the Empire" and Katherine Dunn's *Geek Love* are two such texts. They also both interrogate issues of child labor in relation to the grotesque. In doing so, these texts critique exploitation while simultaneously finding possibilities for new modes of being through feminist resistance. To help contextualize the subsequent analysis of each of these texts, I will first discuss the female grotesque.

The Female Grotesque

The term "grotesque" is etymologically connected to "grotto." The association of the grotesque with the cavern or underground is subsequently linked to the female. Mary Russo writes,

> The word itself . . . evokes the cave—the grotto-esque. Low, hidden, earthy, dark, material, immanent, visceral. As a bodily metaphor, the grotesque cave tends to look like (and in the most gross metaphorical sense be identified with) the cavernous anatomical female body. These associations of the female with the earthly, material, and the archaic grotesque have suggested a positive and powerful figuration of culture and womanhood to many male and female writers and artists. (1)

The associations between the grotesque and the female can carry negative connotations as well. Frances Connelly writes, "The grotto is associated with fertility and the womb, as well as with death and the grave. It is earthy and material, a cave, an open mouth that invites our descent into other worlds. It is the space where the monsters and marvels of our imagination are conceived" (*The Grotesque in Western Art* 1). The grotto or cavern is the womb of the grotesque, where its forms are conceived. It is appropriate that the grotesque grotto is ambivalent and evokes both life and death as the grotesque is the embodiment of cultural tensions. Ewa Kuryluk argues that the cave can both protect and imprison and therefore "because of the association with the womb and the cave, all closed spaces tend to be perceived as female and are associated with both protection and threat" (20). Margaret Miles further emphasizes the threatening nature of the female grotesque. While discussing Bakhtin, she notes, "The association of the female body with materiality, sex, and reproduction in the female body makes it an essential—not an accidental—aspect of the grotesque" (90). This is why "female sexual organs, sexual activity, and behavior are a central object of grotesque figuration" (92–93). Women's bodies and sexuality are threats to patriarchal systems and these threats get subsequently associated with the female grotesque, which folds into the grotesque's often subversive nature; and while men may also be grotesque, that does not make the grotesque gender-neutral. Instead, the grotesque may ascribe attributes associated with women to men's bodies: "[A]s grotesque, male bodies take on precisely the characteristics regularly attributed to women's bodies; they lose form and integrity, become penetrable, suffer the addition of alien body parts, and become alternately huge and tiny" (91).

While the female grotesque may be subversive, in the patriarchal imagination, it is dangerous. Patriarchal societies mitigate against the subversion of the social order by managing women, including their representations (111–12). Miles explains, "In the patriarchal societies of the Christian West, 'woman' was mysterious and ultimately grotesque because women did not represent themselves; lacking conditions for self-representation—collective voice and access to the public sphere—women were represented by men's anxieties, fears, and fantasies" (112). Miles's identification of patriarchal concerns over women's bodies demonstrates that the grotesque can be fearsome to some perspectives and that grotesque depictions or associations can work as a form of cultural discipline. Women, not allowed to manage their own representations, become pigeonholed by men's representations. Miles asserts, "[A]n element of grotesque is present in every woman" (85).

But the female grotesque need not be understood negatively, especially for those who glorify in disorder and subversion of hegemonic institutions. Russo argues that the grotesque offers alternatives and resistance to dominant ideals and expectations. These possibilities extend to feminism itself, which often fails to account for the full complexity of women's bodies and experiences. It is no surprise that Russo, who sees the cave as a positive feminine symbol, finds the potential for emancipation within the grotesque. Russo's association of the grotesque with the feminine coincides with Miles's. Russo notes that "the grotesque—as superficial and to the margins—is suggestive of a certain construction of the feminine" (5). Once again, male grotesques "are produced through an association with the feminine as the body marked by difference" (13). But unlike Miles, Russo focuses on risk and how various spectacles, such as aerial displays or conjoined twins, create the space to resist "oppressive bodily containment" and can ultimately provide a "model of feminist practice" (26). Even more common varieties of spectacle might also be grotesque. Kerry Mallan writes, "The female body as grotesque spectacle is a mark of excess: too much makeup, outrageous clothes, loud laughter, and behaviour which flaunts the limits of physicality, sobriety and sexuality" (26). Such excess marks a refusal to abide by societal restrictions placed on women, and depictions of such transgressive personalities in children's films may provide "pleasure for young female viewers" (26). Approaches like Miles's, Russo's, and Mallan's illustrate that although certain constructions of the grotesque can be understood as distinctly womanly, such associations are not automatically positive or negative. Rather, it depends on a constellation of factors, including who is utilizing, as well as who is encountering, the female grotesque and how.

"Reeling for the Empire," the Japanese Textile Industry, and the Grotesque

In 2013, Karen Russell published her second anthology of short stories, *Vampires in the Lemon Grove.* The stories in this anthology, like much of her fiction, often focus on adolescence and/or transformation. Perhaps the most transfixing story is "Reeling for the Empire." It takes place around the turn of the twentieth century in Japan. The premise of the story is that young women and adolescent girls are recruited to work in a textile factory, where they are imprisoned in the work room. The workers, due to a concoction they are forced to drink after their contracts are signed, gradually transform into human-size silkworms. They begin to produce silk from their own mutating bodies, which they trade for mulberry leaves to eat, which allows them to produce more silk. They become part of a capitalist loop where rather than defining themselves by their work, their work defines and redefines them.

"Reeling for the Empire" utilizes the grotesque transformations of the women and girls as a metaphor that embodies the dehumanizing way that industrial capitalism redefines people as instruments in service to a capitalist ethos. The textile industry is one in which primarily adolescent girls are consigned to physically demanding work, valued not for their individuality but their productivity. "Reeling for the Empire" embodies this abstract value system. While the story is ostensibly about Japan's history, it also critiques contemporary Western culture and its emphasis on productivity, the disintegration of the boundary between work and other aspects of life, and the lack of an adequate social safety net, which provides the impetus for Russell's narrator to unwittingly sign away her life and body. Yet the story also provides emancipatory insight into how the characters are able to escape their dehumanizing environment. This allows for consideration regarding how we might embrace new conceptions of individuality and community while simultaneously rejecting the dehumanization of capitalism.

The economic and social historian Janet Hunter notes that Japan experienced industrialization "from the middle of the nineteenth century to the 1930s" (1). This industrialization was dominated by the textile industry. The "overwhelming majority" of textile work taking place "from the 1880s to the late 1930s" included "silk reeling, cotton spinning, and weaving," and these occupations "drew their workforces mainly from the same group within the Japanese population: young women between the ages of 10 and 25, most of them from rural areas" (2). Textile work was labor intensive, but labor was a resource that industrializing Japan had in abundance (1). Russell's short story does not specifically give a date during which it is set, but it is set during the Meiji period, which was named after Emperor Meiji and ran from 1868 to his death in 1912.

Japan's industrialization was driven in part by a silk export boom after 1850. This transformed much of the silk industry. According to Hunter, "In the wake of the export boom, the silk reeling and spinning industry underwent a process of growth and transformation. While much silk weaving remained in the hands of artisans or farmers' wives, reeling and spinning increasingly moved away from the farm household, becoming concentrated in a range of factories and workshops" (38). One of the ways that the industry was modernized was the advent of mechanical reeling, which was "the major advance of the early Meiji period" (121). The application of steam first and subsequently electricity allowed silk textile workers to focus on extracting and twisting filaments together rather than turning the reel, and it increased the productivity of textile workers by "increasing the number of basins that could be operated by each worker, and the number of threads reeled per worker. The invention of the multi-ends . . . reeling machine in 1903, and its utilisation much later in the interwar period, meant that ten or more threads could be reeled in one basin, whereas previously it had been only a few" (121).

Despite these advances, "the extraction of the filament from the cocoon, and in particular twisting it together with others to form a single unbroken thread, remained largely unmechanised" (122). Yet despite the industrialization of elements of the reeling process, the Japanese silk industry was under pressure from foreign competition. Italian and French reelers introduced reeling machinery in the early 1870s, but the Japanese reeling industry was unable to keep up with technological advancements until they invented and upgraded technology in the 1920s (Tsurumi 47). The Japanese industry compensated by paying their workers less than European or Chinese reelers (48). This coincided with the shift during the Meiji period from reelers who came "from an ex-samurai or well-to-do commoner family [to] a silk worker with a different background, the daughter of marginally independent cultivators or tenant farmers" (47).

So, while the increase in efficiency was good news for those who most profited from the textile trade, there was technological lag compared to other countries, and the workers were not paid well. E. Patricia Tsurumi writes, "The low wage costs of Japanese silk manufacturing were attained and maintained through long working hours, few rest periods, and provision of worker accommodation close to the factory floor so that almost every waking hour could be a working hour" (48). Furthermore, the factory work was difficult. Management at the time considered female labor disposable and sought to control rather than induce workers (Hunter 141). Moreover, the working conditions were wretched. Textile workers in factories worked up to seventeen hours a day, with little time to rest or eat. Factories were loud, dirty, and, in the summer, could be brutally hot. This led to health problems like tuberculosis. The dormitories were crowded and poor quality (90). Workers' activities were monitored so they did not run away. Wages were low and paid in such a way to "put workers in thrall to both employer and family" (91). Due to these conditions, silk reeling mills were "the main locus for protests by female textile workers before the First World War" (254). Sometimes these protests involved strikes, other times they involved "groups of workers absconding together from mills in search of better conditions or wages" (254). However, some Suwa silk manufacturers adopted an agreement that took effect in 1901 that gave members "the exclusive 'right' to reengage his former employees, who remained registered with him after the year's work was finished" (Tsurumi 74). In prior years, many reelers changed mills, but this agreement effectively turned the workers into the property of the manufacturers.

As noted earlier, the Japanese textile industry was heavily gendered, and the majority of textile workers were young women or female children like in many other countries, although it often was not a girl's first job. *Komori* were young girls who looked after their young siblings, and girls from poor families often went to work for richer households until they were able to find jobs as textile workers or housemaids. Harald Salomon notes, "Childhood ended for these girls when they were seven or eight years old, or even earlier" (355). At the time, some argued that girls and young women were ideal for textile work because they were better able to reel and spin thread because their hands were more dexterous, although the requirement that textile workers plunge their hands into near boiling water coarsened their hands to the point that they could damage threads (Hunter 70). Girls and young women were also considered "more docile and less troublesome than men, and over time these qualities of malleability and good behaviour were increasingly believed to reside more in the rural population than in the growing urban one, [which was] seen as corrupted by exposure to new opportunities and dubious moralities" (71). This is not to say urban girls and young women were not hired, but that some felt that growing urban environments corrupted them and made them less appealing workers. Many rural workers were found by recruiting agents who traveled from place to place and attempted to recruit young women and adolescents to sign contracts to work in textile factories. Recruiting agents were a common occurrence in the textile industry during the Meiji period, but their ubiquity did not mean they were safe. Some women were raped or sold into prostitution by their recruiting agents (76). As we will see, "Reeling for the Empire" captures the abuse and control the girls and young women experienced. These abuses are central to the transformation the characters are forced to undergo. The exploitation of the workers is both economic and bodily, as the characters are remade to embody their work, and Russell clearly sees the industrial conditions faced by the silk workers as a form of violation enacted upon their bodies.

"Reeling for the Empire" takes place in a silk reeling mill, which the workers call Nowhere Mill because they are unable to figure out its location. This sets up the story as one that could take place at any of the number of mills, but it also speaks to the notion that these workers are, in effect, kidnapped prisoners. They eat, sleep, and work together in the same room, near the machine that reels the silk. The novel is told through the perspective of Kitsune, who, like her peers, was recruited for the mill. Her father is ill and unable to work, and so Kitsune signs the contract herself and without her father's knowledge, unlike her peers whose contracts are almost always signed by their parents or guardians. To finalize the contract, the recruiting agent takes Kitsune to a secluded place and feeds her an abhorrent concoction that she later learns is what transforms the young girls and women into silkworms. Kitsune, unlike her peers, is the only one who voluntarily drinks the entirety of the liquid. Many have to be violently forced to drink the tea because it is venomous: "Only through the Agent's intervention were they able to get the tea down. It took his hands around their throats" (36).

From the onset of the story, the reader immediately knows something is amiss. The narrator briefly mentions "the polar fur that covers [their] faces" (23) before she bluntly states, "We are all becoming reelers. Some kind of hybrid creature, part *kaiko*, silkworm caterpillar, and part human female" (24). Kitsune describes the process to two new laborers. She says, "The Agent's drink is remaking your insides. Your intestines, your secret organs. Soon your stomachs will bloat. You will manufacture silk in your gut with the same helpless skill that you digest food, exhale" (29). To harvest the silk, the women plunge their hands into boiling water so the skin on their fingertips "softens and bursts," revealing fibers that are subsequently wound together and then fed into the reeling machine (30).

The women exist in a state of transformation, neither fully human nor silkworm. This transformation metaphorically embodies the transition from women who are initially unassimilated into the modernizing economy of

Japan to those who become integrated into it. Kitsune makes this connection overt when she reflects, "All Japan is undergoing a transformation—we *kaiko-joko* are not alone in that respect" (33). The grotesque tends to combine or juxtapose seemingly separate realms or ideas. These combinations and juxtapositions unsettle complacent worldviews because they place seemingly contradictory elements in relation to each other. The emotional resonance of the grotesque is itself complicated, as the grotesque may inspire seemingly contradictory reactions like attraction and repulsion. We can see this in Kitsune's reaction to her transformation, which she calls "a giddy sort of terror" (24). The word "giddy" connotes a sort of almost dizzying excitement, which makes the terror she feels at her transformation one of fear, but also, perhaps, possibility.

The satisfaction Kitsune takes from her transformation surfaces in her appreciation of the volume and color of the silk she produces. She notes, "In spite of everything, I can't help but admire the quantity of silk that we . . . can produce in a single day. The agent boasts that he has made us the most productive machines in the empire" who have eliminated supply problems, don't waste silk, and combine "laborious collection and separation . . . processes in the single factory of our body. Ceaselessly, even while we dream, we are generating thread. Every droplet of our energy, every moment of our time flows into the silk" (30). It is significant that the agent calls them "machines" and Kitsune uses the word "factory." Their bodily factories position them as sites of economic production, and the reference to machines positions them as utilitarian objects with a purpose that ignores their individuality and subjectivity. These references add another metaphorical dimension to the grotesque nature of the women's bodies, which become a way of realizing the relationships between worker, commodity, and capitalist production; the silkworm women become the ultimate efficiency, perhaps. There is no need to even dye the silk they produce because it comes out in colors. Kitsune's silk is green, and we are told "there is no other silk like it on the world market" (31–32). Kitsune also notes, "If you look at [the silk] from the right angle, a pollen seems to rise up and swirl into your eyes. Words can't exaggerate the joy of this effect" (32). We see happiness and pride in what their new bodies can accomplish. It is also notable that Kitsune transforms a human reaction into a more alien one. When she references pollen rising up and swirling into one's eyes, she may be referencing crying. It is not uncommon to hear someone with tears in their eyes downplay it by saying they have something in their eye, but at this point, it is unclear whether Kitsune can even cry or not. The ambiguity of the phrasing and whether or not it is directly referencing tears plays with how the women are transitioning into new forms.

Despite the ambivalent reactions to their transformations, the girls are clearly being exploited. As a result, they end up going on strike. The story references social unrest during the modernization of Japan. Kitsune's grandfather was forced to become a sharecropper on his own land and went into debt. After participating in a farmers' revolt and burning a creditor's office, he hanged himself. Kitsune's father then inherited the debt, which leads to Kitsune's decision to sign the factory contract. At the reeling mill, Kitsune is involved in an accident with the reeling machine and her threads turn black. Due to this adversity, she begins to believe she deserves her fate because she willingly drank the venomous tea. She argues with another worker, Dai. Kitsune exclaims, "Go reel for the empire, Dai. Make more silk for him to sell. . . . Make believe we're not slaves here" (42). This causes Dai to consider her own father's part in a failed rebellion where peasants refused to sow new crops in protest of a tax. Dai takes inspiration from this and decides to go on a hunger strike. But no one joins Dai, and she eventually dies. The agent collects her body to try and salvage the silk and tells the others that Dai was a thief who stole silk from the factory. Even in death, their bodies are not their own.

This incident also inspires Kitsune to rebel. She learns to control the production of her thread and makes a cocoon. Eventually all of the hybrid women make cocoons, and they trick the agent into entering the mill. Once inside, they stuff him inside a cocoon. For the agent, this is death. But for the women, their cocoons contain hope for the future, when they transform into winged moths and are able to escape. By this time, the women look completely alien. Among other changes, they now have white faces, sunken noses, and "insect-huge" eyes (51). Kitsune is excited for her next transformation. She tells the agent, "These wings of ours are invisible to you . . . and in fact you will never see them, since they exist only in our future, where you are dead and we are living, flying" (51). Kitsune's words are especially significant in light of how they have been mistreated and the acknowledgment of the failures of the previous generation's rebellions. In this context, by embracing their transformation into beings unrecognizable to previous conceptions of humanity, they entertain the possibility of escaping from the dehumanizing conditions that value their bodies solely for their economic potential. When redefined and transformed against their will, the women further redefined themselves by rejecting their status as commodities and asserting their independence. The story ends with Kitsune saying the names of the exploited women to their procurer, thus reasserting their individuality. The workers' wings do not exist yet, but they are no less real because they represent the potentiality the future holds for the young women and adolescents now that they have forcefully rejected the exploitative system represented by the now dead factory agent. It is significant that just as Mary Russo sees possibility for freedom in flight, Kitsune and her peers' escape is imagined through flight.

"Reeling for the Empire" asserts that while economies and their champions have the power to violently transform the way we think about ourselves, women, and I believe all exploited workers regardless of gender identity, may find freedom in a complete reconceptualization of themselves outside such systems. It is difficult to make direct comparisons regarding how this might work; however, one element that seems especially important is a sense of community. Alone, Dai dies, but together, the rest of the victims survive, even as they retain their individuality through the final recitation of their names. And, in a way, the final revolution is sparked by Dai, so even her resistance and death were not in vain. The story also suggests that without a shared vision or sense of purpose, it becomes easier for exploitation to continue. Furthermore, it calls for a recognition of the harm that certain systems cause. The dehumanizing labor of textile work, for example, is not something consumers are asked to confront when shopping for clothes. The work to produce textiles becomes abstract or removed from their consumption, but dehumanizing labor has real consequences. By visualizing dehumanization through the workers' transformation, the story helps readers imagine what an overemphasis on labor and productivity does to a person. The characters' (and children and adolescents') futures may be uncertain, but they contain possibilities, which are exemplified by the women's future ability to take flight. Perhaps, like with the silkworm women, our world holds the possibility for the escape from or transformation of real-world systems of exploitation, but surely only by rejecting patriarchal and capitalistic dehumanization.

One kink in the thread of logic emanating from this reading of "Reeling for the Empire" is that it is published in an era where industrial capitalism in the United States has been in decline. The textile industry still exists in the United States and abroad and industrialization is a driving force in many economies, but the current stage of late or neoliberal capitalism in the United

States is dominated by industries of finance, information, service, and technology. However, "Reeling," to my mind, sees similarities in the mistreatment of people at the hands of industry between the present and the past and across borders, which accounts for a contemporary United States novelist placing this narrative in a different historical (though obviously fictionalized) moment and setting. But if one wonders what it might look like to further consider the child worker in the context of a more recent period, *Geek Love* provides us with just such an example.

Geek Love, Fiedler's *Freaks*, and the Grotesque

Geek Love, a novel by Katherine Dunn published in 1989, depicts the Binewski family and their traveling carnival. The Binewski family consists of Aloysius (or Al), his wife Lillian (or Lil), and their children: Arturo, Electra, Iphigenia, Olympia, and Fortunato (or Arty, Elly, Iphy, Oly, and Chick). The story is told from Oly's perspective as a record of the family history for her daughter, Miranda. The Binewskis' history involves the display of their grotesque children in the carnival. Arty's hands and feet are directly connected to his torso and look like flippers; Elly and Iphy are twins conjoined at the torso; Oly has albinism, dwarfism, and a hunchback; and Chick is telekinetic and empathic. He can move things with his mind, even at the molecular level, and he experiences the feelings of others. The inclusion of children in a traveling carnival is in line with actual (and unfortunately named) freak shows and carnivals because they showcased people, often children, for profit (Bogdan 8–9; 112–13). Freak shows, whether in dime museums or traveling circuses, have a long history in the United States and were especially popular between 1840 and 1940 (2).[1] However, the primary difference between these earlier displays of children for profit and the display of children for profit in *Geek Love* is that the Binewski parents engineer their children from conception to be carnival attractions, which informs from birth how the children understand themselves as commodities.

The novel, through the Binewski children, employs grotesque metaphors for the commodification of children while simultaneously providing the rationale for such commodification. The children's bodies are valuable because, except for Chick's, they are physically unique. Furthermore, because the children's bodies are grotesque, they seem to fit in well at the carnival.

While Oly eventually works in the outside world, the children's bodies are the justification for their existence. This dynamic causes the children to define themselves by the patriarchal and capitalistic systems that exploit them. The terminology that dominates the novel is one of "freaks" versus "norms" where the unique freak is desirable and the commonplace norm is not. I will situate the discourse of freaks within the realm of the grotesque and argue that the Binewski children's grotesque bodies are aesthetic embodiments of some of the effects of neoliberal capitalism. This aesthetic disguises itself as one of individuality, but ultimately narrows all possibilities for individual expression because children are valued for their economic worth in the carnival and they are expected to exist within the carnival as part of the family economic unit.

Thankfully, the term "freak" is no longer commonly used, but it was widely used in carnivals. Russo argues that freaks and grotesques share similarities in that both often deviate from physical norms, but freaks may be differentiated from grotesques by the association of freaks with spectacle, such as that which takes place within the carnival (78–79). However, the similarities between the two categories go beyond physical difference. In Leslie Fiedler's 1978 book *Freaks*, he examines extraordinary bodies, like conjoined twins or those with dwarfism, while also discussing their treatment historically, including their relation to the carnival. While he refers to his subject matter as freaks, his discussion resonates with the grotesque, even though he does not specifically engage with theories of the grotesque. Fiedler spends much of his introduction discussing why the term "freak" is the most appropriate for his project. He writes, "Euphemisms lack the resonance necessary to represent the sense of quasi-religious awe which we experience first and most strongly as children: face to face with fellow humans more marginal than the poorest sharecroppers or black convicts on a Mississippi chain gain" (17). This justification is notable because it positions people with disabilities beneath exploited groups like poor sharecroppers, who had to give much of the fruits of their labor to landowners, and prisoners forced to work for the state. This comparison foreshadows the ways such individuals may be exploited. Field also notes that combinations of terror, laughter, and sympathy are reactions people without disabilities have when encountering people with such disabilities (19–20, 24). Furthermore, Fiedler discusses the upending of ontological classifications. "The true Freak," he writes, "challenges the conventional boundaries between male and female, sexed and sexless, animal and human, large and small, self and other, and consequently between reality and illusion, experience and fantasy, fact and myth" before qualifying that "no actual Freak threatens all of these limits at once" (24). Fiedler's association of freaks with marginalized positions, ambivalent reactions, and boundary crossings resonates with theories of the grotesque.

Coincidently, Fiedler notes that childhood is the time when one is most uncertain "about the limits of our bodies and our egos," as well as the boundaries between dreams and reality (27). Children may feel freakish because they are so much smaller than adults but may be quite larger than babies or their previous selves (28). Fiedler also writes, "Born unhousebroken and half wild, dabbling in their own feces and popping into their mouths whatever unlikely objects they can grab, they remain for a long time unsure . . . whether they are beasts or men: little animals more like their pets than their parents" (28). In addition to scale, children may also seem freakish because they are not fully domesticated, so they seem to cross lines between animal and human, civilization and barbarism. The articulation of children as "half wild" aligns with Puritan conceptions of the child as one in need of restraint. Fiedler's discussion of the animality of children is based on an adult perspective. Structural divisions, even ones that may be understandable and helpful in organizing the world and establishing an identity, are learned. It is highly unlikely that children are "unsure . . . whether they are beasts or men" if for no other reason than such classifications are not yet fully ingrained in them. Fiedler's assertion that infants and babies are unsure of their ontological status reveals more about adults than it reveals about children. If anything, parents or adult onlookers may ponder the behavior of a child and whimsically wonder into what realm, animal or human, he or she belongs, thus revealing a small crack in the wall that humans construct between themselves and other animals.

Fiedler's observations regarding feelings of freakishness are more convincingly applicable to adolescents. His most persuasive account of youths as freaks is when they leave childhood behind and enter puberty (30). Entry into adolescence often involves accompanying issues relating to self-perception. Adolescents may feel "monstrously deficient or excessive, too tall, too short, too fat, too thin" (32). His stance that adolescence is a time of freakishness is especially convincing because so many people remember feelings of inadequacy or strangeness from adolescence. Nonetheless, children and adolescents are not freaks. Yet Fiedler's identification of youths' feelings is important because it helps him establish one of the cultural functions of the freak show: "A Victorian institution . . . intended to be finally therapeutic, cathartic, no matter what initial terror and insecurity it evokes. '*We* are the Freaks,' the human oddities are supposed to reassure us . . . 'Not you, Not *you!*'" (31). Fiedler again focuses on multiple reactions, which resonates with the grotesque. Initial feelings of terror or insecurity may give way to feelings of superiority as people with disabilities, in this context, remind the viewer of a social order of which the viewers sit atop, at least compared to those with disabilities.

This reassurance leads to a paradoxical situation in which one of the defining characteristics of people with certain disabilities—the ability to collapse boundaries—is at odds with another characteristic: the ability to alleviate feelings of freakishness in others by creating a boundary. This is because alleviating feelings of freakishness is predicated on the idea that "they" are freaks and "we" are not. Therefore, a boundary is created between, to borrow *Geek Love*'s terminology, "freaks" and "norms." This boundary is reestablished after Fiedler initially collapses the boundary by noting how children and adolescents may appear as, or feel themselves to be, freaks. In the reestablishment of the boundary between people who are different from each other, people with disabilities are placed in emotional service to others, as people with disabilities serve to reassure people without disabilities of their normalcy.

Geek Love and the Commodification of the Grotesque Child

Geek Love, as it overflows with depictions of children with disabilities, is prescient in its exemplification of the dangers of neoliberal capitalism, as it foresaw some of the ways in which children internalize neoliberal logic. Its publication follows the Reagan presidency, which David Harvey notes is instrumental in the rise of neoliberalism (24–26). [2] Anna Mae Duane writes, "The shocking premise in *Geek Love* that parents would create children as explicit commodities starkly dramatizes what, for many theorists, is nothing less than the dominant economic model of the late twentieth century. In an era of affective labor, economic production and human reproduction are inextricable" (111). Engineering children as commodities evokes the tension between the economic and the social under neoliberalism. The tension resonates with discussions of the grotesque children. The Binewskis define the family by market logic and then situate their children in a world where their lives and work are inseparable. The children do not just market their skills; they literally market themselves, not as workers but as beings.

The exploitation of the Binewski children begins before their conception when Al inherits the struggling carnival. To counteract the carnival's decline, Al and Lil Binewski create their own attractions to replace aging and lost ones. Al draws upon traditional American values for perverse means: "Al was a standard-issue Yankee, set on self-determination and independence, but in that crisis his core of genius revealed itself. He decided to breed his own freak show" (7).[3] The word "breed" is evocative of the tension inherent in the Binewski children: they are commodities as well as individuals. The language of breeding evokes both eugenics and breeding animals for profit. The children are ideal carnival workers because their labor is free, and they have familial incentives to stay. If they left, they would abandon their family as well as enter into a world outside the carnival, where their value would be upended and they may no longer fit in. The carnival functions like Kuryluk's cave, as both a shelter and a prison. In the carnival, the Binewski children's bodies are assets, and people come to lavish attention on them. However, outside the carnival, the children lack the protective environment of acceptance the carnival provides. This is evidenced when the family takes a trip to a grocery store, and someone attempts to murder the kids.

Al comes up with the scheme to breed children with physical disabilities, and his wife, Lil, proves a willing partner.[4] During her ovulation and pregnancies, Al doses her with "illicit and prescription drugs, insecticides, and eventually radioisotopes" (7).[5] Although Lil eventually goes blind and loses her memory, she initially avoids health issues. The Binewski parents never concern themselves with the potential consequences for Lil's health or the effect that the desired differences will have on their children. Al and Lil view the differences as gifts. Lil rhetorically asks, "What greater gift could you offer your children than an inherent ability to earn a living just by being themselves?" (7). This is a great question in the neoliberal moment, when society encourages everyone to be unique individuals who are themselves "private owners of their own 'human capital'" (Shaviro 8). Yet Lil's questions, like the ethical issues inherent in neoliberal economic practices, obfuscates or ignores the ethical dimensions of such a question, even as it exhibits a perceptive understanding of the wider world's dominant logic.

Victoria Warren argues that the novel challenges cultural norms by giving subjectivity to those with disabilities rather than those without (329). Part of Dunn's critique of American culture, for Warren, involves Al's creation of his children. Warren observes the exploitive nature of this process with her contention that "Al's product is deformed children" (324) and that his creation and accumulation of these products "underscores the degradation and callousness potentially inherent in individualistic American capitalism" (331). The lack of concern over health risks, as well as the tension in seeing the Binewski children as both subject and object, child and exhibit, resonates with Warren's assertion of degradation and callousness. Al almost abandons one of his newborn children, Chick, because Chick's body is not obviously commodifiable to Al. Rachel Adams notes, "The Binewskis are excellent interpreters of the capitalist system that constructs the body as a commodity" because they "recogniz[e] the significant relationship between the body and the ability to generate income" (280–81). This mentality begins with Al, and although this mentality demonstrates Al's economic intuitiveness, it also resonates with the callousness Warren identifies because Al associates his children's worth with the wealth they can generate. Al's children all internalize this logic, except for Chick. When Chick can no longer take the constant exploitation and subsequent pain and suffering of himself and others, he blows up the carnival. Duane argues that "the Binewskis reflect . . . how extensively the logic of the marketplace permeates the allegedly sacred realm of home and family" (107). Chick especially represents the tension between the merger of the market and the family, and he undermines the notion that the child can be sheltered from such a merger. Duane writes, "As a lovely nineteenth-century cherub stranded in a cutthroat twentieth-century domicile, Chick evokes a past fetishized throughout the 1980s by Christian conservatives—a world in which the child occupies the pinnacle of the private and functions as the affective center of a home ruled solely by love, walled off from the harsh bargains demanded by the outside world" (104). But Chick, Duane teaches us, may undermine this construction. He appears to resist the economic logic that informs his siblings in that he takes pleasure in helping others, not making money. He is "loving, innocent, and seemingly incapable of malice" (108). But this is an illusion, as he represents "a new domestic space reflecting an affective economy that undoes the division between home and work, and between love and money. In the process, the novel chronicles the destruction of the individual subject created by the supposed tension between the home and the market"

(106). Within this domestic space, "the desire to imagine children existing in a state of fetishized innocence, and thereby separate from a primary source of American value—the ability to produce capital—masks the emotional labor that children are expected to do" (110). Chick's emotional labor facilitates the ability of his more overtly capitalistic family members to achieve their desires, and it places Chick at the mercenary whims of his father and brother. While Duane notes that the entrance of the child's affective labor "into the market-place might alter the existing models of value" (118), Chick's destruction of himself and the carnival suggests that "the affective labor of childhood can be as coercive and as destructive as paid labor" (119). Chick demonstrates the illusory nature of the innocent child by revealing how the innocent child cannot be separated from the way that market logic invades the family. Chick provides an effective vehicle for critique because of the rhetorical power of the innocent child. While affective labor is generally associated with women, and specifically mothers, the early twentieth century's attempt to remove children from economic considerations transitioned them more concretely into the domestic sphere.

Duane's argument that Chick undermines the construction of the inno-cent child at a time when market forces permeate the family and that Chick illustrates the destructive capacity of affective labor convincingly illustrates one of the problems of the current economic model, where the work of caring for others is feminized and devalued, supposedly done for its own sake, underpaid and exhausting, both emotionally and physically. Duane need not spend much time on the other children of the novel to construct her argument, yet the other children flesh out the logic of commodification ingrained within the family.

Arty is the oldest living Binewski child and the most invested in his body's economic worth, which is predicated on how he looks. [6] Dunn calls Arty "Aqua Boy" and describes his appearance:

> His hands and feet were in the form of flippers that sprouted directly from his torso without intervening arms or legs. He was taught to swim in infancy and was displayed nude in a big clear-sided tank like an aquarium. His favorite trick at the ages of three and four was to put his face close to the glass, bulging his eyes out at the audiences, opening and closing his mouth like a river bass and then to turn his back and paddle off, revealing the turd trailing from his muscular little buttocks. (7–8)

Arty does not need to be in water to survive, so his learning to swim in infancy is based exclusively on the way Al decides to market him, which is to associate him with aquatic creatures. The words "display" and "trick" reinforce the nature of Arty's status as an object created for the carnival. Arty buys into the role for which his father grooms him. Although he retains identifiably human features, Arty's value to the carnival is based on how nonhuman he appears. But Arty is biologically human. His physical differences are the result of the toxins he was exposed to *in utero*, and these differences do not make him less human. Arty's heredity is not grotesque, but his physicality is: he is marketable because he seems to violate basic categories between human and animal. A typical human in an aquarium is not valuable. An aquatic creature in an aquarium is not necessarily valuable (and a river bass not at all). Arty is valuable because he exists in a state that appears in between, even though logically and biologically he is fully human.

One might expect Arty and his siblings to harbor resentment toward the parents for making them into carnival attractions, but they do not. Oly notes, "Papa would tell us about the hard times and explain that Arty had brought success to the show, and that Elly and Iphy had helped the business and, because he was a kind man, that even Oly had 'done her part.' There was always work but it was good" (47). Al's insistence that the children are integral parts of the family business causes the children to define themselves in those terms. Because the children are told their value is predicated on how much money they can bring in, this becomes how they determine their self-worth. This valuation is so central to their identity that it can register affectively; Oly quivers after being told she is not as economically valuable as her siblings (75).

Oly does take pride in her body but feels inadequate compared to her siblings. Her self-worth is based on how little relative value her unique body holds. She notes, "My father spared no expense in [the] experiments. My mother had been liberally dosed with cocaine, amphetamines, and arsenic during her ovulation and throughout her pregnancy with me. It was a disappointment when I emerged with such commonplace deformities" (8). Oly remarks that her albinism is "the regular pin-eyed variety" and her hump "is not remarkable in size or shape" (8). Albinism and hunchbacks may be uncommon, but they are not so rare that customers would pay to see them. Although her dwarfism "increased [her] value" in her parents' eyes, it does not make her unique enough to headline as her own attraction (8). Oly's disabilities are not scarce enough to generate the types of profit that Arty or the twins generate. She is a unique composite, with a myriad of unusual, but not exceedingly rare, attributes, whereas her siblings' attributes are much rarer and are therefore more commodifiable.

Michael Hardin believes that *Geek Love* "presents a world where the freak-ish is defined as normal, where the mutated body is desired and empowered" (338). But even these celebrated bodies succumb to the crushing weight of exploitation. The female Binewskis experience the tension between agency and vulnerability that Wall observes is so common to childhood (40). However, this tension is heightened due to their bodies. The familial weight smothering the women begins immediately. First, Al commodifies them, and then Arty continues the patriarchal dominance of the family, especially of Elly and Iphy. Most of the Binewski children die in the carnival: more are stillborn or die in infancy than reach adolescence, and every one of Oly's surviving siblings dies immediately before, or because of, Chick's destruction of the carnival.

The children's bodies certainly are "desired and empowered" to various degrees and in various ways. When a journalist following the carnival asks if Oly ever wished to be "normal," Oly responds, "That's ridiculous! Each of us is unique. We are masterpieces. Why would I want us to change into assembly-line items?" (282). Oly's language positions the children as valuable objects with the use of the term "masterpieces" as opposed to the more common "assembly-line items" while comparing birth to a process of manufacturing objects, where norms are easily reproducible while freaks are not. Ironically, the difference that makes the children "masterpieces" is similar to popular parenting rhetoric: rhetoric that valorizes each child as distinctly special. This rhetoric also coincides with neoliberalism's emphasis on entrepreneurship and individuality as opposed to postwar parents' desire for "their children to be normal and average," to "be like the others rather than conspicuous" (Mintz 281).[7]

Historically, people who were carnival attractions were often displayed doing the mundane. Robert Bogdan writes, "Many were presented as 'human wonders,' but they did not sing opera or claim heroic feats; rather, they merely performed pedestrian tasks which the marks assumed were too difficult for them given their physical disabilities. They brandished such mundane achievements as finding a spouse and giving birth" (200). He further notes, "Part of the fascination of joined twins was the puzzle of how they performed such normal activities as walking and sitting" (201). The Binewski twins,

Elly and Iphy, are virtuoso piano players, but they also rely on the interest in the day-to-day workings of people with disabilities that the carnival has historically capitalized on. The twins are also physically attractive, "always beautiful, slim, and huge-eyed" (8), and popular. Oly notes, "The norm crowds loved them. In towns we passed through regularly pairs of young girls would come to the show dressed in a single long skirt in imitation of the twins" (51).

While the performance of the twins revolves around their piano playing, this is not what interests all their fans. Some spectators are interested in how extraordinary bodies engage in the mundane, or knowable, world, but others want to experience it. Fiedler notes, "All Freaks are perceived to one degree or another as erotic, indeed, abnormality arouses in some 'normal' beholders a temptation to go beyond looking to *knowing* in the full carnal sense the ultimate other" (137). Elizabeth Grosz argues that the ability of the freak to inspire multiple reactions like horror and fascination involves their sexuality: "People think to themselves: 'How do they do *it?*' . . . The perverse pleasure of voyeurism and identification is counterbalanced by horror at the blurring of identities (sexual, corporeal, personal) that witness our chaotic and insecure identities. Freaks traverse the very boundaries that secure the 'normal' subject in its given identity and sexuality" (64). The twins understand this and capitalize on such sexual curiosity.

Once Elly and Iphy get older, they attempt to take control of their own destiny by marketing themselves outside the normal carnival acts. They become prostitutes: "'You know what the norms really want to ask?' said Elly. 'What they want to know, all of them, but never do unless they're drunk or simple, is How do we fuck? That and who, or maybe what. Most of the guys wonder what it would be like to fuck us. So, I figure, why not capitalize on that curiosity?" (207). Elly understands that the twins' appeal is in the tension between their difference and similarity to the carnival-goers and revolves around how their bodies are viewed, not their individual subjectivity or less immediately obvious aspects of themselves, such as their personalities.

Elly and Iphy's self-commodification is, in a sense, subversive. It undermines the family dynamic of profits going to the carnival, which is led first by Al and then by Arty. It also gives the twins a sense of ownership over their own bodies. This subversion still treats their bodies as commodities, but now they are commodities for the sake of each other and themselves rather than for the family. For the twins, this has disastrous consequences as Arty reasserts ownership over them, but it also briefly hints at the possibilities for individual expression and the subversive nature of the grotesque, especially in that they are taking ownership of their sexuality, which is traditionally a patriarchal fear. At the same time, however, it reveals the twins' inability, or at least lack of desire, to reimagine themselves as something other than commodities for men. The Binewski family is "highly capitalist and patriarchal" (Worthington 119). Elly and Iphy best embody the harm such systems due to women specifically, as Arty reasserts his dominance over them, in part by reclaiming their bodies by giving them away to his lackey, who rapes and impregnates them.

Even when raised outside the carnival, the Binewskis still exist in a capitalist, patriarchal system, so they cannot fully escape the dehumanizing logic of the carnival. However, the woman who fares the best in the novel grows up outside the carnival. Miranda, Oly's daughter, has a tail that she is able to hide by curling it up and wearing skirts. Miranda works at a strip club that fetishizes difference. As her dance reaches its pinnacle, the reader is led to believe she is going to take off her underwear and reveal her bare buttocks. Instead, the dance's conclusion involves the revelation, both for the strip club patrons and the reader, of her tail:

> She was down to her G-string with the fluffy lace plume on her rump, she had her thumbs hooked in it, looking over her shoulder at the crowd, she was waving her ass in a slow semaphore of invitation . . . she pulled the plume down, unsnapped the G-string and whipped it off with a flourish, waving her ass still, her head tipped up and an unmistakable giggle bubbling out of her as she revealed the thin, curling tail that jutted out from the end of her spine and bounced just above her round buttocks. (17)

The striptease's culmination highlights Miranda's continuation of the Binewski tradition of profiting from physical difference and the twins' acknowledgment that their bodies inspire sexual curiosity. Miranda does not need to work as a stripper because her living expenses and tuition are paid for by a mysterious benefactor (Oly). She chooses to dance. It's ironic that the first Binewski woman completely free from her family's patriarchal control still commodifies herself for, primarily, men. Perhaps the difference is that she makes her own decision, free from certain economic constraints, even as she hones her artistic skills so she can pursue her desire to illustrate medical texts. She cannot, after all, completely escape the broader capitalistic and patriarchal systems beyond the carnival. Miranda hopes to empower herself outside patriarchal directives, and although she has not yet found a way around treating her body as a commodity, she has aspirations to do so.

Conclusion

Within the females of the Binewski family are the seeds of a radical reunderstanding of themselves waiting to bloom. Miranda, who grows up outside the carnival, best embodies such new potentiality. Miranda is an exotic dancer by choice, not necessity. She is able to make her decision without the patriarchal influences of Al or Arty, which is significant and prompts Weese's contention that "Dunn's real interest lies less in physical difference than in gender—in possibilities for female grotesques who must find modes of self-expression outside the literal carnival setting, a space where they are oppressed by the carnival's entirely conventional patriarchal practices" (349). Miranda's uncertainty about whether to have her tail removed suggests she must still negotiate her own sense of self in relation to her body, and her economic freedom provides her advantages the vast majority of people lack, but her decisions are her own.

The complexity of Miranda's feelings about her body also exemplifies the shifting use of the grotesque within literature. David Mitchell writes, "The literary grotesque—those physical and cognitive anomalies, malformations and deformities placed in the service of symbolic social and artistic meanings—is a fantasy that invokes physical aberrancy as a visible symptom of social disorganization and collapse" (348). Although modernist grotesques represent social dimensions, "traditional interpretations of the grotesque in literature end up reinscribing biology, rather than social institutions, as the causal agent of physical aberrancy" (348). In modernist literature, then, even as the grotesque is a metaphor for social collapse, its cause is biological rather than social. Subsequent authors, however, often interrogate the grotesque's use rather than rely on previous conceptions that reinscribe biological rationale, and Dunn's novel is "a caricature of artistic desire to yoke physical aberrancy to metaphors of denigration and perversity" (348). Mitchell is ultimately incorporating postmodern subjectivity into the field of disability studies (349), by arguing that *Geek Love* mediates on the relationship between the constructed nature of freaks and "the conflicted meanings of physical difference in the public and private realms" (357, 360).

Geek Love shows the possibility and danger regarding how children internalize their own commodity status. It shows moments of true economic or emotional self-worth, but it also creates situations where the characters are unable to see beyond their commodity status. This ultimately reifies their assigned identities because they have no understanding of how they might define themselves outside the system into which they were born. Like many economic models, neoliberal capitalism forces children into the market system. But some scholars, like Henry Giroux, understand neoliberal capitalism as especially dangerous because of how little it allows for social welfare. For children under neoliberal capitalism, this means that "youth are denied the ability to define themselves" and "when adult society talks about children, they are usually described as commodities or as threats to society" (14). *Geek Love* demonstrates that children, immersed in an economic system, define themselves by it. Their environment shapes their conceptions before they are consciously aware that there are other alternatives. Of course this makes sense, because for many neoliberals, as Thatcher put it, "There is no alternative" (Blyth 98). At the same time, however, the novel does gesture toward an alternative. It coopts patriarchal and economic dominance by allowing people (females, people with disabilities, the commodified) to define themselves. In the novel, this leads to tragedy for many because of the vise-like grip of patriarchal interests, and it lacks the emancipatory potential of "Reeling," but it allows individuals to assert some of their own agency within a system that exploits them, and offers expressions of transgressive resistance to dominant ideologies, even if such ideologies still shape or constrain such expressions. In doing so, the novel encourages a fuller appreciation of human variety and ability.

CHAPTER 4

Monstrous Soldiers

The Grotesque and Postmodernism in *Elephantmen* and *The Beef*

Another form of child labor, widely and appropriately seen as a scourge, involves child soldiers. Historically, "the active participation of children in armed conflicts is not a new phenomenon" (Collmer 2). In the United States, for example, children have served, oftentimes seemingly by choice, in wars. For example, children and adolescents were active in the lead-up to the Revolutionary War. The minimum age or service was supposed to be sixteen, but demand led many recruiting agents to allow younger boys to serve as half the population was below the minimum age (Mintz 63). Boys were able to lie about their age or find an adult to vouch for them. In fact, "5 percent of Virginia's troops were fourteen or fifteen" (63). During the Civil War, probably about 5 percent of soldiers were under eighteen, and some were only ten. Some children and adolescents also served as scouts and nurses (120). Currently, children fourteen or younger are considered child soldiers for the purposes of war crimes, whereas much international human rights law defines a child as seventeen or younger (Beber and Blattman 67). The efforts to limit the use of child soldiers by the UN and other international organizations has been effective among governments and some nonstate groups, but "child soldiering persists among insurgents, terror groups, and other armed forces" (65–66). In environments with ongoing violence, it may be a rational choice for young people to become child soldiers for the increased protection that a group can bring (Collmer 5). However, the longer an armed conflict takes place, the more likely children will be used as soldiers and the more children will die (7). Furthermore, child soldiers are often forced. Some argue that "overpopulation has made children a cheap, limitless, and renewable resource," although it is also easier to coerce children and cheaper to maintain them than adult soldiers (Beber and Blattman 67–68). The idea that children are a resource as soldiers is also picked up in some fictional narratives. For example, the often-grotesque mutants in *Uncanny X-Men* and related comics first develop powers during puberty. The multiple Marvel lines featuring mutants yoke together the grotesqueness of the mutants' powers, often accompanied by physical changes, with the feelings of grotesqueness many adolescents feel due to their changing bodies. There are a number of mutant storylines in which governments or other state or corporate actors seek to utilize mutants as military assets. Another comic book series, *Elephantmen*, extends the desire for a child soldier to their birth and childhood development so that the entire existence of the child is in service to their future as a soldier. Admittedly, the soldiers fight when they are older and stronger, not when they are young children, but their youth is spent preparing them to be the assets they are created to be.

In this chapter, I argue that *Elephantmen* depicts grotesque dehumanization in the form of the titular characters. The characters specifically draw upon a history of the racial grotesque. This history is bound up in the enslavement of Africans and African Americans, and the comic book engages in a postmodern rendering of this and other atrocities. I connect this postmodern approach to an emphasis on commodification that also exists within the narrative. I also take time to explore the associations between the terms "monster" and "grotesque" as a way of continuing to explore the resonance of the grotesque as well as think about the various ways we disavow humans.

Elephantmen launched in 2006 and is written primarily by Richard Starkings, with art by a variety of creators, including Ladrönn and Moritat.[1] The series takes place more than two hundred years in the future and follows the exploits of male animal-human hybrids who are called Elephantmen. Not all the hybrids are part elephant, but the initial hybrid characters are all created from animals found in Africa.[2] Elephantmen are created in Africa by the transnational MAPPO corporation. The corporation, led by a Japanese geneticist named Nikken, creates the hybrids using kidnapped African women as incubators. After coming to term, the women die as the hybrid children are ripped from their wombs. Because the hybrids are created in

Africa and born from the bodies of African women, they are clearly meant to be understood as Africans. As the hybrids grow, MAPPO trains them to be military commodities. When they are older, the Elephantmen are deployed against Asian forces in a war fought on a European battle front. After the war, the United Nations liberates the hybrids and votes to integrate them into mainstream society, primarily in the United States, and rehabilitates them. While this decision is initially considered altruistic, eventually it is revealed that the Elephantmen are allowed to live because they may be of future use. The series primarily focuses on the adult hybrids after the war. However, the hybrids are shaped extensively by their origins, and the comic books, especially early ones, often depict the circumstances surrounding their birth and childhood.

The grotesque nature of the Elephantmen is multifaceted. Their immense size, for example, is one feature of their grotesque embodiment (Fiedler 14; Miles 91). However, their grotesque elements are most prominently located within their hybridity, which situates them within a tradition of the racial grotesque. Leonard Cassuto argues that the grotesque is culturally constructed and often used to dehumanize other races, and it cannot be understood outside cultural contexts. For example, American Indians were grotesque to American Puritans because American Indians were not "seen consistently as a person in the Western worldview" (*The Inhuman Race* 7). Cassuto, however, focuses on antebellum American literature and culture and the objectification of enslaved Africans and African American by whites who marginalized and dehumanized them so they could exploit them.

This dehumanization involves liminality, and the Elephantmen exhibit liminality through their hybridity. They are, like the hybrids in *Sweet Tooth*, both animal and human and neither animal nor human. They have elements of both but do not fit neatly into either category. This liminality creates the space for the grotesque. The grotesque involves the inability to easily classify something because multiple elements make it impossible to fully belong to a single category (Cassuto, *The Inhuman Race* 6). This does not require literal transformation of the human body; it can be figurative transformation (3). Enslaved African Americans, for example, were classified as property even though they were human. Elephantmen literalize the figurative, dehumanizing objectification of African and African American bodies. Racial objectification, however, "reverberates back to the white subjects, calling their humanity into question in a different way, and thereby making them grotesque also" (6). The ramifications of this statement, that those dehumanizing others end up dehumanizing themselves, is central to understanding the racial grotesque in Cassuto's work and in *Elephantmen*. Racial objectification is never complete; it's always a process, what Cassuto calls "attempted objectification" (16). One can never fully turn a person into an object even if one might treat them as such. Even those who objectify others cannot help but recognize that "human life is at stake" (16). Because humans cannot be fully transformed into objects, the incomplete process provides a gap wherein questions of humanity must be considered.

We witness the grotesque function on two different levels. Those being objectified are grotesque in the categorical sense. They exist in an "ontological netherworld" that denies them complete association with one category or the other (16). Calling enslaved people grotesque, in this sense, is an acknowledgment of the process that dehumanizes them and places them between worlds, not a pejorative aimed at the enslaved themselves. However, the grotesque nature of the objectifiers functions in a different way. They become grotesque for promoting racial objectification. Their actions are repulsive to those who reject their treatment of others. Even in the latter, pejorative sense, the term "grotesque" retains meanings associated with liminality and ontological uncertainty. When used to describe an ugly appearance or behavior, the term functions as an act of disavowal. If someone's appearance or behavior seems monstrous, they become metaphorically grotesque. This is because society often refuses to acknowledge or accept extreme ugliness, both literally and metaphorically, as part of the human condition. We tell ourselves something is wrong with a person who is pejoratively grotesque, and we refuse to allow them complete entry into our shared community. We see them as part human, part monster. They cannot, *must not*, be fully human, yet we cannot ignore that they are human. When the grotesque is used to describe a horrific behavior or appearance, it is also an attempt at separating traits we wish were nonhuman from more acceptable actions and appearances.

Other scholars support the notion that the grotesque is sometimes employed to depict racial objectification. Fritz Gysin argues that certain Black authors use the grotesque to mirror the complexity of African American life. He argues that African Americans live as outsiders in American society and therefore these authors turn to the grotesque to depict this existence. The grotesque is often used to depict outsiders. Frances Connelly observes that the grotesque is "the quintessential voice of the outsider, and it is not surprising that it is embraced by artists concerned with issues of gender or

Figure 4.1. Richard Starkings, Moritat, Ladrönn, et al. *Elephantmen, Vol. 1: Wounded Animals*, Image Comics Inc., 2012, np.

race" (*The Grotesque in Western Art* 23). Even though grotesque bodies can be fearsome or provide estrangement, they can also, for Connelly, encourage empathy, a potentially powerful tool for combating racism and objectification. The transformative aspect of the grotesque is also a fresh way to approach topics because "the grotesque's urge to turn the world upside down and to play among broken boundaries is infectious" (23). Connelly's interest in the grotesque as always being at play figures the grotesque as essentially subversive. It tackles serious issues but glorifies in chaos and disorder.

Elephantmen and Childhood

Although most of *Elephantmen* takes place when the hybrids are adults, their corporate enslavement is established at birth (figure 4.1). The horror of Hip Flask's birth is depicted in a series of early pages. In one panel, drawn from an overhead perspective, the geneticist Nikken triumphantly holds the first hybrid aloft, while the light in the room is centered on them like a stage light. Nikken intones, "Welcome to my world, feeble creature. Breathe deep. With each gasp of oxygen, you will grow **stronger**" (Starkings, Moritat, Ladrönn, et al. np).[3] Referring to the hybrid as a "creature" rather than a "child" emphasizes his otherness, but the hybrid is eerily human. In addition to looking similar to a human child, he is also screaming, something most animals do not do. So the hybrid's first moment outside the womb is a distinctly human one, but this is immediately neglected in favor of Nikken casting him as nonhuman. This panel comes within the midst of movement as the other scientists' hands are suspended in applause and the hybrid's mouth is frozen in a cry. The indefinitely suspended cry of the hybrid is a harbinger of their tortured existence, as the hybrids are dehumanized from the moment of their birth.

The birth of the hybrid is juxtaposed against the violent death of his mother; her womb is ripped apart. She is positioned behind and off to the side of Nikken and the hybrid. This image and its composition demonstrate the lack of sentimental value given to the mother. The scientists all exalt the child as the mother's corpse lies splayed behind the hybrid, ignored. The page that precedes this one explains, "The females indigenous to this region have proven to be excellent engines of **reproduction** . . . The fact that no one has missed them is merely an added bonus" (np). The "engines of reproduction" metaphor and the reference to the fact that no one misses them positions the African women as disposable commodities with no value beyond that which the corporation ascribes. Its rhetoric of science and engineering in relation to human life turns the woman, and others like her, into cogs in a machine; they are not unique individuals with their own wants and needs but objects forced to contribute to the desires of the corporation. Despite the dead mother being largely ignored within the panel, however, the image's perspective connects her to Nikken and her hybrid child. She is forgotten behind Nikken in the narrative, yet the overhead perspective positions her excavated womb between her child and Nikken. From Nikken's perspective, this composition contributes to the sense that the mother is a means to an end. He needs human wombs to bring the hybrids to term, which provides him with the object of his scientific desire. Yet the placement of the forgotten mother also creates the sense that Nikken cannot completely separate the hybrid child from its human origin. This scene also serves as a perverse metaphor for the unacknowledged and unappreciated labor of Black women in a Western context. Writ large, this corporate commodification and enslavement of African women and hybrid children is a perverse reflection of how "bio-capitalism relies on reproduction as a racializing process that creates human biological commodities and itself functions as a commodity" (Weinbaum 13).

The subsequent pages continue with the dehumanization of hybrids (figure 4.2). These pages are comprised of three symmetrical panels stacked on top of one another against a black background with small gutters between them. The left panels focus on the hybrid, but gradually home in on the corporate brand seared into his flesh. Nikken says, "These animals are completely **unique**. Perhaps the term 'animal' no longer even applies. Brand it" (Starkings, Moritat, Ladrönn, et al. np). The middle panel shows the hybrid screaming as his flesh steams. Nikken intones, "MAPPO shall name them. MAPPO will own them" (np). The brand reinscribes the hybrids as property rather than individuals and triply evokes branding: the branding of some enslaved people in relation to the hybrid's human elements, the branding of livestock in relation to the hybrid's animal elements, and the idea of a corporate brand and a corporation's obsession over asserting and retaining control over its trademarks and assets. The reader feels empathy for the hybrid screaming out in pain but does not connect with the detached scientists in their scrubs who are harming the child. This empathy is built on the powerlessness of the hybrid, which, at this moment, is tied up in its status as an individual in pain, and as a newborn child, which further mobilizes the readers' desire to protect children. Nick Sousanis notes that comic book readers make connections "not just from one panel to the next, but across the page and back and forth, in all directions" (Paragraph 2). The images from the branded child to the traditional image of a swaddled newborn on the next page present themselves simultaneously and sequentially. When viewing these panels collectively, the hybrid is in the process of both being denied and asserting his humanity, which is a tension throughout the series.

The dehumanization of the Elephantmen continues further with the indoctrination they experience during their formative years (figure 4.3). A man tells the hybrids that "thinking for himself is the nature of **man**" but that the hybrids, whom he refers to as "monkeys," are beneath man. When one of the hybrids tries to ask a question, he is punished. The trainer says, "There is no sense of self outside of MAPPO. No independent thought. . . Your lives are not your own, Monkeys. You have been born into servitude . . . and your master is MAPPO" (Starkings, Moritat, Ladrönn, et al. np). The final panel is an image of a child or adolescent hybrid imprisoned in a cell

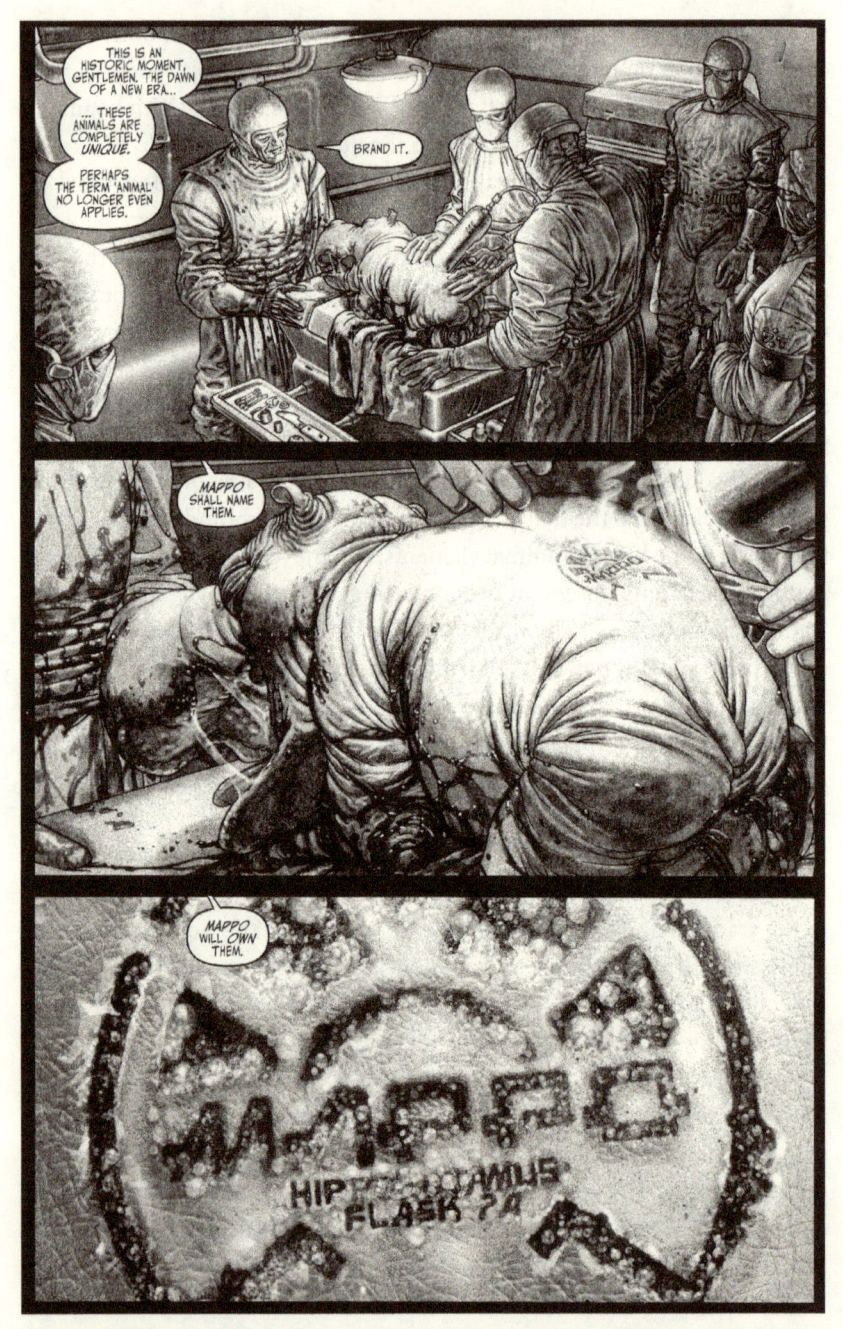

Figure 4.2. Richard Starkings, Moritat, Ladrönn, et al. *Elephantmen, Vol. 1: Wounded Animals*, Image Comics Inc., 2012, np.

Figure 4.3. Richard Starkings, Moritat, Ladrönn, et al. *Elephantmen, Vol. 1: Wounded Animals*, Image Comics Inc., 2012, np.

clearly designed to hold adult hybrids. The child is sitting in the corner of his cage, positioned centrally and looking outward, as if to directly challenge readers regarding their complicity in processes of dehumanization. This page depicts the relegation of the hybrids as inferior to humans, but it also subverts the hybrid's objectification by making MAPPO and their trainer the metaphoric monsters.

The trainer uses racist language that dehumanizes and also evokes slavery: "monkey," their "lives are not their own," "master," etc. He focuses on the hybrids' potential as assets rather than their status as individuals with their own wants and needs. The trainer's emphasis on what the hybrids will be rather than what they are provides a perverse take on the developmental discourse of childhood, which emphasizes the gradual accumulation of knowledge and acclimation to the world and focuses on children-as-becoming. John Wall argues this discourse is problematic because it assumes a similar life path and end result for individuals, which results in a lack of "moral diversity" (29). Wall notes that Western thought has evolved developmental approaches to childhood throughout its intellectual history. Thinkers as disparate as Aristotle and John Locke believed that parents (for Aristotle) and society (for Locke) could help children realize and master their potential over time (25–27). This approach has its benefits, specifically "its temporality and realism. It refuses to either demonize or sentimentalize childhood but instead assumes a starting position of ethical neutrality. This allows it to recognize children's dual goodness and potential for harm" (28). However, the emphasis on the end result of the child—the type of adult a child will be—opens up developmental approaches to criticism. For example, "Childhood, as Rousseau complained, is given value chiefly as a means to adulthood. Childhood is interpreted through the lens of what children are not yet, namely, developed adults. What it means to be a child is paradoxically secondary, for children, to becoming an adult" (29). While it makes sense to prepare children to become productive members of society, Rousseau's concern is that the emphasis on preparation can sometimes lead to the future overshadowing the present. This is what the trainer, acting on behalf of Nikken and his corporation, wants. He wants all the hybrids to be remorseless, killing machines who will obey orders without question, and he values them only for what they become. This is why the hybrids are dehumanized; not because they lack independent thought, but because MAPPO wants to suppress such thought to better turn them into objects by placing them outside the bounds of humanity, along with the rights people might attribute to *human* hybrids, as opposed to *animal* hybrids. This is why the trainer refers to Hip by his number rather than his name. Furthermore, theoretically, discourses of childhood apply equally to all children, yet practically, we know this is not true. Black children are not afforded the same protections and expectations of innocence that other children in the United States are, for example. While these hybrids are coded as African, the comics are produced within the United States. Historically, childhood innocence in the United States is often associated with white children, and Black children were and are often not viewed as children at all (Bernstein 8, 16; Wanzo 139). This racist exclusion reverberates today in the way that Black children are often viewed as threats by authority figures such as teachers and police officers.

Yet this entire page of the comic fundamentally reasserts the humanity of the hybrid children in the midst of their dehumanization. Immediately after the trainer tells the hybrids they lack the "capacity to have an **original** behavioral impulse," Hip raises his hand to ask a question. The act of asking a question is itself a direct rebuttal of the trainer's logic because it shows Hip is thinking for himself. This second panel would be delightful out of context: six young hybrids, all gangly and awkward. Their eyes are large. Some, like the giraffe and camel hybrids, seem particularly skinny. Some, like the elephant hybrid, are chubby. They all look awkward and simultaneously cute and ugly in that strange adolescent way. These are a far cry from the sleek and often sexualized bodies of the adult hybrids, who get fetishized. For example, the cover of the third trade collection features an adult Hip in a loincloth, holding a spear, wearing jewelry, with tribal tattoos covering his body. He dwarfs Miki, his girlfriend, a human woman who is pressing her topless body against him. In the pages of the comic, another example of the fetishization of Black bodies is the occasional reference to what humans assume must be the large size of the hybrids' genitalia, a stereotype sometimes attributed to Black men. The fetishization of the hybrids' bodies is another form of dehumanization in that it treats them as sexual commodities and again values them for their physicality rather than their individuality.

But the adolescent hybrids exist in a state prior to this fetishization. They capture the awkwardness many experience in youth even as they embody a youth drastically different from our own. Hip's "huh" carries with it so much uncertainty, discomfort, and awkwardness. Their humanity asserts itself even in the most dehumanizing circumstances, as the hybrids contradict the trainer in both their behavior and appearance. In fact, as we saw with Nikken, it is often the humans themselves who are monstrous, and this theme continues as the narrative unfolds.

Animals, Humans, Monsters

Elephantmen draws upon the reprehensible treatment of African and African American bodies as it illustrates what commodification does to people: it attempts to transform them into nonhumans. The hybrids are a metaphor for objectification. David Punter writes, "[T]he control of public metaphor is a way of gaining and securing power" (47). By creating hybrid super soldiers rather than human ones, MAPPO ends up creating creatures who metaphorically embody their own dehumanization because they are literally hybrids, and it is no coincidence that minority groups and people from different cultures or places are often dehumanized by being compared to animals. The hybrids' embodiment of their dehumanization relies on how dissimilar the hybrids are from humans. Dissimilarity, like similarity, is also part of metaphor: "Although metaphor undoubtedly deals in likeness, similarity, it also deals in unlikeness and dissimilarity" (9). This makes it difficult for human characters to interpret their bodies due to their simultaneous similarities and differences. Punter argues, "Where the classical metaphor posits the possibility of furthering the search for meaning through aligning one object, word or phenomenon with another, this variant on the postmodern metaphor takes as its ground the impossibility of assigning meaning" (61). It is impossible to assign definitive meaning in the hybrids' case because their bodies are in a constant state of tension. While the comic itself and sympathetic readers may emphasize the humanity of the characters due to the ontological uncertainty of the hybrids, the diegetic world has a more ambiguous relationship as some characters consider the hybrids monstrous.

Scholars occasionally discuss monsters when writing about the grotesque. Wolfgang Kayser, for example, notes that all monsters are grotesque (181). Mark Dorrian provides a more comprehensive accounting for the similarities and differences between the monstrous and the grotesque. Dorrian uses the classical world and its ideals of beauty and form to discuss these "closely aligned" terms (315). Initially using the terms almost interchangeably, Dorrian understands monsters via Platonic metaphysics: as beings that transgress nature through either fragmentation of the body, such as a being with two heads, or combination, such as man-beasts or hermaphrodites (310). Monsters undermine the cosmic order by transgressing accepted forms, a description that resonates with discussions of the grotesque. As Dorrian explains, "The operative principle of monstrosity might be described as the coming together of what should be kept apart" (313). While "what should be kept apart" is open for debate and culturally contingent, in their joining of the animal and human kingdoms, the hybrids are monstrous. More specifically, humans are part of the animal kingdom, but the joining of disparate animals (human/elephant, human/giraffe, human/hippo, etc.) is where boundaries collapse. For Dorrian, "The grotesque enfolds the monstrous," but the terms diverge when "power changes to paranoia" and the monstrous seems to collapse representational distance and appear as if it may enter into the viewer's world (316). Dorrian is referring to the collapse of representational distance between viewers and art, but this makes sense in relation to the diegetic world of *Elephantmen*. When the hybrids become immigrants or refugees who integrate into the Western world, they cease to be an unknown fear that resides far away and instead force those human characters who fear or despise them to confront such feelings head-on. The monsters, in this case, force others to confront their grotesque embodiments.

Noël Carroll believes that monsters "are beings whose existence science denies" ("Horror and Humor" 148). This is an elegant conception of the monster, but it feels inadequate for *Elephantmen*. It might be more accurate in this case to say that the hybrids are beings whom *current* science denies. Even though there is a scientific explanation for them in the series, it is not available to us. Jeffrey Jerome Cohen locates the monster within the realm of culture. He writes, "The monstrous body is pure culture" and that monsters "are disturbing hybrids whose externally incoherent bodies resist attempts to include them in any systematic structuration. And so the monster is dangerous, a form suspended between forms that threatens to smash distinctions" (4, 6). Cohen's definition of the monster is reminiscent of the grotesque, which is not surprising given their close relationship. Grotesque bodies are anomalous and "'monster' is the oldest word in our tongue for human anomalies" (Fiedler 16). For Cohen, the monster's importance, like the grotesque itself, is to discover what it reveals about society: "These monsters ask us how to perceive the world, and how we have misrepresented what we have attempted to place. They ask us to reevaluate our cultural assumptions about race, gender, sexuality, our perception of difference, our tolerance toward its expression. They ask us why we have created them" (20). In the Elephantmen's case, they also force people to consider *how* they could have been created in the first place. The hybrids were not created fully formed like militaristic Adams. Instead, they were gestated, birthed, and raised over the course of years with the express intent to create monsters capable of dominating opposing armies. The hybrids are products of their childhood abuse. They redefine themselves in many ways, but they are all shaped by their childhood objectification: the culmination of a process of commodification that shapes their existence from (and before) childhood.

Cohen's monsters follow the logic of the Gothic monster whose "body . . . produces meaning and can represent any horrible trait that the reader feeds into the narrative. The monster functions as monster, in other words, when it is able to condense as many fear-producing traits as possible into one body" (Halberstam 21). The way the hybrids become repositories of a cavalcade of fears over immigration and race while also blurring various racial atrocities is bound up in their status as monsters. However, Gothic monsters in the nineteenth century combined "the features of deviant race, class, and gender," whereas contemporary monsters emphasize "deviant sexualities and gendering but [show] less clearly the signs of class or race" (3–4). Yet *Elephantmen* is a contemporary narrative whose "monsters" clearly signal its interest in race. Furthermore, while the physical difference in the hybrids' being manifests as ontologically confusing bodies, the fundamental reason some consider them nonhuman may include the way hybrids are created and brought into the world and the intent behind their creation. The hybrids' conception and birth are strange and horrifying. This coincides with Peter Brooks's understanding of what makes Frankenstein's monster monstrous:

> The creation of the Monster . . . takes place on the borderline of nature and culture. The Monster is a product of nature—his ingredients are 100 percent natural—yet by the process and the very fact of his creation, he is unnatural, the product of philosophical overreaching. Since he is a unique creation, without precedence or replication, he lacks cultural as well as natural context. (217)

In their science fictional world, the lack of cultural and natural precedent for the hybrids is fearsome. This fear is then displaced onto the chimerical bodies of the hybrids. But just as Elephantmen may appear human despite their monstrosity, so, too, as we have seen and will continue to see, can humans become monsters.

In the opening pages of an issue that follows Trench, a zebra/human hybrid, during his time as a police officer immediately following integration into the United States, Trench narrates, "MAPPO's engineers took sovereignty of the animal kingdom even further, they made us **like** man, but not man. We remained creatures to conquer or fear once again, not brothers they could relate to. Better Products. . . . We became Elephantmen, neither one nor the other" (Schweikert et al. np). Trench articulates a conception of the hybrids that directly coincides with Cassuto's observation that grotesque bodies are neither human nor object. While Cassuto is dealing with objectification based on race, not species, the animal aspect of the Elephantmen resonate with the racial grotesque because, in addition to their African heritage, they provide a metaphor for one of the ways humans are dehumanized: by comparisons to animals. It is for this reason that their status of "**like** man" is emphasized with bolding.

Trench is called to a crime scene where an African American man high on cough syrup has murdered a child relative. This leads to a panel that captures the horror of people in dehumanizing circumstances. The panel encompasses approximately two thirds of the page. A dead African American child is in bed, his throat cut. This panel juxtaposes what should be a safe space, the child's bedroom, with the horrors of his circumstance. The boy, were it not for his cut throat, appears peaceful, almost as if he is asleep. His dog is lying quietly by him, and the boy's hand is touching a stuffed animal. Yet the boy is murdered; blood covers the sheets. There is dog excrement on the bed. Unpacked boxes sit in the corner of the room, while a large bong is on the nightstand. A human police officer enters and says, "What kind of **animals** are they breeding, out here?" This moment contributes to the human becoming grotesque through his own behavior. Trench responds, "Animals. We call them that when we don't understand. When we're afraid of what a man can become" (np). The emphasis on what a man or woman can become resonates with the grotesque as transformation. Trench also demonstrates that fear can be a factor in the grotesque. Society may dehumanize or objectify that which scares it so that it becomes unrecognizable. The other officer's question creates a gap between himself and the people he wants to distance himself from, which allows him to project the blame for their heinous circumstances onto the victims rather than the structural issues at play, like poverty and racial discrimination. By seeing the individual or a small group of individuals as grotesque, he can ignore the larger ramifications of grotesque inequality. Generally speaking, some people, rather than embracing the idea that the grotesque can force us to explore more fully what it means to be human and/ or embrace incongruity, instead reject it.

While Trench's experience illustrates a way that humans might be compared to animals, one woman transforms herself into a monster. Yvette is a French resistance fighter who faces the Elephantmen before their emancipation, when they fight in Europe. Yvette lost family and friends to the Elephantmen, so she fights for her homeland against the foreign military presence. The Elephantmen, engines of death and destruction, fear her. Years after the war, Yvette travels to the United States and begins murdering Elephantmen before confronting her ultimate target, Obadiah Horn. During the war, Horn made it his mission to kill Yvette. During their final confrontation after the war, Yvette appears to commit suicide rather than be spared by the hybrids and their allies. She would rather die than be used as "evidence" of the hybrids' humanity (Starkings, Medellin, Kane, et al. np). Yvette's inability to put aside her vengeance signifies how she has been reshaped by her circumstances. Shun-Liang Chao writes,

> Grotesque *trans*-formation is an *excessive* pursuit of incompleteness and contradiction: it transgresses the natural order of things and produces within itself a self-contradictory (or in-between) physical structure, one that, as we shall see, displeases classicists because of its ability to feed the feelings of (dis) pleasure and to obscure the borderline between life and death, beauty and deformity, the central and peripheral. (26)

Even though contradictory topics like life and death often help inform each other, classicists prefer they be kept separate. This is why the grotesque can be so displeasing. Classicists reject, for example, animal/human hybridity because the classical human body is predicated on its adherence to proportion and symmetry and altering them makes the sacred into something profane. To excessively pursue incompleteness and contradiction warps a person so that his or her incongruity becomes written on the body.

Chao's emphasis on grotesque transformation as an excessive pursuit contextualizes Yvette's experience as her excessive pursuit of vengeance causes her to forsake all else and changes her into the living embodiment of death. Yvette is initially depicted as a French freedom fighter who can somehow go toe-to-toe with the Elephantmen. In an early recollection of Yvette, the narrator reflects on the Elephantmen's presence in Europe: "We were confronted by enemies just as ferocious as ourselves, some were perhaps even more deadly" (Starkings, Medellin, Kane, et al. np). This seems absurd. While the ferocity of the humans may be equal to the Elephantmen, how could a human be more deadly than a being bioengineered for war? Yet this is the case. Hip Flask later recalls, "[Yvette] was the scourge of the Elephantmen. . . . We marched into Europe with the most sophisticated state-of-the-art weaponry known to man. . . . We could have easily brushed **armies** aside. . . . But when we were confronted by a young French girl who had lost **everything**. . . . [w]e may as well have raised bows and arrows against the **lightning**" (np). This description transforms Yvette into a force of nature. All the Elephantmen's advanced weaponry is for naught, as it gets technologically reduced from bullets to arrows. Of course, bullets are also no good against lightning, but the metaphor of bows and arrows against lightning highlights, even more so, the futility and power differential between Yvette and the hybrids.

A few pages later, after a description of Yvette surviving being shot and falling hundreds of feet, a panel that captures Yvette's grotesque transformation coincides with Chao's description of the blurring of the border between life and death (figure 4.4).[4] Yvette is depicted on the left half of the panel from the shoulders up, against a black backdrop. The left half of her face has three tears streaming down it. The right half is a skull, with an empty socket incapable of tears. The left side of the panel includes the narration "[i]t was as if Yvette had become death itself" above the image (np). The panel shows a contradiction within Yvette as a simultaneously living and dead being. The right half of her face is fully fleshed but juxtaposed against the skull on her left half. This evokes contradictions between life and death and beauty and deformity. She becomes the embodiment of death, at least to the Elephantmen. The right half of the panel is wreathed in flames that seem to be born of, and partially framed by, Yvette's flaming red hair. Her beret also blends into the right half of the panel as it burns. Within these flames is an image of Yvette walking out of a firestorm as she fires her rifle. She is unburned, an avenging angel or rising phoenix, seemingly immune to and unfazed by the fire she walks out of, come to deliver death and retribution to her attackers. The narration "[t]he hunted became the hunter" repositions Yvette from a position lacking power to one containing power. Both sides of

Figure 4.4. Richard Starkings, Axel Medellin, Shaky Kane, et al. *Elephantmen, Vol. 5: Devilish Functions*, Image Comics Inc., 2012, np.

this panel capture Yvette's transformation: a moment of metaphorical rebirth where Yvette redefines herself as the Elephantmen's enemy.

Yvette becomes a monster when she pursues her vengeance after the war. When Yvette follows the hybrids to the United States to finally kill Horn, she engages in a campaign of terror where she kills other Elephantmen and leaves behind the phrase "No Mercy." This harkens back to her days as a freedom fighter when she carved her name into the flesh of at least one dead hybrid. In the United States, Yvette begins wearing the skull of the Elephantman Tusk. In doing so, Yvette is reflecting back to the hybrids the image of their own death as she delivers it. But she is also transforming herself. She remains human but becomes so consumed by her role that she transforms a part of

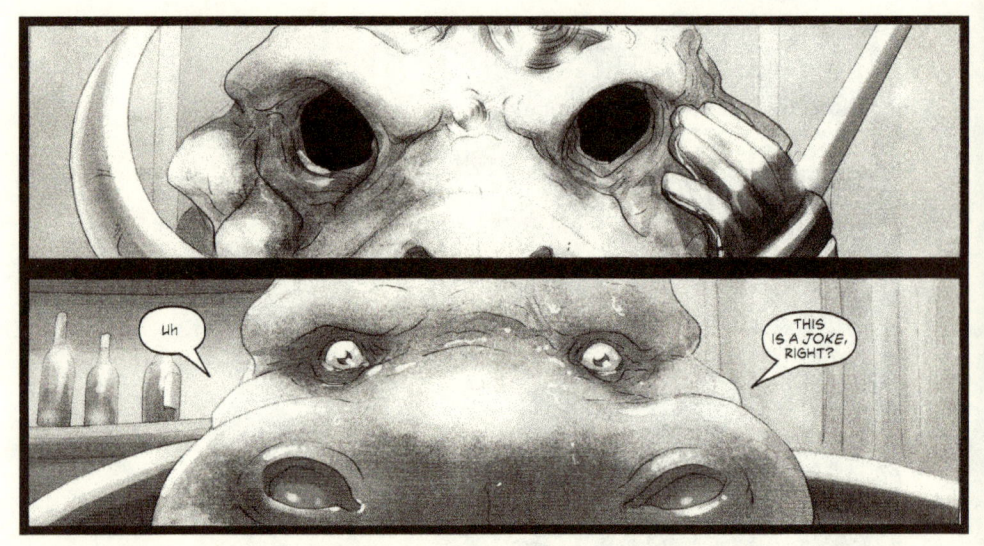

Figure 4.5. Richard Starkings, Axel Medellin, Shaky Kane, et al. *Elephantmen, Vol. 5: Devilish Functions*, Image Comics Inc., 2012, np.

herself into something that is less recognizably human. Her excessive pursuit of vengeance requires her to sacrifice much of her humanity and transforms her into a reaper. Two (of six) panels take this even further (figure 4.5). The emphasis on the eyes of Yvette and her victim creates the impression that they are of the same kind. The dimensions of them are the same, and the reader is denied a view of any of Yvette's actual human body and is instead forced to confront the mask she wears. The mask is unable to convey emotion; even the eyeholes are inscrutable pits of darkness with no indication of what lies beneath. This is in contrast to the clearly frightened hybrid. He is sweating and appears incredulous. The subsequent panels show Yvette killing him. The living creature of the second panel is dead meat with no future, whereas the creature in the first panel, wearing a mask of bone, lives. The mask completes the grotesque transformation that Chao describes. Rather than being half human and half death, Yvette is now all death.

Yvette's transformation into an angel of death is reinforced when Yvette murders another hybrid in his bedroom (figure 4.6). In the first panel, Yvette stands against a backdrop of the sky, her bloody axes in hand, as the dead hybrid collapses on the floor. But the background of Yvette, rather than depicting a discernible daytime skyline, instead looks like a flaming backdrop. It thus resonates with the image of Yvette emerging from flames, gun blazing.

Figure 4.6. Richard Starkings, Axel Medellin, Shaky Kane, et al. *Elephantmen, Vol. 5: Devilish Functions*, Image Comics Inc., 2012, np.

Here, she also emerges from flames, but wearing a full skull. In the bottom panel of the page, the image emphasizes the impenetrability of her eye socket, which also resonates with the earlier figures that also contain an empty eye socket, of the mask or Yvette herself. Yvette's ability to become an instrument of destruction is predicated on her ability to take on the characteristics of that which she kills, which is the Elephantmen at the peak of their war years. She does not just hunt Elephantmen; she becomes an agent of their death by embracing the violence she abhorred in them, which the hybrid skull she now wears represents. Just as Elephantmen were created to be perfect military specimens, Yvette has turned herself into a perfect specimen for hunting and killing them. Her self-imposed mission completely defines her.

When Yvette finally confronts Horn, he says, "I know who you are. Yvette. The freedom fighter. At least you were then. Now? Now you are nothing. Look at yourself. You are little more than an animated cadaver. A spectre clinging to delusions of morality" (np). Horn's references to her as an "animated cadaver" and a "spectre clinging to delusions of morality" recognize the transformation of Yvette into a manifestation of death animated by her vengeance. Horn says, "I will be **mourned** by the society that celebrates me now and they will marvel at my achievements **long** after I am gone.... **You** will be **executed** as an assassin, a **psychopath**. An **animal**" (np). In some respects, it is remarkable that Horn, having been dehumanized throughout his life, calls Yvette an animal. Biologically, Yvette is more human than Horn, and their capacity for logic and emotion is equal. Horn, like Yvette, taps into the pejorative connotations of the grotesque, the unwillingness to associate extremely distasteful behavior with humanity. Yvette rejects this: "I am not an animal! I am a human being and none of your **bullshit** will stop me from exterminating you" (np). This exclamation, ironically, takes place in a panel that showcases Yvette's mask, which complicates her defense. In the comic book, "not," "human being," and "exterminating" are printed using red ink. This red ink connotes rage, more powerful for its relatively rare use in comics. The words shift from a rejection of Yvette's animality to an assertion of her humanity before ending with a dehumanization of Horn as "extermination" is primarily used when referring to insects or rodents.

This refusal to give into her own dehumanization, even as she dehumanizes others, connects to Cassuto's notion of the dialectical interplay between the objectifier and objectified. It also demonstrates how the grotesque involves perspective. Yvette's behavior is monstrous, but not to her. To her, the Elephantmen are the monsters for what they did. To Horn, she is the monster due to her murderous tendencies occurring outside the theater of war. This is why a person can be made grotesque by others with the power to redefine them, but it is also how a person can become grotesque through their own behavior. If others see this behavior as abhorrent, they seek to expunge it. Of course, the grotesque most clearly describes images and bodies that trouble dominant paradigms or structures, but its ambivalent nature allows for multivalent possibilities. Even though the Elephantmen's ambiguous forms embody a lifetime of commodification, Horn's assertion that Yvette is the true grotesque challenges MAPPO's early dominance over the hybrids' lives. The hybrids can be more than soldiers, and Yvette's inability or unwillingness to recognize this transforms her into a monster.

Elephantmen and Racial Objectification

The hybrids' origins position them as African even if the beings themselves are bioengineered to be unlike anything humanity has seen up to that point. This connection to African bodies is placed into an American context when the hybrids are brought to the United States. Upon entering the United States, however, the hybrids are coded as immigrants. This duality can be jarring at times, as the narrative refuses to settle on a historical antecedent.

The Elephantmen's passage to the United States mirrors that of enslaved Africans, millions of whom died when crossing the Atlantic in slave ships. Elephantmen are ferried to the United States in chains and are kept in cells that further restrict their movement (figures 4.7 and 4.8). The pages shown here visualize their transport to the United States. On the page preceding these, the narration says, "Obadiah Horn came to America in chains . . . like a slave" (np). One might argue that Horn and the others are in chains because they are dangerous military assets, which is reasonable, but they are also meant to be released upon entrance into the United States, so their imprisonment also feels gratuitous. This moment draws upon the historical reality of slavery even as it redeploys it. While Obadiah says he came to the United States "like" a slave, which leaves some comparative distance, the image of chained African bodies crossing the Atlantic along with the word "slave" is clearly evoking the specific historical record of the transatlantic enslavement of Africans even as it fictionalizes what comes next. For example, the hybrids are enslaved from their birth in Africa, but the United States becomes a place of new, though limited, opportunities for them, so their existence there does not entail slavery. There are immigrants and refugees who have endured forms of enslavement before coming to the United States. But whatever else this moment does, clearly, the African bodies combined with the crossing of the Atlantic in chains also associates them with the United States' abject history of slavery. Readers are meant to fold this awareness into our understanding of the Elephantmen's dehumanization, but it is severed from its historical context.

There are other moments that recall the dehumanization of African Americans. The Elephantmen are given toxins as they are trained for warfare, and those who are unable to survive the toxins are killed. Tusk is a human/warthog hybrid who survives the toxins but not without them ravaging his mind. Tusk's name and the unethical experimentation on him (and others) evoke the Tuskegee syphilis experiment that was conducted on African

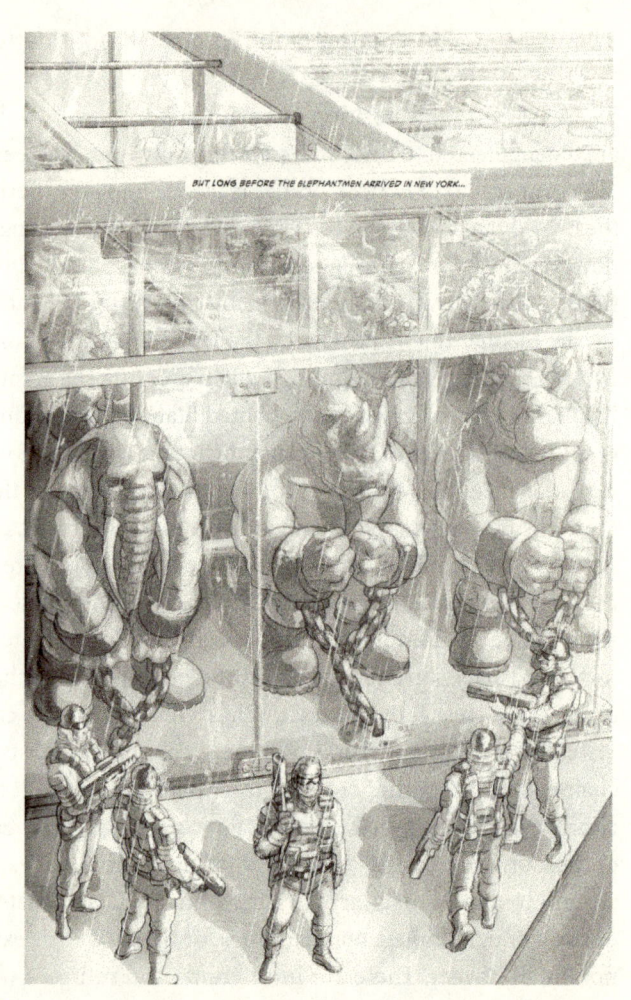

Figure 4.7. Richard Starkings, Axel Medellin, Shaky Kane, et al. *Elephantmen, Vol. 5: Devilish Functions,* Image Comics Inc., 2012, np.

American men without their knowledge or consent. In this experiment, African American men were not told they had syphilis and lied to about their condition. They were left untreated, and the doctors observed the progression of the disease. In the context of the narrative, the atrocities were committed in Africa by a corporation prior to the hybrids' transition to the United States, after which the narrative transitions the Elephantmen to immigrants.

One issue in particular shows Elephantmen in a variety of mostly working-class positions, positions oftentimes accessible to immigrants. For example, we can see images of Elephantmen as construction workers as they recreate an iconic image of early American immigrant workers (figure 4.9). We also see them as agricultural and service workers. These are just a few

Figure 4.8. Richard Starkings, Axel Medellin, Shaky Kane, et al. *Elephantmen, Vol. 5: Devilish Functions*, Image Comics Inc., 2012, np.

of many examples from this issue. These images are accompanied by the narrator's reflection on his arrival in the United States and the reception the hybrids received as they tried to integrate into a new society. Starkings talks about how his experience as an immigrant from England has influenced his approach to the series ("Strange Times, Stranger Heroes"), although it is fair to say that the experience of a white immigrant from England is fundamentally different than a person of color from Africa.

What are we to make of characters who are meant to evoke the experience of those enslaved and brought to the United States and then transitioned into immigrants? After all, Ben Carson was rightfully criticized for suggesting enslaved Africans were immigrants (Lartey). *Elephantmen*'s dual logic

Figure 4.9 Richard Starkings, Axel Medellin, and Gabriel Bautista. *Elephantmen, Issue 50*, Image Comics Inc., 2013, np.

of both the enslaved and the immigrant is part of a postmodern aesthetic cultivated throughout the comic. Fredric Jameson associates the postmodern with depthlessness and an emphasis on commodification. The depthlessness involves a "weakening of history" (19). Nostalgia films, for example, don't actually reflect a specific time in our past, but rather an aesthetic or style that invokes a nostalgia for the idea of the past. They imagine the past but redeploy it as an aesthetic for consumption. This is why pastiche is such a prominent aspect of the postmodern. It is the invocation of various forms and styles but without the satiric bite of parody (17). Pastiche is about commodification rather than critique or insight. Barry Lewis calls "pervasive and pointless pastiche" one of the "dominant features" of postmodernism (171). On the other hand, John Storey believes that pastiche and nostalgia are inadequate for fully understanding the intertextual nature of postmodern texts. He writes, "The intertextual understood as a form of borrowing from what already exists is always also (at least potentially) a making new from combinations of what is old. In this way, popular culture is, and has always been, about more than a pastiche or a nostalgic recycling of what has been before" (209). Pastiche alone cannot account for the ways the postmodern recycles old forms or ideas into new ones.

Another aspect of postmodernism is its ahistorical nature. Linda Hutcheon notes, "One of the few common denominators among the detractors of postmodernism is the surprising, but general, agreement that the postmodern is ahistorical" (87). Postmodern approaches consider history and fiction as "human constructs," which provides "the grounds for its rethinking and reworking of the forms and contents of the past" (5). Hutcheon names texts that engage in this tendency "historiographic metafiction." She writes, "Historiographic metafiction always asserts that its world is both resolutely fictive and yet undeniably historical" (142).

Others also discuss the relationship between postmodernism and history. Christopher Butler writes, "History was just another narrative, whose paradigm structures were no better than fictional, and was a slave to its own (often unconsciously used) unrealized myths, metaphors, and stereotypes . . . even its causal explanations could be shown to derive from, and hence to repeat, well-known fictional plots" (32). This doesn't mean that "*anything goes*," but that we should be more cognizant of "the theoretical assumptions which support the narratives produced by all historians" (35). This coincides with the rationale for historiographic metafiction: it can rework and rethink the past because it recognizes the narratives of the past are constructed by people. This emphasis on the past as construct makes it less likely to see history as linear progress. According to Simon Malpas, " [P]ostmodern fiction frequently treats history ironically as a site of fragmentation rather than a progressive structure" (101).

Elephantmen incorporates its grotesque hybrids within a postmodern environment of history, pastiche, and commodification. It draws on fragments of specific atrocities even as it dissolves boundaries between atrocities. Nikken, speaking to a United Nations court, says, "So much **blood** has been spilt. . . . So many **people** have died. So many **atrocities** have been committed. So many **monsters** have walked the earth. But you are looking for just **one**" (Starkings, Moritat, Churchill, et al. np). Certainly Nikken's assertion metatextually speaks to the series' practices: the series gives us one atrocity, the abuse of the hybrids, to stand in for multiple atrocities and one group, the hybrids, to stand in for multiple marginalized groups. The UN trial of the hybrids' creator, which is juxtaposed against images of mass graves, draws upon the Holocaust and its aftermath, which adds another atrocity to *Elephantmen*'s plethora of references. The comics often include quotes on a variety of topics from real people, like George W. Bush, Marshall McLuhan, and Josef Mengele, but there is also an opening quote by Dr. Nikken. This pastiche of atrocity and of real and fictional people are elements of how the narrative consciously recalls a variety of events and perspectives without fully affirming a historical narrative. At the same time, by placing fictional Nikken's voice among nonfictional people, the narrative subsequently calls into question the authenticity of all the voices. Readers may question if other quotes are contrived or not.

Starkings describes *Elephantmen* as pulp science fiction in the vein of precursors like the "great 60s Marvel comics and 70s issues of *2000 AD*" (Starkings, "Pulp Science Fiction!" np). Pulp science fiction is, to Starkings, "[a]ction and adventure with a SF [science fiction] twist" (Starkings, interview). The pulp influences of the comic can be found in the pastiche of imagery and styles within the comic books. This contributes to its postmodern aesthetic. The series often switches genres and is prone to referencing influences. For example, one title page embodies the emphasis on detective fiction. The Elephantmen Hip Flask and Ebony Hide work as detectives after the war. The title page depicts Ebony Hide as a gumshoe with his trench coat and flashlight. The comic's title, "*The* **Elephant** *in the* **Room**," in addition to being an idiom for something obvious that goes undiscussed, is also a joke that references the hybrid skeleton on display, Ebony Hide himself, and the mystery the detective is investigating. In addition to drawing on tropes and images from the pulp detective genre, *Elephantmen* also references specific genre texts like *Blade Runner*.

Sometimes the characters within *Elephantmen* read comics themselves, and these comics are often another source of homage. One of these comics-within-a-comic, "The Victory of Sammy Thrace," is an homage to Will Eisner's famous detective comic *The Spirit* (figure 4.10). Part of Eisner's fame is due to his innovative and meticulous title pages, which incorporated the name of the series into the architecture of the page in stunning ways. *Elephantmen* mimics this by spelling "Hip" with the laundry hanging on the clothesline and "Flask" painted perpendicular on the building. Contributors' names are integrated into the cityscape with "Busiek Arms" and "Immonen Barber Shop." The "Created by Richard Starkings" signature mirrors the appearance of Eisner's credits in *The Spirit*, down to the circles atop the I's. There are other moments of homage, too. Ebony Hide gets cast as Conan the Barbarian during his drug-induced dreams and hallucinations, an homage to Robert E. Howard's pulp sword and sorcery creation and the focus of the 1970s Marvel comics by Roy Thomas. The title of one such comic, "The Power of the Elephant," is a riff on an actual Conan story, "The Tower of the Elephant," and the introduction is meant to mimic the sound of Conan stories. It begins, "Welcome, my lord, to a world only dreamed of. . . . Hither comes **Ebony, the Barbarian,** dark-eyed, axe in hand, ready to become a prince among thieves, a ruthless mercenary, and slaughterer of demons." (Starkings, Medellin, Kane, et al. np). These examples do not account for the complexity of each individual image or the sheer volume of all the references. Rather, they illustrate the propensity of the comic series to directly reference and mash together its influences and play with their styles in a postmodern fashion.

The multitude of references also coincides with a variety of aesthetic styles used in the comics. While it is not surprising that a comic book series that has employed a number of artists has differences in styles, the aesthetic differences are often drastic, and while sometimes the changes in style coincide with diegetic reasons (to depict a dream or comic or story within the overarching narrative), oftentimes the changing aesthetics do not coincide with a temporal or spatial shift in the diegetic world. The comics' art sometimes has realist details, although bodies and guns are usually exaggerated. It alternates

Figure 4.10. Richard Starkings, Moritat, Ian Churchill, et al. *Elephantmen, Vol. 2: Fatal Diseases*, Image Comics Inc., 2011, np.

between dark, noir settings and vivid, energetic scenes. It is usually full of kinetic energy and movement, but not always. In some instances, the art is lush, full of watercolors. Some stories are done in bright pastels. *Elephantmen* more freely blends aesthetics than most other comics. This artistic promiscuity is in line with its pastiche in that it constantly draws attention to itself (through its references/through its art) and its constructed nature.

The comics also commodify the characters in various ways, which contributes to the series' postmodernism sensibility. After the Elephantmen come to the United States and despite the fear and derision some people feel toward them, Ebony Hide capitalizes on the fascination the public has with them by commodifying their likeness. They are featured in comics within the comic, turned into toys, and placed on clothing and television. The awe and fear the hybrids generate as grotesque beings give them cultural appeal. The toys, specifically, seem to have a further purpose than simply commodification as they make imposing creatures diminutive and cute (figure 4.11). Ngai argues that "cute" is a prominent aesthetic category that emerged over the course of the twentieth century. In terms of *Elephantmen*, what seems most important about Ngai's argument is that "cuteness solicits a regard of the commodity as an anthropomorphic being less powerful than the aesthetic subject appealing specifically to us for protection and care" (60). With regard to the hybrids, their imposing bodies are turned into huggable objects in need of protection. The Elephantmen toys recast the intimidating beings as objects in need of support and protection from the general public or at least the toy owner. This reverses the actual power differential between hybrid and human by repositioning the hybrid as the less powerful one. This power differential is key to "cute" as "the subject's affective response to an imbalance of power between herself and the object" is what determines whether something is cute or not (54). The appeal of the cute commodity, which implores its subjects to buy and care for it, also inspires feelings of sadism in the consumer (64–65). The rough treatment toys may receive can theoretically be a way for consumers to vent their fears over the Elephantmen, but ultimately, the toys, by appealing to sentimentality through their cuteness, metaphorically resituate the hybrids, turning them into creatures to be protected rather than feared. The emphasis on the commodification of the hybrids coincides with the history of the main character. Before *Elephantmen* was a comics series, Hip Flask was used as a mascot to advertise Richard Starkings's burgeoning comics fonts company (Starkings, "Pertinent Points"). Starkings has faced accusations

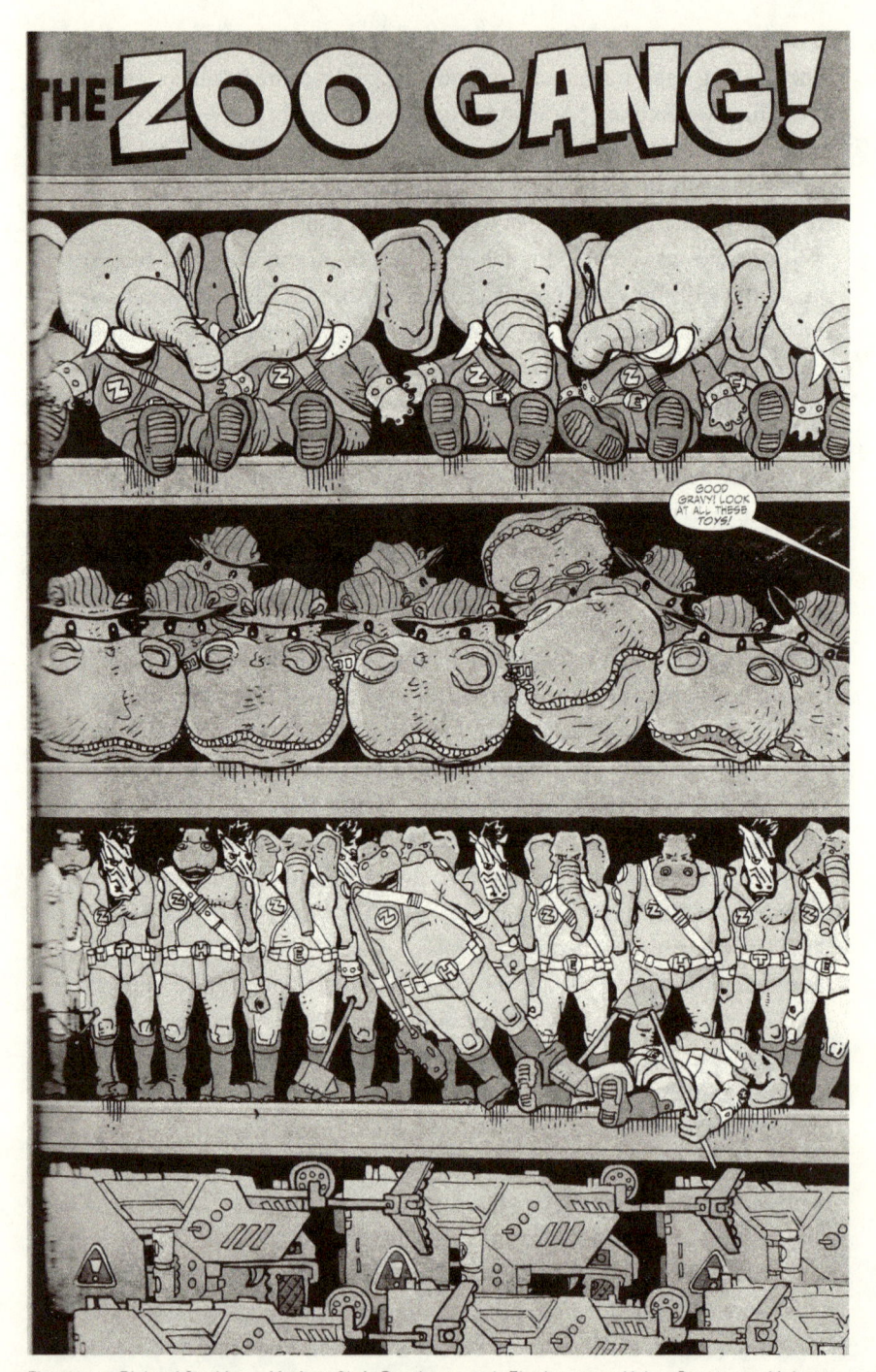

Figure 4.11. Richard Starkings, Moritat, Chris Burnham, et al. *Elephantmen, Vol. 3: Dangerous Liaisons*, Image Comics Inc., 2010, np.

of plagiarism for the similarities of Hip Flask to Jason Paulos and Bodine Amerikah's character, Hairbutt. Starkings rejects the accusations (Brice np).

The actual bodies of the hybrids, in addition to their plush and commodified likenesses, contribute to the postmodern tone of the narrative. The hybrids' bodies challenge human/animal binaries and ontological determinism. This often occurs in the intersections between postmodernism and science. Simon Malpas notes, "The cultural productions that engage with the developments and challenges of science and technology frequently present pictures of a future in which human subjectivity and identity have become profoundly problematic" (75). Iain Hamilton Grant situates "the hybrid" as one of the dominant figures of "postmodern science" (105). Ursula K. Heise notes that the line between animal and human (and human and machine) is becoming unstable and that

> the fact that technoscientific advances are beginning to make such border crossings more than mere hypotheses, combined with a willingness, at least in some quarters, to put in question conventional definitions of humanness, do mark a point of departure from the modernist conviction that human beings stand apart, and should remain apart, from other forms of existence. (144)

The relationship between these three points is that postmodernism in science often involves questions regarding what it means to be human, and these questions are often evoked through hybrid figures like in *Elephantmen*, but such forms and questions may also end up reinscribing the human.

We can see a similar interest in the grotesque and postmodern approaches to consumerism, if not cultural trauma and identity, within Richard Starkings, Tyler Shainline, and Shaky Kane's 2018 comic series, *The Beef*. *The Beef* is an aggressive critique of industrial farming that parodies the superhero genre. It focuses on Chuck Carter, a meatpacker in love with a strawberry picker named Mary-Lynn (after Marilyn Monroe). When Mary-Lynn is threatened, Chuck transforms into the Beef: a grotesque giant whose muscle and fat are on the outside of his body.[5] This transformation is attributed to all the time Chuck spends around cattle as well as his lifelong diet of beef and thus his consumption of large amounts of excitotoxins. Critic Tegan O'Neil astutely reads *The Beef* as a modern superhero take on *The Jungle* and notes that the artwork is influenced by Gilbert Hernandez along "with a bit of Kirby's grotesque mannerisms" (np). This is especially prevalent in images of the Beef himself, who looks like a skinned version of Kirby's renditions of Beast or The Thing. As O'Neil also notes, the comic can be difficult to look at (np). It is full of images of brutality and viscera, and its villains demean and dehumanize others.

Issues of genetics and eugenics take a backseat in *The Beef*, although there is reference to the genetic modification of food as well as excitotoxins within the beef. No one actively creates cow/human hybrids, yet a different type of connection is made between the two creatures. The event that inspires his initial transformation comes when a bull is released by some racist and sexist bullies to scare Mary-Lynn, so the bullies can save her and appear as protectors. After the Beef intervenes to save Mary-Lynn, he collapses in a pasture, his face buried in mud and, presumably, shit. Flies surround him. He rises and proceeds to puke in the midst of onlooking cattle. Within the first three panels, as he lies in the mud until the point at which he pukes, his thoughts are with him: "What has he been eating? What has rendered him this way? What has left him with this **taste** in his mouth—?" (np). Of course he has been eating beef. Yet the page also subtly shifts his identity to connect with the cows. The use of the word "rendered" is one often used in conjunction with meat products and reinforces his presence among the cattle. His placement among the cows inside a pasture foregrounds how later on the cows will respond to him when he is changed into his superhero persona as they share his pain. After the transformation, his body starts to change in other ways. The comic reads, "He felt bloated, **heavy** . . . and his nipples felt **sore**" (np). He then notices that, like a cow, he has grown four milk-producing breasts or udders. Soon after, he is walking next to the holding pens for the cattle. He looks at a cow inside a cage and the cow looks back at him. The perspective of these two panels makes it seem as if Chuck may also be behind bars. The narration notes, "He's eaten so many **double-double burgers** at **The Beef** [a diner], he often wondered how much more he is **cow** than he is **human**" (np). Later on, he feels more cow than human.

What we see in these details is the grotesque transformation of Chuck from human to cow that is not just relegated to extreme moments but is the result of his ubiquitous day-to-day decisions and now impacts his regular, not just superhero, body. There is another grotesque image at play. At one point, a cow questions why some humans call women "cows," and, tongue-in-cheek, provides the option that a woman being called a cow might be considered "a life-giving mother" (np). Then we are presented with a panel of a human/cow

Figure 4.12. Richard Starkings, Tyler Shainline, and Shaky Kane. *The Beef*, Image Comics Inc., 2018, np.

hybrid (figure 4.12). She is sitting on a couch with a controller in hand. A large soda is next to her. The background of the panel is part of an American flag. The hybrid has small horns and big cow ears. She is nude, with large breasts and elongated nipples suggesting breastfeeding. She has cow udders obscuring her genitalia. She is visibly pregnant. She asks, "Do I make you horny, baby?" (np). Under the panel is an acknowledgment of Ariana Reines's poetry collection, *The Cow*. This grotesque image, with its Austin Powers reference, shocks with its gratuity as it forces readers to think about the grotesque nature of their food consumption in new ways. The cow asks rhetorically, "Oh? You don't like it when it's about **your** species?!" (np). Readers grasp the grotesque nature of the comic, which prominently features a breakdown in the divide between animals and humans, as it critiques a capitalist system of animal exploitation and human consumption. Unlike *Elephantmen*, the grotesque hybrid bodies in the comic are not themselves commodified, or rather, the commodification they experience under capitalism is not because they have grotesque bodies; it is because the system is grotesque.

This commodification, like in *Elephantmen*, is present in the postmodern way that the comic plays with the idea of creatures and objects as commodities, and, to some degree, with the history of comics, a commodity, selling cheap products in their pages. When Chuck's superhero name is mentioned, the font shifts to one that looks like it is part of a corporate logo of some sort.

In some instances, characters are drawn as cutouts or cardboard figures as if they were meant to be played with. Of course, to cut it out would destroy the next page. Perhaps such an image was intended to be cut out after the comic was fully read, as if to provide a partial reuse for a formerly cheap and disposable commodity. However, comics today can be expensive and are now likely to be saved rather than disposed of, so this moment toys with the preservation mindset of such a reader/collector.

Gandhi appears in the narrative and quotes a film about himself. The covers of the individual comics, which are collected in the trade, all reference materiality. The first cover depicts canned meat with an image from *The Beef* on it. The second issue shows part of a calendar with a buxom woman in an American flag bikini eating a hamburger. The third includes a milk carton with pictures of the Beef on it, as if he were a missing child. The fifth is drawn as if a comic book was lying on a surface. The final image is an overhead perspective of packaged cuts of meat that are instead pieces of the character the Beef (figure 4.13). This final cover especially resonates in that there are five packages, just as the comic itself is originally spliced into five issues.[6]

What the comic consistently does, then, is continue Starkings and his collaborators' interest in emphasizing the material status of the commodity and of the commodity within the commodity, the characters and properties within the pages of the comic book. In this tale, this emphasis foregrounds how the grotesque process of consumption shapes our lives and our bodies.

With all this in mind, *Elephantmen* is a staunchly postmodern comics series that glorifies in its pulp roots, and its combination of enslavement and immigration may be understood as part of a postmodern, ahistorical rendering of identity that coincides with the comics' overall sensibility and its interest in the grotesque treatment of humans and animals. Critics of postmodernism believe it lacks meaningful commentary on that which it references. And in some ways, that might apply to these comics. For example, the later commodification of the hybrids goes largely unremarked upon, and the comic references its influences in terms of cultural identity without substantially reimagining or commenting upon them. One might argue there is relevant commentary on the hybrids as immigrants and enslaved people in that the series articulates the struggles of a marginalized population, the hybrids, and asserts their humanity in the face of dehumanization. This continuous assertion potentially generates empathy for the marginalized. But it also mashes together various atrocities and dehumanization in a way that

Figure 4.13. Richard Starkings, Tyler Shainline, and Shaky Kane. *The Beef*, Image Comics Inc., 2018, np.

gives it an ahistorical bent. Slavery and the mistreatment of immigrants are the two most common examples, although not the only ones.

Moments meant to galvanize empathy for the hybrids are not uncommon, so despite *Elephantmen*'s ahistorical and sometimes heavy-handed approach to the struggles of marginalized people, it does seek to emphasize the humanity of those who have been othered by society. Kate Polak argues that for empathy to have value it must be active rather than passive (16–17). It is not enough to feel empathy; rather, we must use that feeling to actually go out into the world and work to help others. In such a context, might the attempt to build empathy for marginalized people by referencing numerous mistreatments ultimately be inadequate? Maybe. Such a range of references may prevent us from reacting to the specific inequalities that arise from a given situation, and the comic does not actually give voice to the victims of the atrocities it draws upon. But I do believe that the more we humanize others and make visible the horrors of dehumanization, both historical and fictive, the more we create the conditions where action becomes possible. It is not the end, but the beginning. *Elephantmen*, though problematic, exists in that area before action, where empathy may be galvanized, but before it becomes productive. There is ambivalent but unrealized potential.

CHAPTER 5

Never Let Them Go

The Government and Children in *One of Us* and *Never Let Me Go*

Biopolitics and *One of Us*

In a biopolitical sense, children provide an opportunity for states "to secure a future for the populations they govern" (Lee 1). As a result, states may fund societal goods like children's healthcare or education in part so that children are more likely as adults to become "net contributor[s] to state finances" (1). There has been pushback to identifying children with the future, specifically from social constructionists who argue that this association has the effect of silencing children in the present because of their formulation as future adults. Thus, social constructionists tend to emphasize children's agency and voice (4). Despite children's capacity to exert agency, however, they still lack institutionalized political power. Their symbolic association with the future is thus hard to dislodge. Nonetheless, even though society may consider the investment in children ethically important, regardless of whether children eventually become net contributors or not, it is certainly the case that funding education and healthcare for all citizens is increasingly scrutinized, especially under austerity governments.

Even a future return on investment in an economic sense is often not good enough justification for those wringing their hands over the present costs, although, on an individual or familial level, the monetary costs of raising children are often justified due to their emotional worth, both in the present and future. Indeed, in modern times, children are generally considered emotional and psychological investments for families rather than economic ones (Katz, "Cultural Geographies" 10). On a governmental level, while some fret over the cost of funding education and childhood, a neoliberally infused biopolitics sometimes goes so far as to assume that those who do receive governmental support in childhood, whether directly or indirectly, may at some point *owe* the state. This imagined debt is not simply the idea that in the future a citizen's taxes both pay back and pay forward any potential economic spending that benefited the adult as a child. Instead, the hope that an adult become an economic net contributor transforms into the assumption that the adult become one, perhaps even beginning in their youth. If not, the adult or child who received investment may be considered waste. Of course, as this manuscript suggests, economic valuations of people is problematic and dehumanizing, and there are excellent moral and ethical reasons to invest in everyone, regardless of background or circumstance. Yet this chapter charts a trend in viewing people, dating back to their childhoods, as indebted to their government.

This is evident in Craig DiLouie's *One of Us*. The novel draws heavily from comics like *Uncanny X-Men* and *Spiderman* and their emphasis on the angst of youths with extraordinary abilities. The premise is that beginning in 1968, an STD creates a generation of children with different forms and abilities, many of whom manifest superpowers. The STD is considered a sort of plague and those born to infected individuals are referred to as "plague kids." The narrative is set in and around a Home[1] for infected children in Georgia in 1984. During the course of the narrative, an adult murders an adolescent girl and blames it on one of the plague kids, which sparks an uprising on the part of the plague children and adolescents that then threatens to extend beyond the small town it begins in.

From the start of the novel, the kids are shown to be ostracized from the larger community and their humanity is often questioned. For example, they are described as both animals and monsters (11, 12), and comparisons are frequently drawn between the children and those who experience racial discrimination. For example, the real name of Dog, the narrator, is Enoch, but another adolescent, Brain, believes Enoch is Dog's "slave name," even though Dog likes the name because many of the uncanny children were not named by their parents (6). Later, Brain argues that the marginalized individuals will be placed on reservations like the Creek Indians before altering the comparison to reference Auschwitz (26). Comparisons to the racism that African Americans experienced and continue to experience are most common, however. Brain even wonders at one point if one of his Black teachers sees him as Black "because of the color of his skin and curly fur, though his mother was White, and such distinctions didn't matter to monsters" (28). The book's amalgamation of comparisons to the various abuses suffered by a number of racial and cultural groups is a bit heavy-handed, and it is a narrative choice that is reminiscent of the previous chapter on *Elephantmen*. Like *Elephantmen*, the purpose of the referenced atrocities is to position the youths in relation to those whose mistreatment by governments is and was predicated on their dehumanization and othering. In each case, it involves people whose discrimination was, and often still is, sanctioned and enforced by the state.

Early in the novel, a government agent comes to the Home to interview the kids. Originally, these interviews were meant to determine whether the kids were threats or not. Recently, however, special abilities have begun to manifest in some of the kids, and the government wants to utilize these abilities. Agent Shackleton, from the Bureau of Teratological Affairs, tells Dog, "You're a ward of the state. More than a million of you. Living high on the hog for the past fourteen years in the Homes" (6–7). Such a large number of kids certainly must require a significant government investment, but the kids are definitely not living well. The residence in which the main characters live is housed on a former plantation with ruined buildings on the premises (72). Dog notes, "The Home was run-down and overcrowded, the beds infested. The room leaked brown water on the floor," and Brain believes that the adults who worked there were also unwanted within broader society (23, 24). The dilapidated environment in which the children live indicates that even though the Homes may be costly to run, they are certainly not getting the sort of investment necessary to make them livable in terms of comfort or quality. Rather, the infested and leaking facilities suggest a lack of commitment that can be attributed in large part, if not solely, to the lack of value placed on the children by the government and society writ large. Even if the youths were living in vastly improved conditions, it would be difficult to quantify what, if anything, they would owe in return when they have little agency at this point in their lives: agency that is circumscribed by the government oversight of their day-to-day lives; oversight that includes violence against kids who do not conform.

What education the kids do receive is second-rate at best. It consists of "mostly forced labor and social conditioning" (221). Despite the lack of adequate housing and education, the kids' labor is extracted and commodified. Dog and some of his friends work for a local farmer, where cotton, peanuts, and vegetables are grown. The kids also work with some of the farm animals. While the children are initially little help, they learn under threat of violence, and the farmer, Pa Albod, comes to see them as indispensable (40). Despite their value, however, the compensation for their labor goes to the government. Albod pays work fees, although he believes "[t]he Home should have been helping him for free considering all the taxes he paid to Washington" (40). This entitlement is especially disconcerting in that he believes that taxes mean he should be able to benefit from the work of others for free. The children are told they are getting an education through their work and Dog wants to do such work as a career later in life, but Brain explains to Dog that they work for free, without a choice, and that any future pay for the pounds of peanuts and cotton they pick will not be enough to live on: "It's slavery by another name" (44).

The military, as represented by Agent Shackleton, is also interested in commodifying the kids as assets to fight the Soviets, who have their own superpowered children. Individual members of the military also use such children as crutches for their careers. Agent Shackleton discovers that the character Goof, who has an upside-down face, has the power to compel people to do what he says. He takes Goof to a government facility and notes, "This little freak was his ticket.... Finding a hot one could get an agent promoted upstairs to management" (68). Shackleton also believes that the children require too many government resources and thus owe a debt:

> As far as Shackleton was concerned, it was about time the freaks gave something back to the USA. For the past fourteen years, the economy had limped through one recession after another. The cost of keeping them all alive was a constant drain on tax dollars even with funding cuts to the bone. Millions had been spent on a cure that never materialized.... Who would have ever guessed these kids might be the key to America reclaiming its status as a superpower? (68–69)

Shackleton's viewpoint illustrates the relatively straightforward idea that citizens are a national resource but places it within a neoliberal and biopolitical context centered on debt. Furthermore, Shackleton sees a scenario where the government finds a way to duplicate and synthesize the children's capabilities so that they might give the powers to others (69–70). In this case, the military spends additional money on their military programs involving kids with special abilities. This spending is referred to as an "investment" (319). This attitude takes the unique attributes of a child and subsequently extracts and distills the individual into those components most valued by the government. This would also conveniently allow the government to take for themselves the potentially valuable genetic material of these children while presumably making the children less valuable because their powers would no longer be unique. In such an event, the government could, if they chose, eventually dispose of the children, whose physical attributes often disturb those around them, and put the powers in more typical bodies. The desire to extract value from the bodies of certain children is an example of an ideology that cares for such children only to the extent that they can provide recompense to the government and support its interests.

The real irony is that were the government not so consumed by present costs and military applications and people not so afraid of the differences of the kids, the children would be a future boon. The unimaginatively named super-genius, Brain, in the midst of leading a violent uprising, imagines a different possibility:

> He envisioned a vehicle that ran on water and sunlight, a truck that would never die, a once-removed cousin to a perpetual motion machine. An all-purpose vehicle that outlived its owner, scalable and modularized for easy future upgrades. On the fly, he imagined materials and methods, tools and parts, machines and processes, new scientific fields that would revolutionize everything. He saw entire industries rise up out of nothing, manufacturing and service, new business models, halo disruption as his technologies rippled across other industries, tearing them down and replacing them with fresh marvels. . . . He could build dreams if only he weren't a monster. (264–265)

What this unrealized vision suggests is the xenophobic dehumanization and exploitation of these children in the present, as opposed to a societal embrace and genuine investment in their well-being, sacrifices the potential for future greatness. The novel, overall, fails to address issues of racism and exploitation in nuanced ways, but its acknowledgment of the damage caused by a biopolitics that assumes a relationship of debt between children and state is insightful in that it accurately asserts that this approach leads to a lack of adequate investment, it dehumanizes those not deemed worthy of investment, and it creates a society where citizens feel abandoned by and disconnected from their government. All unsustainable elements. One might argue that the government had no way of knowing the positive impact that Brain could have on society writ large because he actively hides his intelligence from his caretakers, as a means of protecting himself, but that is precisely the point. One can never know what a given child will be capable of contributing down the road, much less predict who will make or contribute to breakthroughs that fundamentally improve society. Even if one could make such predictions, these valuations do not supersede the notion that everyone has basic rights and responsibilities. To deny someone their rights, even as they make claims upon the person, is problematic.

What the novel posits, ultimately, is a biopolitics that, like other texts I have examined, commodifies children for the sake of the present at the expense of the future but which does so specifically through the justification of governmental intervention in childhood and its associated costs, even when said costs are not specifically quantified and even if such expenditures are inadequate to provide a reasonable level of care. Of course, what constitutes a reasonable level of care is open for debate, though it is certainly not the standard the government in *One of Us* sets for itself. But, to me, a reasonable level of care for children involves access to health care, education, shelter, proper food and hygiene, and emotional support from caretakers, all delivered in an environment or environments that are conducive to their function.

The government in *One of Us* is reacting to a calamity in a shortsighted and callous way, but they did not create the calamity, at least as far as we are aware. This does not absolve them of responsibility, yet the biopolitical governmental response is a reaction to a crisis that originates outside state control. What happens, however, when the state uses technology to craft a class of children whose sole purpose is to serve the interests of the government and its preferred citizens?

Children as State Resources in *Never Let Me Go*

Rebekah Sheldon argues that the capacity of technological advances to harness nonhuman vitality results in the possibility for a "reciprocal recognition" that such vitality might escape its constraints (5). She also asserts that the child informs the way we consider future catastrophe and is "literally . . .

a matter of reproduction and not just . . . a disciplinary tool toward social reproduction" (6). Sheldon's emphasis on the biopolitics of reproduction, which she terms *somatic* capitalism, as well as its relationship to neoliberal capital, is applicable here (19). Sheldon defines "somatic capitalism":

> the intervention into and monetization of life-itself. . . . It siphons vitality rather than exerting discipline, swerves and harnesses existing tendencies rather than regulating their emergence. . . . Its accelerant is capital, and it rides on the profits to be reaped from catastrophe. It is an expression of the move from state biopolitics with its rhetoric of concern to neoliberal speculation. (118)

Within this paradigm, the child remains a sentimental figure, but rather than mobilizing the desire to protect it, somatic capitalism under neoliberalism instead seeks to "extract and monetize" it (177).

This is precisely the vision which Kazuo Ishiguro imagines in his novel *Never Let Me Go*, which takes place in Britain in the "late 1990s" (np). The novel follows clones raised from childhood to become organ donors for humans. Kathy H. narrates the story and remembers growing up with her friends, Ruth and Tommy. They are raised at an English boarding school named Hailsham before moving into transitional housing called cottages, where they live together without adult supervision. After leaving the cottages, they become carers and donors. The reader gradually learns that Kathy and her friends are all clones and are raised and trained to donate their organs. In this sense, although the government is not monetizing the clones' organs, they are extracting what they see as the value of the clones, and as this is done, the clones lose their vitality: they often become bedridden before their death. The tension between the clones as humans and objects captures the tension between liberalism and neoliberalism, and the novel registers a shift "from disciplinary institutions to networks of prosthetic control" (Johnston 34, 35).

This shift is metaphorically embodied in the transition of the clones from carers to donors, and the use of euphemisms to mask these roles mirrors how the structures that control our lives often operate outside our immediate perception. In the novel, clones serve as caretakers for other donating clones before they must donate their own organs. As children, the characters have a general sense of their role in society but do not seem to fully grasp the ramifications, and the mistreatment of the clones is not immediately obvious to the reader because their horrific fate is couched in euphemistic terms. The titles "carer" and "donor" are initially confusing. The novel gives few clues as to what these positions entail. It begins, "My name is Kathy H. I'm thirty-one years old, and I've been a carer now for over eleven years. . . . My donors have always tended to do much better than I expected. Their recovery times have been impressive, and hardly any of them have been classified as 'agitated,' even before fourth donation" (3). Because the reader is not yet familiar with the terms Kathy uses, the ramifications of Kathy's introduction are unclear. The reality under which the clones live is slowly revealed so that by the time the whole process is visible, the clones are already firmly established in their roles. Furthermore, euphemisms make these roles seem positive. Carers sound like social workers. Kathy's work sounds laudable. Perhaps it is. However, because the narrator assumes knowledge on the part of the reader, Kathy does not explicate the fact that by excelling at her work, she allows donors to move more quickly through their donation process and increases the likelihood they will live through multiple donations. From the government's perspective, this allows more organs to be harvested before the donations kill the clones or, as some clones fear, the clones become conscious but unresponsive and their bodies continue to be harvested.

Sheldon asserts that the harvesting of the clones' organs is part of "the movement from a biopolitics of population reliant on aggregates of whole persons to a new biopolitics of subindividual, modular, and extractable parts" (18). Because of the immediate introduction of euphemistic terms to obfuscate the reality of the clones, the reader initially fails to understand that donors are not given a choice. The clones' creation predetermines their donations. Scholar Mark Currie argues that the euphemisms create a space between the closed world of Hailsham and the "brutal domain of inequality and social injustice" (103). This space is imperative to consider, as the clones grow up in Hailsham under the protection of guardians but are shaped for a future of forced organ extraction. In addition, this liminal space between worlds also mirrors the grotesque status of the clones, as they reside within the space between human and nonhuman.

Rocío Carrasco argues that the film adaptation of *Never Let Me Go* recognizes the power the wealthy and powerful hold over marginalized bodies of the clones, which are commodified and disposable. This is justified by those in power by the clones' "non-human status" (2, 6). This chapter makes a related argument but explicates it further in relation to the novel, and, as in other chapters, situates the grotesque as a means to understand this otherness. In the novel, the tension between the clones' status as humans deserving of dignity and agency and their intended purpose as organ stock takes the form of the grotesque. According to Philip Thomson, the grotesque is *"the unresolved clash of incompatibles in work and response"* or *"the ambivalently abnormal"'* (27). The grotesque often involves bodies that juxtapose various forms like human and insect or human and animal. This incongruity leads us to question what it means to be human. *Never Let Me Go* subtly utilizes the grotesque in its exploration of personhood. The clones are grotesque, but because the clones look exactly like nonclone humans, they are not immediately identifiable as grotesque. Their grotesque nature, however, is present in their ontological uncertainty: they exist between human and nonhuman, person and object, because of how they are created. The clones were initially thought of as medical supplies, as "shadowy objects in test tubes" (Ishiguro 261). Paul Sheehan asserts, "[Clones] show sameness to be a form of monstrous otherness; not a monstrosity of appearance, however, but of ontology" (253). Clones have monstrous, or grotesque, bodies not because of their differences but their similarities. Their bodies unsettle ontological classifications of the human. Humans in the novel reject clones as human simply by naming them clones, thus foregrounding their difference in origin. At the same time, the tenuous nature of this difference is evident because humans are unable to recognize clones outside the confines of the clones' residences and roles.

Sheehan's associations of clones with ontological uncertainty positions the clones as grotesque bodies paradoxically predicated on sameness rather than difference. To be grotesque, a body must be both familiar and strange, but usually the difference is physical. Not so for the clones. This is significant because it is the clones' ability to experience a wide range of human emotions that convince the reader that their origins do not make them less human than humans who are not clones. The ability of the novel to elicit recognition of the clones' humanity and condemnation regarding the way in which they are treated places the text within a tradition of eighteenth- and nineteenth-century sentimental and abolitionist literature (Shaddox 448; 450), which was used to humanize people who were consistently dehumanized in public and private spheres.

The clones' work as carers is one of the ways they illustrate their humanity. Carers may help prepare donors for death, but they also genuinely *care* for the donors. They help donors meet death with a semblance of dignity and provide them with a witness to the end of their life. Jill Casid argues that novels like *Never Let Me Go* give us a space to entertain tough but necessary possibilities relating to death and care (132). For her, the novel combines issues of human and nonhuman with the commodification of bodies and additional questions relating to power, reproduction, and economies. She argues that "love makes a difference" even though the carers cannot save the donors (129). Her argument emphasizes the precarity of the world, or the lack of social support for systems of care in a time of great economic inequality (122). For Casid, a "good" death can still exist in such a world. Although an individual may be diminished in a world that fails to allow them adequate economic opportunity or support, he or she can still assert dignity.

Besides the emotional value of the carers' work, caring causes two additional effects. One effect is it also prepares carers to die. Caregiving is brutal and difficult labor that emotionally drains the carer. Kathy notes, "Carers aren't machines. You try and do your best for every donor, but in the end, it wears you down. You don't have unlimited patience and energy" (4). Kathy's assertion that she and her peers are not machines can be read, in part, as a rejoinder to emphases of their posthuman nature over their human nature. The emotional grind Kathy mentions alludes to the fact that many clones, after initially serving as carers, request to become donors. However, this emotional labor has another effect: requiring that clones' care for donors helps to shelter the outside world from the clones. While the doctors and nurses are surely not clones, having other clones assist donors helps minimize the contact between clones and humans. This has the effect of keeping clones separate from other humans, which makes it easier for humans to commodify clones without requiring them to confront the consequences of their actions. Of course, clones might also provide better care because they can relate with the donors, but this does not negate the other structural benefits of having clones care for clones.

Although serving as carers prepares clones for their eventual organ harvesting, this preparation begins when they are children. It is at Hailsham that Kathy and her peers internalize the logic of their own objectification. This internalization helps facilitate the transformation of the clones into commodities, which is why Hailsham is also where the grotesque nature of the clones first surfaces. The boarding school is the source of their earliest memories. It is much like any other school: brimming with laughter and pain. The narrator's first description of Hailsham involves Kathy, Ruth, and their friends watching some boys pick soccer teams, and it foregrounds the novel's interest in the grotesque. As a great soccer player, Tommy expects to be picked early, if not first, but no one picks him. Kathy narrates, "'Look at him,' someone behind me said. 'He's completely convinced he's going to be first pick. Just look at him!' There *was* something comical about Tommy at that moment, something that made you think, well, yes, if he's going to be that daft, he deserves what's coming" (8–9). As other players are picked, Laura, Ruth's friend, pantomimes Tommy's facial expressions, and outside, "Tommy is left standing alone, and the boys all began sniggering" (9). This turns to laughter and the boys run off, leaving Tommy alone. This leads Tommy to explode: "He began to scream and shout, a nonsensical jumble of swear words and insults" (9). This soon escalates into the novel's first grotesque image: "[Tommy] was just raving, flinging his limbs about, at the sky, at the wind, at the nearest fence post. Laura said he was maybe 'rehearsing his Shakespeare.' Someone else pointed out how each time he screamed something he'd raise one foot off the ground, pointing it outward, 'like a dog doing a pee'" (10). This scene is grotesque because students take pleasure in the pain and humiliation of Tommy, secure in the knowledge that they are in no danger of similar abuse. Kathy's use of the word "comical" and Ruth's pantomime adds a comic element to the scenario, as cruel as it may be. For Tommy, the horror of this situation reveals itself as he realizes that not only will he not be picked first, but he will not be picked at all. For the others, Tommy's gradual realization serves to build up to the culmination of the joke: the explosive outburst. Tommy's inability to articulate his pain and frustration, as evidenced by the "nonsensical jumble," leads him to indiscriminately lash out at everything: "sky . . . wind . . . fence post" (10). Laura turns this into a joke by comparing this inarticulate expression of rage to Shakespeare. This comparison yokes together high culture and low culture, the greatest playwright in Western history and a bullied teen screaming in a field, whose gestures are compared to a urinating dog. The joining of high and low culture in a scene of this nature conjures images of the Bakhtinian carnivalesque. But whereas Bakhtin's conception of the carnivalesque is subversive in that it suspends hierarchy and emphasizes equality (10), here the low is kept low through mockery. This moment reinforces hierarchical social status instead of undermining it. The kids are punching down.

Tommy's constant rage is brought on by his abuse, but it also reflects his ability to intuit his own fate. As adults, Kathy tells Tommy, "I was thinking maybe the reason you used to get like that was because at some level you always *knew*." Tommy initially disagrees, but then considers it: "[T]hat's a funny idea. Maybe I did know, somewhere deep down. Something the rest of you didn't" (275). Tommy's rage is a very human reaction, and it contributes to the sense that the clones are essentially indistinguishable from humans. Scholar Shameem Black notes that "the question of what it means to be human pervades" the novel and that the "clones struggle to comprehend the significance of their own circumscribed personhood" (785). Tommy's rage is part of his struggle to understand his role in the world; it is a reaction against the unfairness of his circumstance. Whether it is his own isolation from, and bullying by, his peers or the isolation of the clones from the rest of society, Tommy is equally frustrated. Both demean and demoralize him. As heartbreaking as Tommy's abuse is, it is important that we recognize that this also demonstrates his humanity. Emotions like cruelty or rage are just as human as those of empathy and love, even if we might work to restrain the former and spread the latter. In the context of the novel, any emotional display is an argument for the humanity of the clones.

One of the ways that Hailsham prepares the clones for their lives of giving is by taking their art. Students are constantly producing art and the best is taken away to be displayed in the Gallery. Though the clones do not know this at the time, their art is used in the outside world to try and encourage people to recognize the souls of the clones. This appeal is empowered by the idea of childhood itself. The appeal to recognize the souls of the children is buttressed by the notion that children are innocents in need of protection from exploitation. The appeal fails, perhaps, because the protection one owes to the idealized child or children requires a recognition of one's own responsibility to such a group, but most adults apparently do not feel a responsibility to the clones. The ability to take the clones' art, without recompense, also foreshadows their positions as forced organ donors, where they are expected to give of themselves until it kills them.

The work produced for the Gallery and the way it systematically trains the children to selflessly give are reinforced by two other aspects of Hailsham: Exchanges and Sales. The Exchanges occur four times a year. Students produce different forms of art for the Exchanges: "paintings, drawings, pottery," etc. (16). Students are given "Exchange Tokens" for what they enter into the Exchanges, which they then use to purchase art from each other. Guardians give tokens based on how many they feel a particular item is worth. Participation in the Exchanges is used as a way to solidify communal bonds among the students, as the Exchanges, along with the Sales, are the "only means . . . of building up a collection of personal possessions" (16). Much of the popularity of students also depends upon their ability to create (16).

The reliance of the students on each other for many of their sentimental objects has a "subtle effect" on the students because, as Kathy puts it, "being dependent on each other to produce the stuff that might become your private treasures—that's bound to do things to your relationships" (16). Kathy is correct, but her sense that it does "something" is vague. A more specific description might be that it teaches the students to value each other based on what they can produce, which is how the wider world values them. The entire structure of Hailsham is designed to place students together, even as it separates them as much as possible from the humans. Students spend all their time together. They eat, play, and learn together. They sleep together in dorm rooms. And the Exchanges make them rely on each other for almost all the objects to which they may become attached, as well. This constant reification of the bonds of the students sets the stage for their future as they gradually move out of Hailsham and begin becoming carers and donors. When the students move beyond Hailsham's walls and segue into their new roles, they are supposed to keep themselves separate from humans and care for each other. It may be that the absence of any attempt to escape their fate and their willingness to take care of each other are predicated on how tightly the tapestry of their lives is woven.

The clones' best art is taken by a woman named Marie-Claude for the Gallery. This creates tension as the clones grow up. Kathy remembers, "By the time we were ten, this whole notion that it was a great honour to have something taken by Madame collided with a feeling that we were losing our most marketable stuff" (39). For all the institutional training the Exchanges and tokens provide for the clones, they also give them an awareness of exchange value. Some students take this up with Miss Emily, the headmistress of Hailsham, who subsequently gives students tokens for their art but not as many tokens as students might like because Miss Emily still believes it's an honor to be associated with the Gallery (39–40). Despite Miss Emily's compromise, the reimbursement for art is not a sacrifice on the part of the guardians. It still involves the students giving up what they are taught to cherish for tokens that hold no value outside Hailsham. Thus, the clones are trained to give of themselves without any real sort of compensation outside their own social circles, and their training as future donors is still intact. Alys Eve Weinbaum argues that the tokens are a symbolic payment in relation to the theft of their organs and lives and that the exchange "amounts to a pedagogical exercise that adjusts clones to exchange of something for nothing and, more important, to (mis)perception of a surface injustice (theft of their art) for the deep injustice: theft of life itself through a process by which human biological life is abstracted and integrated into the exchange relationship" (158). Similarly, the various ways artwork circulates, according to Shameem Black, mirrors "the circulation of vital body parts" and "repress[es] the students' possible resistance" by cultivating a reliance on community for a sense of self, by tying their value to their ability to produce art, and by making the clones feel as if "they actually partake in a real exchange" as opposed to being part of "an economy of . . . extraction" (795). The Gallery and Exchange systems are thus troubling in that they prepare the clones for lives of exploitation while masking their intended goals. Black understands the novel as a metaphor for the inequality of "national and global economies systems" where "First World economies desire labor without the inconvenient presence of human laborers" (796).

The circulation of goods at Hailsham shows up in another event: Sales. During Sales, students use tokens to purchase personal possessions from the outside world. Once a month, a white van arrives with items from the outside. Kathy remembers, "It's where we got our clothes, our toys, the special things that hadn't been made by another student" (41). These vans are always greeted with excitement, and yet the Sales seem to generate disappointment. Kathy explains, "There'd be nothing remotely special and we'd spend our tokens just renewing stuff that was wearing out or broken with more of the same" (41). The number of tokens the students accumulate is barely enough to cover the replacement of items. Perhaps this is part of a larger effort to keep the clones used to living their lives with little in the way of commodities, but it also demonstrates the precarity in which so many struggle just to maintain. The clones value the Sales items even though the items are mundane: clothing or unused items one can find in most households. The possibility that they find something of value fills them with hope and excitement. This seems in line with contemporary consumerism in that the excitement produced by the possibility of a purchase often leads to a letdown after the purchase, a process which may then repeat itself. One also gets the sense that the items at the Sales are the castoffs of humans (Black 796). They arrive in cardboard boxes and seem random, as the students never know what will be there. If this is the case, the students are exchanging their tokens, worthless to the outside world (though, admittedly, not to them), for the items that humans do not want.

The clones get so worked up at the prospect of finding something they can treasure at the Sales that things get violent. Whereas the Exchanges have a "hushed atmosphere," the Sales are "crowded and noisy," a place where "pushing and shouting was all part of the fun . . . Except . . . every now and then, things would get out of hand, with students grabbing and tugging, sometimes fighting" (42). The atmosphere is reminiscent of a shopping mall or store during Black Friday as reports often indicate violence among customers (Piccoli). The fighting at a sale leads to an admonishment by Miss Emily: "[W]e were all very special, being Hailsham students, and so it was all the more disappointing when we behaved badly" (43). The students at Hailsham are, we learn, treated better than most other clones; although it is unclear exactly how less-fortunate clones are treated or what their homes are like. But in relation to the wider world, a world of both clones and humans, describing the clones as special is not like describing a nonclone human child as special. For clones, "special" becomes another euphemism, like "carer" or "donor," and helps to ennoble their future roles by obfuscating the reality of what will happen to them because of their special status.

The euphemistic use of "special" to describe the clones comes up in other places, too. The teacher Miss Lucy is asked about whether she ever smoked. She says yes, "but what you must understand is that for you, all of you, it's much, much worse to smoke than it ever was for me. . . . You've been told about it. You're students. You're . . . *special*. So keeping yourselves well, keeping yourselves very healthy inside, that's much more important for each of you than it is for me" (68–69). The clones are not special because they are children, of course, but because of the unspoken reality of their origins. Children are often called "special" in Western societies. We exalt them and they are special, each being a unique individual. However, the clones are not special because they are unique; they are special because they are commodities. In this context, clones are warned not to smoke, not to keep them healthy so they might live to a ripe old age, but to prevent them from damaging the goods, so to speak.

It is an encounter with Marie-Claude when Kathy is a child that most directly exposes Kathy to how special she truly is and situates the clones themselves in the realm of the grotesque, as opposed to their earlier encounter with Tommy where he is turned into a grotesque object of derision. The young clones intuit that Marie-Claude fears them. To test this hypothesis, Ruth, Kathy, and others contrive to quickly and suddenly come upon Marie-Claude and then walk closely past her. Kathy recalls Marie-Claude's reaction: "I can still see it now, the shudder she seemed to be suppressing, the real dread that one of us would accidentally brush against her. And though we just kept on walking, we all felt it. It was like we'd walked from the sun right into the chilly shade" (35). The horror which Marie-Claude feels toward the clones is palpable, expressing itself both in her bodily reaction and the clones' ability to feel Marie-Claude's dread. This is confusing for them. They have no idea what the Gallery is truly for and no idea why an adult would fear them, as their origin and future are minimized at Hailsham. Marie-Claude's fear gets even stranger: "Madame *was* afraid of us. But she was afraid of us in the same way someone might be afraid of spiders. We hadn't been ready for that. It had never occurred to us to wonder how *we* would feel, being seen like that, being the spiders" (35). Spiders are often associated with the grotesque due to their ability to unsettle people (Kayser 182; McElroy 8–9), and the connection of the clones to arachnids forces the children to consider their own dehumanization. Their grotesque ontology is innately terrifying for Marie-Claude. Not because she thinks them inherently dangerous, but because she knows they are inherently different even though the clones' difference in origin leaves no distinguishable trace, or, more precisely, *because* the clones' biological differences leave no distinguishable trace.

As I noted earlier, this seems contrary to the grotesque, which often registers itself on the body. Noël Carroll notes, "The grotesque subverts our categorical expectations concerning the natural and ontological order" ("The Grotesque Today" 297). This, in turn, has the potential "to elicit certain affective states, such as horror, comic amusement, and awe" (298). Furthermore, for Carroll, the grotesque is embodied. He writes, "Something is grotesque only if it is an image, whether verbal or visual, of an animate being that violates our standing biological or ontological concepts and expectations" (297–98). While the clones are animate beings, their images are of conventional humans. If the cloned humans had some sort of striking differences between their bodies and non-cloned humans' bodies, they might still be grotesque. But Marie-Claude is terrified precisely because of the normalcy of their bodies; she is terrified because they look like her but upset her notion of what's natural pertaining to the "biological [and] ontological" categories of the human. Even as Marie-Claude is repulsed by the children, however, she is drawn to try and help the clones, which gets at the convoluted way that the grotesque registers upon a person.

Kathy connects her experience with Marie-Claude to the reader's experience:

> I'm sure somewhere in your childhood, you too had an experience like ours that day; similar if not in the actual details, then inside, in the feelings. Because it doesn't really matter how well your guardians try to prepare you... . So you're waiting, even if you don't quite know it, waiting for the moment when you realise that you really are different to them; that there are people out there, like Madame, who don't hate you or wish you any harm, but who nevertheless shudder at the very thought of you—of how you were brought into the world and why—and who dread the idea of your hand brushing against theirs.... It's like walking past a mirror ... and suddenly it shows you something else, something troubling and strange. (36).

The troubling mirror image here evokes the familiar yet repressed inherent in the uncanny, which is itself connected to the grotesque by a number of scholars. This connection is made, in part, because they "both reflect an ambiguity that relates to an interior condition and can produce a range of responses, from alienation and estrangement to terror and laughter" (Edwards and Graulund 5–6). Here, by looking in the mirror, we can understand the troubling and strange aspect of Kathy as her ontological difference is manifested in her reflection. She is both familiar (she looks like a nonclone human) yet strange (a human clone). Kathy and her peers carry their differences inside them, so to speak, in that they are intangible and immaterial, yet their differences end up materially shaping their entire lives. The mirror reference, then, is a slippage where Kathy briefly sees herself from the perspective of a nonclone human.

While it is true that in the novel the "debate [about whether to harvest the clones' organs] has been defused by the logic of a common welfare that must sacrifice individuals for the health of the greater whole" (Holmes 391), the sacrificed are isolated and objectified to make it more palatable. The exploited look no different from the rest of the populace, yet the populace understands them as different and thus exploitable. A proponent of the way clones are treated might argue that clones are different and exist for one purpose, but, under neoliberal capitalism, we all suffer from a narrow set of options that are circumscribed in large part by the precarity under which so many people live. Chris Holmes understands the clones' function less as science fiction and more "as a novelistic expression of the contemporary state of corporate thinking and intentionality" (391). In this context, to truly free ourselves is to recognize the harmful logic of corporate neoliberal thinking and demand better for everyone underneath the system but especially for the most marginalized.

To return to the neoliberal and biopolitical understanding of clones as objects, these elements are further elucidated when Tommy cuts his elbow. Another student tells Tommy that moving his elbow too quickly can cause his arm to "unzip like a bag opening up" and that this has happened to another student who "[woke] up to find his whole upper arm and hand skeletally exposed, the skin flopping about next to him" (85–86). Tommy eventually discovers the joke, but the notion of "unzipping" stays with the clones. Kathy remembers that it "[became] a running joke among us about the donations. The idea was that when the time came, you'd be able just to unzip a bit of yourself, a kidney or something would slide out, and you'd hand it over" (87–88). At the time, this scene is the most direct connection the clones make between themselves and their future use, even though it is done as a joke. The joke also masks the horror of the clones' future, as it elides the organ transplant process by taking the corporeal effect of scalpels on bodies and making it comically simple. But from the perspective of most humans in the novel, clones are body bags who carry the organs humans need but are otherwise faceless and unknowable.

The emphasis on the grotesque and interiority continues as the clones get older. After Hailsham, the clones spend a transitional period at some cottages. There, the clones mix with some older peers as well as peers who grew up outside Hailsham. Their only contact with the wider world is a man who occasionally brings them supplies. At the cottage, Kathy worries about her sexuality. She tells Ruth, "There might be something not quite right with me, down there" (128). The irony of this moment is that her struggles with understanding her sexuality convey Kathy's humanity because, like many people, she is unsure how to process these new feelings. Because she does not understand them, Kathy believes they are *wrong*. She thinks herself grotesque. This moment exemplifies Leslie Fiedler's assertion that when adolescents enter puberty, their bodies seem either "monstrously deficient or excessive" (32). While Fiedler is generalizing, this description coincides with Kathy's feelings. She sees her urges as monstrously excessive or unnatural, as evidenced by the fact that she thinks something might be wrong with her. Kathy believes this may be a result of her "possible," the woman she was cloned from. Kathy recalls, "The basic idea behind the possible theory was simple. . . . Since each of us was copied at some point from a normal person, there must be, for each of us, somewhere out there, a model getting on with his or her life" (139). However, the clones are uncertain as to what age their possibles should be. Humans could be cloned at any age. For some clones, the "models were an irrelevance, a technical necessity for bringing us into the world, nothing more than that. . . . At the same time, whenever we heard reports . . . we couldn't help getting curious" (140). The possibles are a mirage. Nowhere in the novel does a clone meet their possible. The one trip to get a better look at Ruth's potential possible ends with the certainty the potential possible is not it. The clones believe that glimpsing a possible is like "glimps[ing] your future" (140). But this is incorrect. Theoretically, a possible may give a clone a sense of what the clone would look like later in life, but they cannot give a clone a glimpse into a future because the clone's future is predetermined. A more accurate articulation of what the possible would reveal is an *alternative* future, a might-have-been. It is emblematic of the clones' world that their fantasy of viewing their future through their possibles is also one that sees the future as predetermined.

The clones' attitude toward the possibles connects with Kathy's feelings of being sexually grotesque because she believes that if her possible is a sex worker, this accounts for her sexual urges. As readers, we understand this to be a red herring. But, to some, pornography might be an appropriate place to look, considering the social stigma attached to it. Ruth, upon learning that the office worker she went to look at is not her possible, explodes,

> We're modeled from *trash*. Junkies, prostitutes, winos, tramps. Convicts, maybe, just so long as they aren't psycho. That's what we come from. We all know it, so why don't we say it? . . . If you want to look for possible, if you want to do it properly, then you look in the gutter. You look in rubbish bins. Look down the toilet, that's where you'll find where we all came from. (166)

There's logic to Ruth's diatribe. As a disposable body, Ruth sees herself as part of a heritage of "disposable" groups who are kept outside the bounds of "civil" society and often refused the type of social support they would benefit from, as Western societies like the United States often emphasize the punitive over the rehabilitative. Ruth is speaking from a position of powerlessness, and she thus situates herself within a community or heritage of the powerless. She is a disposable commodity whose organs will be harvested until she expires. Ruth's acknowledgment that "psychos," whether mental or moral, would be unfit to be cloned is not because they are socially stigmatized but because the clones need to be pliable, and thus the state seems unwilling to risk cloning people who most deviate from societal norms. Leonard Cassuto notes that the grotesque can be used to depict the iniquities heaped upon the lower classes. He writes,

> [Jack] London uses the grotesque to try to make a visceral impact on an order that links humanity to social station, and which keeps the lower orders from living like the human beings they are. . . . The grotesque in London's hands therefore becomes a hard-hitting social tool with which to attack the money-eyed interests who are ruining the lives of the innocents. In effect, London is willing to sacrifice the humanity of some of these innocents, a loss taken in the interest of exposing the inequities of the system. ("Jack London's" 123–24)

In this context, Ruth and her peers, who associate their possibles with the lower classes and who are considered undesirable among humans, are metaphorically sacrificed to highlight an environment wherein the lower classes are considered expendable.

As we know, the clones are not actually harvested until they are adults. This may be partially because it would be more difficult for humans to countenance the use of child clones, but it may also be because the organs of children are not yet fully developed (although this does not explain why the clones' organs are not taken during their adolescence or young adulthood). Kathy and Tommy eventually reunite and seek Marie-Claude. There is a rumor that Hailsham students in love can defer donations for a few years to be with each other. When they confront Marie-Claude, they also encounter their old headmistress, Miss Emily. Miss Emily reveals that she and Marie-Claude were part of a movement to treat clones more humanely. She argues that they protected the Hailsham clones from the "worst of those horrors" involving the deplorable conditions other clones are raised in (261). She states, "Most importantly, we demonstrated to the world that if students were reared in humane, cultivated environments, it was possible for them to grow to be as sensitive and intelligent as any ordinary human being" (261). But in spite of the temporary accomplishment of Hailsham and institutions like it, they ultimately fail to effect any large-scale changes. In fact, by this time in the narrative, Hailsham and other humanist schools have closed. All that's left are "those vast government 'homes,' and even if they're somewhat better than they once were . . . you'd not sleep for days if you saw what still goes on in some of those places" (265).

In spite of her support of the clones, Miss Emily, like Marie-Claude, fears them. Miss Emily explains, "We're *all* afraid of you. I myself had to fight back dread of you almost every day I was at Hailsham. There were times I'd look down at you from my study and I'd feel such revulsion. . . . But I was determined not to let such feelings stop me doing what was right" (269). The revulsion Miss Emily feels, like Marie-Claude, demonstrates the grotesque nature of the clones in the eyes of humans. The clones are positioned as inferior to human to justify how the clones are used. At the same time, they clearly are human, or at least resemble humans so thoroughly that it makes humans uncomfortable with the clones. This is why they must be kept in the shadows, so that people can forget about the ways in which the clones challenge their definitions of humanity and the widespread exploitation of the clones. Miss Emily is able to work with the clones in spite of her feelings of revulsion because she focuses on their rights. Perhaps Miss Emily does not see clones as fully human, but the better life Miss Emily sought to win for the clones would not have been a goal if the clones did not remind Miss Emily and her supporters of humans. Black notes that the novel expresses "concerns about the state of England and . . . transnational fears about rising inequality" (785).

The clones represent a permanent underclass locked into roles as exploited caregivers, whose ability to make decisions is circumscribed by their environment (Elliot). Scholar Lisa Fluet observes that immaterial laborers, those who work but do not produce tangible products, have "no future in Ishiguro's novels" but that this "enables their more ethical approach to the demands of the present" (268). This also allows readers to consider our own immaterial labor in the present without hope for a better future (285). In this sense, the inevitability of Kathy's death and the accompanying loss of her memories of Tommy and Ruth speak to a harsh truth outside the novel: a world that accepts the governmental commodification of individuals and their subsequent disposability is a cruel world indeed.

CODA

What Next?

After the exploration of worlds where children are sacrificial lambs at the altar of commodification, it may seem as if there is, despite some of the texts' endings, little hope. This feeling is heightened in a world that is in the midst of biological, ecological, and economic insecurity. In this context, reproduction, both biological and societal, seems daunting. In some ways, one might think about the texts under analysis as warnings about a decline in reproductive futurity. They involve a series of narratives that suggest concern over the ways some adults treat children. These children are ontologically or physically different than previous generations, but all texts make clear the children and adolescents are as emotionally and intellectually complex as those who preceded them. What happens when adults not only refuse to safeguard the future of subsequent generations but actively see children as exploitable resources? The texts we've considered note a variety of possibilities. In some cases, new communities arise; in other cases, things seem to go on largely as they did before. At their most dire, humanity seems to end or be on the verge of ending.

Natasha Hurley argues that nonreproduction "is the repository of reproduction's negativity" but that it should be positioned "not simply against but also within and beside reproduction in an effort to map new avenues of thought and new sites of inquiry for the field" (148). Many people who choose to forego children or are unable to have them still exist in social spaces with children or encounter them, and because social reproduction exists alongside biological reproduction, for Hurley, even those without children are part of reproduction. That is, adults without children also help reproduce social behavior and expectations in children, even if they do not add to the population. Yet even as the nonreproductive still assist in social reproduction, they also provide for "alternative modes of social relations to the child" (156). Hurley also notes, "Reproduction is the fantasy and the issue (literally) of the adult" (157). The notion that reproduction is also social, coupled with the emphasis on reproductive futurity as an adult fantasy or concept, which was touched on in the introduction, enables us to speak more directly to issues of nonreproduction.

The texts I write about include biological reproduction but largely reject the incorporation of grotesque children into mainstream society via social reproduction. They mostly do not want these children to partake in society in the same way that children who are not viewed as commodities might be allowed or encouraged. If the grotesque children are allowed to grow up, they exist (mostly) apart and are marked as other. Here then we have reproductive nonreproduction or nonreproductive futurity. Of course, adults do pass on social values to the children and adolescents they exploit throughout this analysis, but these values are the dark undercurrent of what Western society likes to believe. Adults will choose whom to protect, whom to exploit—their neoliberal darlings—and whom to abandon to the wolves.

Of course, biopolitical and economic thought often focus on growing the population to increase workers, consumers, and capital. Nina Power questions this approach: "What does it mean to 'keep human life going' when to do so also entails keeping capitalism going? When to have children is to also . . . generate workers and to generate work?" ("Brief Notes" 2). Seeing people as resources is not particularly new, and certainly precedes capitalism in numerous ways. For Power, it becomes a matter of scale: "If we want to protect certain forms of labour—love, care, sustainability—but refuse others—those that generate profit for others, that cause un/intentional harm, we must decide on this question of scale" (3). The potential of non-reproduction, then, is not about a refusal to biologically reproduce but a refusal of certain elements of society that benefit "the ruling class that treats the continued existence of everyone else as mere fodder for its own self-perpetuation" (3).

Power also explores some of these issues regarding capitalist reproduction in an earlier essay, "Non-Reproductive Futurism," wherein she critiques Lee Edelman's strident denunciation of reproductive futurism through a reading of Jacques Rancière's discussion of rational equality. She writes, "If there has in fact been a widespread feeling of 'no future' it is because it has been impossible to imagine anything different; capitalism depends upon the reproduction of sameness in the guise of difference, the idea that there is no alternative, and no future (in the sense of new ways of living) is possible" (2). Power's "no future" is a future that lacks any substantive changes to the current economic order. It lacks hope for something different. No future beyond a continuation of the present. There are tensions within the system because "if the image of the child and the fantasy of futurity are shared by both politics and the economy, it is not necessarily in the same way. Capitalism may in the long run need future workers, but in the short term, the conflict between paying for maternity leave, for example, and making a profit are frequently at odds" and that "politics is so pro-child in theory because it is so anti-child (and anti-woman) in practice" (4, 5). Because the present is so hypercapitalistic, this means an unwillingness to invest long-term in children, which coincides with an unwillingness to invest in women and families, whatever those family structures may look like. In some respects, then, the idealization of children is currently a drastic overcompensation for our refusal to take care of them or an unwillingness to leave the world (the economy, the environment, etc.) better for future generations. Better as in more equalitarian and less profit-driven, healthier, and more sustainable. If done thoughtfully, such a movement would also improve conditions for many or most adults too. So what happens when this idealistic possibility is foregone in favor of a doubling-down on destructive behavior to such an extent that not only do those in power stop actively asserting they care for all children, but they start to actively harm them? We get the type of nonreproductive futurity present in the narratives within this book.

Power leaves us with a new possibility. She ultimately argues for a queer rationalism that would allow for the coexistence of reason and queerness. This includes a reconceptualization of children: "In place of a sentimental, vitalist understanding of children as bearers of the future, it would treat them as nothing special, but in a positive way" (15). I would not only treat children as nothing special and therefore unburden them from the responsibilities that adults displace onto children but also consider them more seriously. Earlier, I outlined John Wall's enunciation of three traditional approaches to childhood: top-down, bottom-up, and horizontal. Yet Wall rejects all these views in favor of a society where the child would be equal to the adult. This type of society would emphasize the needs of its most vulnerable citizens and lead to more social inclusiveness. He asserts, "The underlying moral obligation is to expand rather than contract the sphere of social inclusiveness in light of those most easily left out of it" (104). This begins with children but also expands to include everyone, children and adults. This attitude toward social justice would be socially reproduced by teaching it to children (103). I think it is here, in the space between discussions of social reproduction and social justice, that we see the possibility for societal redemption, for an expansion and strengthening of social safety nets, of resources for the most vulnerable, of respect and appreciation of difference, and of resistance to structures that dehumanize and incentivize extraction over sustainability. The texts throughout this manuscript warn us about the dangers we face and how they change and estrange us and subsequently turn our progeny and ourselves grotesque, but it is up to us to heed those warnings.

NOTES

Introduction: Childhood, Commodification, and the Grotesque

1. The figure of the Athenian child has been introduced to reflect the agential, participatory child (Smith 5). This sort of active child is what many childhood studies scholars who research actual children emphasize.

2. The number of children of color tried as adults for various crimes compared to white children also speaks to the ways in which innocence and childhood is often associated with whiteness.

3. Wall also outlines a horizontal/developmental approach to childhood that he associates with Aristotle and Locke that emphasizes the child's progression over time.

4. Sacralization and the social conditions that allowed it probably also paved the way for the reemergence of the Romantic conception of childhood in contemporary times as economic imperatives for urban, middle-class childhoods lessened and children's emotional value became the point of emphasis.

5. Whether childhood might or should be kept separate from the market is an open question. For example, Kathryn Bond Stockton notes that some believe children are more vulnerable in our society because they lack money, though she questions whether having more money would make children more or less vulnerable (38).

6. While some of the texts include a developmental discourse of childhood, the characters aren't really encouraged to develop in ways that enable them to make large-scale decisions or gain autonomy due to the systems that constrain them.

Chapter 1. Innocent and Grotesque: The Child in *Sweet Tooth* and *The Girl with All the Gifts*

1. Although Lemire has worked with many comics publishers, including DC Comics and Marvel Comics, his most innervating work involves original characters and worlds such as *Essex County*, *Descender/Ascender*, and *Family Tree*.

2. José Villarrubia is the colorist. Pat Brosseau is the letterer. Other contributing artists include Matt Kindt, Emi Lenox, Carlos M. Mangual, and Nate Powell.

3. To borrow Shun-Liang Chao's wording on classification: the hybrids are both human and animal and neither human nor (a recognizable) animal (45). This wording mirrors that of Leonard Cassuto, who writes that the grotesque is "a breach of fundamental categories surrounding the definition of what is human. Neither one thing nor another, the grotesque is instead a distortion, conflation, or truncation that is simultaneously both and neither—and it thus questions the image of the human" ("Jack London's Class-Based Grotesque" 115).

4. This approach also takes one of the elements of chaotic children, animality, and destigmatizes it. It coincides with the idea that both animals and children are closer to nature than adults due to the divide between nature and culture (Höing 65).

5. On the forest side, where trees are so neatly rowed they were clearly planted by human hands, is the space where Gus's parents are buried, as evidenced by the graves and the dead buck. The placement of the graves by the highway seems counterintuitive: Gus's father hid from others, and so it is strange that he would initially bury his wife by the highway because it seems more visible to travelers than if the grave was hidden further in the trees. One explanation for this might be that the grave was put farther away from the home.

6. Similar, perhaps, to how narratives critiquing the commodification of youths are also commodifying (fictional) youths. This point is not meant as a critique so much as a lament over the seeming inescapability of economic imperatives under late-stage capitalism.

7. The alternating series of panels is established on the preceding page.

8. While the villains would argue that they are working toward the long-term good, the narrative undercuts such an argument by showing the butchery the adults commit without any noticeable strides toward curing the plague. Furthermore, in flashbacks, Abbot, the leader of the compound, is depicted as a brutal man before the experiments.

9. Although the children of hybrids sometimes contain multiple animal aspects, depending on their heritage. One of Gus and Wendy's children has antlers and a pig nose, for example.

10. Melanie provides an example of this in the help she provides the humans. Sergeant Park even comes around to her.

Chapter 2. "I'm Not an Animal": Grotesque Description and Chaotic Children in *The Power* and *The Flame Alphabet*

1. Leonard Cassuto observes this dual application of the grotesque in Antebellum American literature and culture (*The Inhuman Race* 6).

2. Leslie Fiedler asserts that early Christians initially encounter "[f]reaks not as creatures from elsewhere but as monstrous children born into their own families" (229). Though the children in *The Flame Alphabet* are not coded as atypical (eventually, everyone's language is toxic), the notion that parents might initially encounter the monstrous other in "their own families" resonates.

3. Williams discusses how the body of the zombie metaphorically embodies the effects of capitalism, as zombies represent capitalism's poor and needy: "[T]he sick repetition of want let loose on a global scale" (74).

4. In the novel, characters that look like zombies are often positioned as victims, while the vampiric connotations are often applied to victimizers. Perhaps this is due to the intellectual passivity of zombies as compared to vampires. Sami Khatib notes that capitalism itself is vampiric as it sucks labor and time from the proletariat zombie-laborers (109).

5. The draining of vitality also speaks to the often difficult nature of parenting: emotionally, financially, and physically.

Chapter 3. "We Are Masterpieces": Child Labor in "Reeling for the Empire" and *Geek Love*

1. Going back even further, Leslie Fiedler notes that "human Freaks have, in fact, been manufactured for ritual aesthetic and commercial purposes ever since history began," and, more specifically, that "the bodies of children [were] stunted and twisted in late Renaissance Europe so that they could be used as props by beggars or peddled to exhibitors" (251).

2. Two portions of *Geek Love* were published earlier, in 1983 and 1988, during the Reagan administration.

3. Al's Polish or Eastern European last name suggests he came from a family of immigrants, though it is never commented upon. Lil's maiden name is Hinchcliff, and she leaves behind her aristocratic Boston family to run away with Al.

4. It cannot be overstated that Al and Lil are not just hoping for any disability. They desire extremely unique physical differences.

5. This may recall the thalidomide crisis.

6. Al and Lil had six children who did not survive. Four were stillborn or died during childbirth. Two died early in childhood. Arty killed one because his parents wanted to make them a dual act, but Arty wanted to have his own show. The parents display the bodies of their dead children in jars of formaldehyde in a tent of oddities that costs one dollar to enter.

7. Although Oly's perspective that they are masterpieces would align well with a Bakhtinian emphasis on the carnivalesque and its ability to subvert hierarchies, I believe that ultimately the Binewski carnival is much more confining due to the reliance of the characters on their bodies as commodities.

Chapter 4. Monstrous Soldiers: The Grotesque and Postmodernism in *Elephantmen* and *The Beef*

1. Contributors to the series, including colorists and letterers, include Monifa Aldridge, Blond, Steve Buccellato, Chris Burnham, Greg Capullo, J. Scott Campbell, Keu Cha, Marian Churchland, Boo Cook, Ian Churchill, Camilla D'Errico, Jenny Frison, Brandon Graham, Peter Gross, David Hine, Stuart Immonen, Shaky Kane, Ryan Kelly, Ladrönn, Tula Lotay, Eric Larsen, Ed McGuinness, Axel Medellin, Fiona Meng, Moritat, Tony Parker, Nei Ruffino, J. G. Roshell, Dave Sim, Rob Steen, André Szymanowicz, Shannon Wheeler, and Gregory Wright.

2. The comic *WE3* follows animals bioengineered to serve as soldiers. They develop extremely limited forms of speech. However, *WE3* focuses more on the commodification of animals by humans, not the metaphor of the grotesque human whose form is used as evidence for and of their dehumanization.

3. *Elephantmen*, both the individual comic books and collected trades, lack page numbers.

4. Figure 4.4 appears after figures 4.5 and 4.6 in the comics but takes place earlier in the characters' lives as it describes her time in Europe.

5. Of course, chuck also refers to a cut of beef.

6. This image is reproduced from the trade collection. The original cover has some additional markings in the upper left corner.

Chapter 5. Never Let Them Go: The Government and Children
in *One of Us* and *Never Let Me Go*

1. The capitalization of "Home" mirrors the novel.

WORKS CITED

Abate, Michelle Ann. "'They're Quite Strange in the Larval Stage': Children and Childhood in Gary Larson's 'The Far Side.'" *International Journal of Comic Art*, vol. 21, no. 1, 390–422.

Adams, James Luther. "The Grotesque and Our Future." *The Grotesque in Arts & Literature: Theological Considerations*, edited by James Luther Adams and Wilson Yates, William B. Eerdmans Publishing Group, 1997, 69–74.

Adams, Rachel. "An American Tail; Freaks, Gender, and the Incorporation of History in Katherine Dunn's Geek Love." *Freakery; Cultural Spectacles of the Extraordinary Body*, edited by Rosemarie Garland Thomson, NYU Press, 1996, 277–90.

Alderman, Naomi. *The Power*. Little, Brown and Company, 2016.

Bakhtin, Mikhail. *Rabelais and His World*. Translated by Helene Iswolsky, MIT Press, 1968.

Barasch, Frances K. *The Grotesque: A Study in Meanings*. Mouton, 1971.

Barton, Chris. "Book Review: 'The Flame Alphabet' by Ben Marcus." *Los Angeles Times*, February 24, 2012. http://articles.latimes.com/2012/feb/24/entertainment/la-et-book-20120224.

Beber, Bernd, and Christopher Blattman. "The Logic of Child Soldiering and Coercion." *International Organization*, vol. 67, no. 1, Winter 2013, 65–104.

Becker, Gary S., and Kevin M. Murphy. *Social Economics: Market Behavior in a Social Environment*. The Belknap Press of Harvard UP, 2000.

Berger, Arthur Asa. *The Comic-Stripped American*. Walker and Company, 1973.

Bernstein, Robin. *Racial Innocence: Performing American Childhood from Slavery to Civil Rights*. New York UP, 2011.

Bhabha, Jacqueline. "The Child—What Sort of Human?" *PMLA*, vol. 121, no. 5, October 2006, 1,526–35.

Bhagwati, Jagdish. *In Defense of Globalization*. Oxford UP, 2004.

Black, Shameem. "Ishiguro's Inhuman Aesthetics." *MFS: Modern Fiction Studies*, vol. 55, no. 4, Winter 2009, 785–807.

Blum, Virginia L. *Hide and Seek: The Child between Psychoanalysis and Fiction*. University of Illinois Press, 1995.

Blyth, Mark. *Austerity: The History of a Dangerous Idea*. Oxford UP, 2013.

Bogdan, Robert. *Freak Show: Presenting Human Oddities for Amusement and Profit*. University of Chicago Press, 1990.

Bohlmann, Markus P. J., and Sean Moreland. "Introduction: Holy Terrors and Other Musings on Monstrous-Childness." *Monstrous Children and Childish Monsters: Essays on Cinema's Holy Terrors*, edited by Markus P. J. Bohlmann and Sean Moreland, McFarland & Company Inc., 2015, 9–25.

Bombaci, Nancy. *Freaks In Late Modernist American Culture: Nathanael West, Djuna Barnes, Tod Browning, and Carson McCullers*. Peter Lang, 2006.

Brice, Jason. "Sentinels, Not Senators." Silver Bullet Comics, August 7, 2007. https://web .archive.org/web/20070807200031/http://www.silverbulletcomicbooks.com/rage /99230093664723.htm.

Brooks, Peter. *Body Work: Objects of Desire in Modern Narrative*. Harvard UP, 1993.

Brown, Wendy. *Undoing the Demos: Neoliberalism's Stealth Revolution*. Zone Books, 2015.

Bruhm, Steven. "Nightmare on Sesame Street: Or, the Self-Possessed Child." *Gothic Studies*, vol. 8, no. 2, 2006, 98–113.

Buckingham, David. "Constructing Children as Consumers." *The Routledge International Handbook of Children, Adolescents, and Media*, edited by Dafna Lemish. Routledge, 2013, 54–60.

Butler, Christopher. *Postmodernism: A Very Short Introduction*. Oxford UP, 2002.

Carey, M. R. *The Girl with All the Gifts*. Orbit, 2014.

Carrasco, Rocío. "The Commodified Body and Post/In Human Subjectivities in Frears's *Dirty Pretty Things* and Romanek's *Never Let Me Go*." CLCWeb: Comparative Literature and Culture, vol. 21, no. 1, 2019, 1–9.

Carroll, Noël. "Horror and Humor." *Journal of Aesthetics and Art Criticism*, vol. 57, no. 2, Spring 1999, 145–60.

Carroll, Noël. "The Grotesque Today: Preliminary Notes Towards a Taxonomy." *Modern Art and the Grotesque*, edited by Frances S. Connelly, Cambridge UP, 2003, 291–311.

Casid, Jill H. "Handle with Care." *TDR: The Drama Review*, vol. 56, no. 4, Winter 2012, 121–35.

Cassuto, Leonard. "Jack London's Class-Based Grotesque." *Literature and the Grotesque*, edited by Michael J. Meyer. Rodopi, 1995, 113–28.

Cassuto, Leonard. *The Inhuman Race: The Racial Grotesque in American Literature and Culture*. Columbia UP, 1997.

Castro, Ingrid E. "The Emergence of Agency after Bionuclear War: Posthuman Child— Animal Possibilities." *Child and Youth Agency in Science Fiction: Travel, Technology, Time*, edited by Ingrid E. Castro and Jessica Clark. Lexington Books, 2019, 251–72.

Chan, Kara. "Children and Consumer Culture." *The Routledge International Handbook of Children, Adolescents, and Media*, edited by Dafna Lemish. Routledge, 2013, 141–47.

Chaney, Michael. "Animal Subjects in the Graphic Novel." *College Literature*, vol. 38, no. 3, Summer 2011, 129–49.

Chao, Shun-Liang. *Rethinking the Concept of the Grotesque: Crashaw, Baudelaire, Magritte*. Legenda, 2010.

Clark, John R. *The Modern Satiric Grotesque*. UP of Kentucky, 1991.

Cohen, Jeffrey Jerome. "Monster Culture (Seven Theses)." *Monster Theory: Reading Culture*, edited by Jeffrey Jerome Cohen. University of Minnesota Press, 1996, 3–25.

Colas, Alejandro. "Neoliberalism, Globalisation and International Relations." *Neoliberalism: A Critical Reader*, edited by Alfredo Saad-Filho and Deborah Johnston. Pluto Press, 2005, 70–79.

Collmer, Sabine. "Child Soldiers—An Integral Element in New, Irregular Wars?" *Connections*, vol. 3, no. 3, September 2004, 1–12.

Connelly, Frances S. "Introduction." *Modern Art and the Grotesque*, edited by Frances S. Connelly. Cambridge UP, 2003, 1–19.

Connelly, Frances S. *The Grotesque in Western Art and Culture: The Image at Play*. Cambridge UP, 2012.

Cook, Daniel Thomas. *The Commodification of Childhood: The Children's Clothing Industry and the Rise of the Child Consumer*. Duke UP, 2004.

Csicsery-Ronay, Istvan Jr. "On the Grotesque in Science Fiction." *Science Fiction Studies*, vol. 29, no. 1, March 2002, 71–99.

Csicsery-Ronay, Istvan Jr. *The Seven Beauties of Science Fiction*. Wesleyan UP, 2008.

Currie, Mark. "Controlling Time: *Never Let Me Go*." *Kazuo Ishiguro: Contemporary Critical Perspectives*, edited by Sean Matthews and Sebastian Groes. Continuum, 2009, 91–103.

Diamond, Jason. "'Flame Alphabet': Are Your Kids Making You Sick?" NPR.org, January 31, 2012. http://www.npr.org/2012/01/31/145703545/flame-alphabet-are-your-kids-making -you-sick.

DiLouie, Craig. *One of Us*. Orbit, 2018.

Dorrian, Mark. "On the Monstrous and the Grotesque." *Word & Image: A Journal of Verbal/ Visual Enquiry*, vol. 16, no. 3, 2000, 310–17.

Duane, Anna Mae. "The Angel and the Freak: The Value of Childhood and Disability in Katherine Dunn's *Geek Love*." *Studies in American Fiction*, vol. 39, no. 1, 2012, 103–22.

Dunn, Katherine. *Geek Love*. Vintage Contemporaries, 2002.

Edelman, Lee. "The Future Is Kid Stuff." *No Future: Queer Theory and the Death Drive*. Duke UP, 2004, 1–31.

Edwards, Justin, and Rune Graulund. *Grotesque*. Routledge, 2013.

Elliot, Jane. "Suffering Agency: Imagining Neoliberal Personhood in North America and Britain." *Social Text*, vol. 31, no. 2, 2013, 83–101.

Fass, Paula S. *Children of a New World: Society, Culture, and Globalization*. NYU Press, 2007.

Fass, Paula S. "The Child-Centered Family? New Rules in Postwar America." *Reinventing Childhood After World War II*, edited by Paula S. Fass and Michael Grossberg. University of Pennsylvania Press, 2012, 1–18.

Fearnow, Mark. *The American Stage and the Great Depression: A Cultural History of the Grotesque*. Cambridge UP, 1997.

Fiedler, Leslie. *Freaks: Myths and Images of the Secret Self*. Simon and Schuster, 1978.

Fluet, Lisa. "Immaterial Labors: Ishiguro, Class, and Affect." *NOVEL: A Forum on Fiction*, vol. 40, no. 3, Summer 2007, 265–88.

Flynn, Richard. "The Intersection of Children's Literature and Childhood Studies." *Children's Literature Association Quarterly*, vol. 22, no. 3, Fall 1997, 143–45.

Flynn, Richard. "What Are We Talking about When We Talk about Agency?" *Jeunesse: Young People, Texts, Cultures*, vol. 8, no. 1, 2016, 254–65.

Földváry, Kinga. "In Search of a Lost Future: The Posthuman Child." *European Journal of English Studies*, vol. 18, no. 2, 2014, 207–20.

Foucault, Michel. *The Birth of Biopolitics: Lectures at the Collège de France, 1978–1979*, edited by Michel Senellart, translated by Graham Burchell. Palgrave MacMillan, 2008.

Friedman, Milton. *Capitalism and Freedom*. University of Chicago Press, 1962.

Gaiman, Neil, et al. "Babycakes." *Taboo 4*, edited by Stephen R. Bissette. Spiderbaby Grafix & Publications, 1990, 9–12.

Gill-Peterson, Jules. "The Value of the Future: The Child as Human Capital and the Neoliberal Labor of Race." *Women's Studies Quarterly*, vol. 43, no. 1–2, 2015, 181–96.

Giroux, Henry. *Disposable Youth, Racialized Memories, and the Culture of Cruelty.* Routledge, 2012.

Grant, Iain Hamilton. "Postmodernism and Science and Technology." *The Routledge Companion to Postmodernism*, edited by Stuart Sim, 3rd ed. Routledge, 2011, 94–107.

Grosz, Elizabeth. "Intolerable Ambiguity: Freaks as/at the Limit." *Freakery: Cultural Spectacles of the Extraordinary Body*, edited by Rosemarie Garland Thomson, NYU Press, 1996, 55–66.

Grylls, David. *Guardians and Angels: Parents and Children in Nineteenth-Century Literature.* Faber and Faber, 1978.

Gubar, Marah. "Risky Business: Talking about Children in Children's Literature Criticism." *Children's Literature Association Quarterly*, vol. 38, no. 4, Winter 2013, 450–57.

Gysin, Fritz. *The Grotesque in American Negro Fiction: Jean Toomer, Richard Wright, and Ralph Ellison.* Francke Verlag Bern, 1975.

Halberstam, Jack. *Skin Shows: Gothic Horror and the Technology of Monsters.* Duke UP, 1995.

Hale, Kimberly Hurd, and Erin A. Dolgoy. "Humanity in a Posthuman World: M. R. Carey's *The Girl with All the Gifts.*" *Utopian Studies*, vol. 29, no. 3, 2018, 343–61.

Hardin, Michael. "Fundamentally Freaky: Collapsing the Freak/Norm Binary in *Geek Love.*" *Critique*, vol. 45, no. 4, Summer 2004, 337–46.

Harpham, Geoffrey Galt. *On the Grotesque: Strategies of Contradiction in Art and Literature.* Princeton UP, 1982.

Harris, Richard Legé, and Melinda J. Seid. "Critical Perspectives on Globalization and Neoliberalism in the Developing Countries." *Critical Perspectives on Globalization and Neoliberalism in the Developing Countries*, edited by Richard Legé Harris and Melinda J. Seid. Brill, 2000, 1–26.

Harvey, David. *A Brief History of Neoliberalism.* Oxford UP, 2005.

Hayek, Friedrich A. *Individualism and Economic Order.* Henry Regnery Company, 1972.

Heilbroner, Robert, and William Milberg. *The Crisis of Vision in Modern Economic Thought.* Cambridge UP, 1995.

Heimermann, Mark. "Old Before Their Time: The Impossibility of Childhood Innocence in *The Walking Dead.*" *Journal of Graphic Novels and Comics*, vol. 5, no. 3, 2014, 266–83.

Heise, Ursula K. "Science, Technology, and Postmodernism." *The Cambridge Companion to Postmodernism*, edited by Steven Connor. Cambridge UP, 2004, 136–67.

Higonnet, Anne. *Pictures of Innocence: The History and Crisis of Ideal Childhood.* Thames and Hudson, 1998.

Hindman, Hugh D. *Child Labor: An American History.* M. E. Sharpe, 2002.

Höing, Anja. "Animalic Agency: Intersecting the Child and Animal in Popular British Children's Fiction." *Representing Agency in Popular Culture: Children and Youth on Page, Screen, and In Between*, edited by Ingrid E. Castro and Jessica Clark. Lexington Books, 2019, 65–84.

Holmes, Chris. "Ishiguro at the Limit: The Corporation and the Novel." *NOVEL: A Forum on Fiction*, vol. 52, no. 3, 2019, 386–405.

Hornblum, Allen M. *Acres of Skin: Human Experiments at Holmesburg Prison.* Routledge, 1998.

Hume, Kathryn. *Aggressive Fictions: Reading the Contemporary American Novel.* Cornell UP, 2012.

Hunter, Janet. *Women and the Labour Market in Japan's Industrialising Economy: The Textile Industry Before the Pacific War.* Routledge Curzon, 2003.

Hurley, Natasha. "Reproduction/Non-Reproduction." *Jeunesse: Young People, Texts, Culture*, vol. 7, no. 2, 2015, 148–61.

Hutcheon, Linda. *The Poetics of Postmodernism: History, Theory, Fiction.* Routledge, 1988.

Ishiguro, Kazuo. *Never Let Me Go.* Alfred A. Knopf, 2005.

Jackson, Kathy Merlock. *Images of Children in American Film.* The Scarecrow Press Inc., 1986.

Jaques, Zoe. *Children's Literature and the Posthuman: Animal, Environment, Cyborg.* Routledge, 2015.

Jenks, Chris. *Childhood.* Routledge, 1996.

Johnston, Justin Omar. *Posthuman Capital and Biotechnology in Contemporary Novels.* Palgrave Macmillan, 2019.

Katz, Cindi. "Cultural Geographies Lecture: Childhood as Spectacle: Relays of Anxiety and the Reconfiguration of the Child." *Cultural Geographies*, vol. 15, 2008, 5–17.

Katz, Cindi. *Growing Up Global: Economic Restructuring and Children's Everyday Lives.* University of Minnesota Press, 2004.

Katz, Cindi. "Vagabond Capitalism and the Necessity of Social Reproduction." *Antipode*, vol. 33, no. 4, 2001, 709–28.

Kayser, Wolfgang. *The Grotesque in Art and Literature.* Translated by Ulrich Weisstein, Indiana UP, 1963.

Kelp-Stebbins, Katherine. "Hybrid Heroes and Graphic Posthumanity. Comics as a Media Technology for Critical Posthumanism." *Studies in Comics*, vol. 3, no. 2, 2012, 331–48.

Khatib, Sami. "The Drive of Capital: Of Monsters, Vampires, and Zombies." *Coils of the Serpent*, vol. 8, 101–13.

Kincaid, James Russell. *Child-Loving: The Erotic Child and Victorian Literature.* Routledge, 1992.

Kincaid, James Russell. *Erotic Innocence: The Culture of Child Molesting.* Duke UP, 1998.

Krugman, Saul. "The Willowbrook Hepatitis Studies Revisited: Ethical Aspects." *Reviews of Infectious Diseases*, vol. 8, no. 1, 1986, 157–62.

Kuryluk, Ewa. *Salome and Judas in the Cave of Sex.* Northwestern UP, 1987.

Lartey, Jamiles. "Ben Carson Incorrectly Suggests African Slaves Were 'Immigrants' to US." *The Guardian*, March 6, 2017. https://www.theguardian.com/us-news/2017/mar/06/ben-carson-african-slaves-immigrants-housing-speech.

Latham, Rob. *Consuming Youth: Vampires, Cyborgs, and the Culture of Consumption.* University of Chicago Press, 2002.

Lee, Nick. *Childhood and Biopolitics: Climate Change, Life Processes, and Human Futures.* Palgrave Macmillan, 2013.

Lemire, Jeff. Email to Mark Heimermann, December 4, 2014.

Lemire, Jeff. *Sweet Tooth, Vol. 1: In Captivity.* DC Comics, 2010.

Lemire, Jeff. *Sweet Tooth, Vol. 2: Out of the Deep Woods.* DC Comics, 2010.

Lennon, Robert J. "When Children's Speech Turns Lethal." *New York Times*, January 20, 2012. http://www.nytimes.com/2012/01/22/books/review/the-flame-alphabet-by-ben-marcus-book-review.html?_r=0.

Lewis, Barry. "Postmodernism and Fiction." *The Routledge Companion to Postmodernism*, edited by Stuart Sim, 3rd ed. Routledge, 2011, 169–81.

Lezard, Nicholas. "The Flame Alphabet by Ben Marcus—Review." *The Guardian*, April 30, 2013. http://www.theguardian.com/books/2013/apr/30/flame-alphabet-lezard-review.

Mallan, Kerry M. "Witches, Bitches and Femmes Fatales: Viewing the Female Grotesque in Children's Film." *Papers: Explorations into Children's Literature*, vol. 10, no. 1, 2000, 26–35.

Malpas, Simon. *The Postmodern*. Routledge, 2005.

Marcus, Ben. *The Flame Alphabet*. Alfred A. Knopf, 2012.

Marcus, Ben. "Why Experimental Fiction Threatens to Destroy Publishing, Jonathan Franzen, and Life as we Know It: A Correction." *Harper's Magazine*, October 2005, 39–52.

McClanahan, Annie. "Serious Crises: Rethinking the Neoliberal Subject." *Boundary 2*, vol. 46, no. 1, 2019, 103–32.

McElroy, Bernard. *Fiction of the Modern Grotesque*. Macmillan, 1989.

Meindl, Dieter. *American Fiction and the Metaphysics of the Grotesque*. University of Missouri Press, 1996.

Miles, Margaret. "Carnal Abominations: The Female Body as Grotesque." *The Grotesque in Arts & Literature: Theological Considerations*, edited by James Luther Adams and Wilson Yates. William B. Eerdmans Publishing Group, 1997, 83–112.

Mintz, Steven. *Huck's Raft: A History of American Childhood*. The Belknap Press of Harvard UP, 2004.

Mitchell, David. "Modernist Freaks and Postmodern Geeks." *The Disability Studies Reader*, edited by Lennard J. Davis. Routledge, 1997, 348–65.

Morgenstern, Naomi. *Wild Child: Intensive Parenting and Posthumanist Ethics*. University of Minnesota Press, 2018.

Muller, Gilbert H. *Nightmares and Visions: Flannery O'Connor and the Catholic Grotesque*. University of Georgia Press, 1972.

Nevárez, Lisa. "Playgrounds in the Zombie Apocalypse: The Feral Child." *Gothic Studies*, vol. 21, no. 1, 2019, 85–99.

Ngai, Sianne. *Our Aesthetic Categories: Zany, Cute, Interesting*. Harvard UP, 2012.

Nieuwenhuys, Eva, and Joop de Kort. "The Challenges of Social Sustainable Globalisation." *Neo-Liberal Globalism and Social Sustainable Globalisation*, edited by Eva Nieuwenhuys. Brill, 2006, 1–11.

Nodelman, Perry. "Inventing Childhood: Children's Literature in the Last Millenium." *Journal of Children's Literature*, vol. 26, no. 1, 2000, 8–17.

Nodelman, Perry. "The Disappearing Childhood of Children's Literature Studies." *Jeunesse: Young People, Texts, Culture*, vol. 5, no. 1, 2013, 149–63.

Nussbaum, Martha C. "Objectification." *Philosophy and Public Affairs*, vol. 24, no. 4, 1994, 249–91.

Olson, Debbie, and Giselle Rampaul. "Representations of Childhood in the Media." *The Routledge International Handbook of Children, Adolescents, and Media*, edited by Dafna Lemish. Routledge, 2013, 23–30.

O'Neil, Tegan. "Reviews: The Beef #1." *The Comics Journal*, March 2018. tcj.com/reviews/the-beef-1.

Penn, Helen. "Gambling on the Market: The Role of For-Profit Provision in Early Childhood Education and Care." *Journal of Early Childhood Research*, vol. 9, no. 2, 2011, 150–61.

Piccoli, Sean, and Post Wires. "Black Friday Violence Erupts Across Country." *New York Post*, November 29, 2013. http://nypost.com/2013/11/29/cop-shoots-shoplifter-near-chicago-amid-black-friday-chaos-others-hurt-around-country/.

Pieris, Pamela. "The United States." *Child Labor: A Global View*, edited by Cathryne L. Schmitz et al. Greenwood Press, 2004, 185–98.

Pifer, Ellen. *Demon or Doll: Images of the Child in Contemporary Writing and Culture*. UP of Virginia, 2000.

Polak, Kate. *Ethics in the Gutter: Empathy and Historical Fiction in Comics*. OSU Press, 2017.

Power, Nina. "Brief Notes Towards a Non-Nihilistic Theory of Non-Reproduction." *Studies in the Maternal*, vol. 6, no. 1, 2014, 1–3.

Power, Nina. "Non-Reproductive Futurism." *Borderlands*, vol. 8, no. 2, 2009, 1–16.

Pressler, Shirley J. "Construction of Childhood: The Building Blocks." *Key Issues in Childhood and Youth Studies*, edited by Derek Kassem et al. Routledge, 2010, 14–26.

Punter, David. *Metaphor*. Routledge, 2007.

Renner, Karen J. "Evil Children in Film and Literature." *The "Evil Child" in Literature, Film and Popular Culture*, edited by Karen J. Renner, Routledge, 2013, 1–27.

Rosenberg, Chaim M. *Child Labor in America: A History*. McFarland & Company Inc., Jefferson, North Carolina.

Russell, Karen. "Reeling for the Empire." *Vampires in the Lemon Grove*, Alfred A. Knopf, 2013, 23–52.

Russo, Mary. *The Female Grotesque: Risk, Excess and Modernity*. Routledge, 1994.

Saad-Filho, Alfredo, and Deborah Johnston. "Introduction." *Neoliberalism: A Critical Reader*, edited by Alfredo Saad-Filho and Deborah Johnston. Pluto Press, 2005, 1–6.

Sainato, Michael. "'Dumb and Dangerous': US Sees Surge in Efforts to Weaken Child Labour Regulations." *The Guardian*, May 1, 2023. https://www.theguardian.com/law/2023/may/01/us-surge-efforts-reduce-child-labor-regulations.

Sainato, Michael. "US Labor Department Condemns Surge in Child Labor after Teen Dies on the Job." *The Guardian*, July 27, 2023. https://www.theguardian.com/us-news/2023/jul/27/child-deaths-labor-department.

Salomon, Harald. "'A Paradise of Children': Western Perceptions of Childhood in Meiji Japan (1868–1912)." *Journal of the History of Childhood and Youth*, vol. 11, no. 3, Fall 2018, 341–62.

Schmitz, Cathryne L., et al. "Introduction." *Child Labor: A Global View*, edited by Cathryne L. Schmitz et al. Greenwood Press, 2004, 1–12.

Schor, Juliet B. *Born to Buy: The Commercialized Child and the New Consumer Culture*. Scribner, 2004.

Schulz, Andrew. *Goya's Caprichos: Aesthetics, Perception, and the Body*. Cambridge UP, 2005.

Schweikert, Mark, et al. *Elephantmen, Issue 56*. Image Comics Inc., 2014.

Shaddox, Karl. "Generic Considerations in Ishiguro's *Never Let Me Go*." *Human Rights Quarterly*, vol. 35, no. 2, May 2013, 448–69.

Shaikh, Anwar. "The Economic Mythology of Neoliberalism." *Neoliberalism: A Critical Reader*, edited by Alfredo Saad-Filho and Deborah Johnston. Pluto Press, 2005, 41–49.

Shaviro, Steven. "Introduction to Accelerationism." *No Speed Limit: Three Essays on Accelerationism*, University of Minnesota Press, 2015, 1–24.

Sheehan, Paul. "Posthuman Bodies." *The Cambridge Companion to the Body in Literature*, edited by David Hillman and Ulrika Maude. Cambridge UP, 2015, 245–60.

Sheldon, Rebekah. *The Child to Come: Life after the Human Catastrophe*. University of Minnesota Press, 2016.

Smith, Karen M. *The Government of Childhood: Discourse, Power, and Subjectivity*. Palgrave Macmillan, 2014.

Sonu, Debbie, and Jeremy Benson. "The Quasi-Human Child: How Normative Conceptions of Childhood Enabled Neoliberal School Reform in the United States." *Curriculum Inquiry*, vol. 46, no. 3, 2016, 230–47.

Sousanis, Nick. "Grids and Gestures: A Comics Making Exercise." *SANE Journal: Sequential Art Narrative in Education*, vol. 2, no. 1, September 2015.

Starkings, Richard. Interview: Richard Starkings. Interview by Cameron K., web, May 26, 2009. http://www.denofgeek.us/books-comics/11376/interview-richard-starkings.

Starkings, Richard. "Pertinent Points Pertaining to Pilots, Pieces and Pulchritude." *Elephantmen, Vol. 2: Fatal Diseases*, Image Comics Inc., 2011.

Starkings, Richard. "Pulp Science Fiction! Are You Ready to Believe?" *Elephantmen, Vol. 1: Wounded Animals*. Image Comics Inc., 2012

Starkings, Richard, Axel Medellin, and Gabriel Bautista. *Elephantmen, Issue 50*. Image Comics Inc., 2013.

Starkings, Richard, Axel Medellin, Shaky Kane, et al. *Elephantmen, Vol. 5: Devilish Functions*. Image Comics Inc., 2012.

Starkings, Richard, Moritat, Chris Burnham, et al. *Elephantmen, Vol. 3: Dangerous Liaisons*. Image Comics Inc., 2010.

Starkings, Richard, Moritat, Ian Churchill, et al. *Elephantmen, Vol. 2: Fatal Diseases*. Image Comics Inc., 2011.

Starkings, Richard, Moritat, Ladrönn, et al. *Elephantmen, Vol. 1: Wounded Animals*. Image Comics Inc., 2012.

Starkings, Richard, Tyler Shainline, and Shaky Kane. *The Beef*. Image Comics Inc., 2018.

Stearns, Peter N. *Childhood in World History*, 2nd ed. Routledge, 2011.

Stobbe, Mike. "AP IMPACT: Past Medical Testing on Humans Revealed." *Washington Post*, February 28, 2011, 1–5.

Stockton, Kathryn Bond. *The Queer Child, or Growing Sideways in the Twentieth Century*. Duke UP, 2009.

Storey, John. "Postmodernism and Popular Culture." *The Routledge Companion to Postmodernism*, edited by Stuart Sim, 3rd ed. Routledge, 2011, 204–14.

Tarr, Anita, and Donna R. White. "Introduction." *Posthumanism in Young Adult Fiction: Finding Humanity in a Posthuman World*, edited by Anita Tarr and Donna R. White, UP of Mississippi, 2018, ix–xxiv.

Thomson, Philip. *The Grotesque*. Methuen & Co. Ltd., 1972.

Tsurumi, E. Patricia. *Factory Girls: Women in the Thread Mills of Meiji Japan*. Princeton UP, 1990.

Uruburu, Paula M. *The Gruesome Doorway: An Analysis of the American Grotesque*. Peter Lang, 1987.

Wall, John. *Ethics in Light of Childhood*. Georgetown UP, 2010.

Wanzo, Rebecca. *The Content of Our Caricature: African American Comic Art and Political Belonging*. NYU Press, 2020.

Warner, Marina. "Little Angels, Little Monsters: Keeping Childhood Innocent." *Six Myths of Our Time: Little Angels, Little Monsters, Beautiful Beasts, and More*, Vintage Books, 1994, 43–62.

Warren, Victoria. "American Tall Tale/Tail: Katherine Dunn's *Geek Love* and the Paradox of American Individualism." *Critique*, vol. 45, no. 4, Summer 2004, 323–36.

Webb, Janeen, and Andrew Enstice. "Domesticating the Monster." *Seriously Weird: Papers on the Grotesque*, edited by Alice Mills, Peter Lang, 1999, 89–103.

Weese, Katherine. "Normalizing Freakery: Katherine Dunn's *Geek Love* and the Female Grotesque." *Critique*, vol. 41, no. 4, Summer 2000, 349–64.

Weinbaum, Alys Eve. *The Afterlife of Reproductive Slavery*. Duke UP, 2019.

Williams, Evan Calder. *Combined and Uneven Apocalypse*. Zero Books, 2011.

Wolfe, Carey. *Before the Law: Humans and Other Animals in a Biopolitical Frame.* The
    University of Chicago Press, 2013.

Woodrell, Daniel. *Winter's Bone.* Back Bay Books, 2006.

Worthington, Marjorie. "The Texts of Tech: Technology and Authorial Control in *Geek
    Love* and *Galatea 2.2." Journal of Narrative Theory*, vol. 39, no. 1, Winter 2009, 109–33.

Zelizer, Viviana. *Pricing the Priceless Child: The Changing Social Value of Children.*
    Princeton UP, 1994.

INDEX

ABOUT THE AUTHOR

Mark Heimermann is assistant professor of English at Lakeland University. He coedited the anthology *Picturing Childhood: Youth in Transnational Comics*, which was nominated for the Eisner Award for Best Academic/ Scholarly Work. His research interests include childhood studies, comics studies, and contemporary literature.

www.ingramcontent.com/pod-product-compliance
Lightning Source LLC
LaVergne TN
LVHW050011020825
817679LV00033B/835